Young Children Learning

Understanding Children's Worlds
Series Editor: Judy Dunn

The study of children's development can have a profound influence on how children are brought up, cared for and educated. Many psychologists argue that, even if our knowledge is incomplete, we have a responsibility to attempt to help those concerned with the care, education and study of children by making what we know avalable to them. The central aim of this series is to encourage developmental psychologists to set out the findings and the implications of their research for others – teachers, doctors, social workers, students and fellow researchers – whose work involves the care, education and study of young children and their families. The information and the ideas that have grown from recent research form an important resource which should be available to them. This series provides an opportunity for psychologists to present their work in a way that is interesting, intelligible and substantial, and to discuss what its consequences may be for those who care for, and teach children: not to offer simple prescriptive advice to other professionals, but to make important and innovative research accessible to them.

Children doing Mathematics
Terezhina Nunes and Peter Bryant

Children and Emotion
Paul L. Harris

Bullying at School
Dan Olweus

How Children Think and Learn, 2e
David Wood

Making Decisions about Children, 2e
H. Rudolph Schaffer

Children's Talk in Communities and Classrooms
Lynn Vernon-Feagans

Children and Political Violence
Ed Cairns

The Work of the Imagination
Paul Harris

Children in Changing Families
Jan Pryor and Bryan Rodgers

Young Children Learning
Barbara Tizard and Martin Hughes

Young Children Learning

Barbara Tizard and Martin Hughes

With a new foreword by Judy Dunn

Blackwell
Publishing

BLACKWELL PUBLISHING
350 Main Street, Malden, MA 02148-5020, USA
108 Cowley Road, Oxford OX4 1JF, UK
550 Swanston Street, Carlton, Victoria 3053, Australia

First edition published 1984 by Fontana Original
Fontana Press edition published 1986
Second edition published 2002 by Blackwell Publishing Ltd
Reprinted 2004

Transferred to digital print 2005

Library of Congress Cataloging-in-Publication Data

Tizard, Barbara.
  Young children learning / Barbara Tizard and Martin Hughes ; with a new foreword by Judy Dunn.—2nd ed.
    p. cm.—(Understanding children's worlds)
Includes bibliographical references and index.
  ISBN 0–631–23615–5 (pbk. : alk. paper)
  1. Learning, Psychology of. 2. Children—Language. 3. Cognition in children. 4. Home and school. 5. Mother and child. 6. Nursery schools. 7. Teacher–student relationships. 8. Speech and social status. I. Hughes, Martin, 1949 May 15– II. Title. III. Series.
  BF318 .T59 2002
  155.42'3315—dc21

                                                    2002008001

A catalogue record for this title is available from the British Library.

Set in 10 on 12.5 pt Sabon
by SetSystems Ltd, Saffron Walden, Essex
Printed and bound in Great Britain by
Marston Book Services Limited, Oxford

For further information on
Blackwell Publishing, visit our website:
www.blackwellpublishing.com

Contents

Foreword – *Judy Dunn*   vii

Preface   xiii

1. Why we studied children learning   1

2. How we carried out this study   11

3. Learning at home: play, games, stories and 'lessons'   22

4. Learning at home: living and talking together   54

5. The puzzling mind of the four-year-old   80

6. Working-class verbal deprivation: myth or reality?   107

7. An afternoon with Donna and her mother   132

8. How the children fared at nursery school   149

9. The working-class girls, including Donna, at school   179

10. The gap between home and nursery school   197

11. Young children learning   209

Statistical appendix   227

Notes   236

Index of children   241

General index   242

Foreword

What do young children learn, at home? What kind of thinkers are four-year-olds, and how do they try to make sense of their world? Do working-class children suffer from home environments that are 'deprived', in terms of their language experiences? And how do children's learning experiences differ at home and at nursery school?

Clearly these questions are highly relevant and of social importance now, just as they were in the 1980s, when this fascinating book was first published. Barbara Tizard and Martin Hughes, with their colleagues Helen Carmichael and Gill Pinkerton, set out to investigate what children were learning at home with their mothers; they studied the social contexts in which this learning took place, and the kind of thinking and curiosity that the young children showed in their conversations with their mothers. Their findings – and the messages that they chose to highlight from these results – aroused great attention and interest among psychologists and educationalists when the book was published (and some agitation among those who taught young children!). Why is it important that we should now read again what they found, and welcome the re-publication of this classic study? Two messages of the research are particularly important.

Learning experiences at home

The first message is that everyday experiences at home can be valuable educational learning experiences. For most of the children in the study, formal 'lessons' were relatively rare, but through their daily conversations, their questions, arguments, jokes and stories, the children were involved in talk with their mothers about the social world, in which general knowledge about why people behave the way they do, about their cultural world, and indeed the early stages of literacy and numeracy were explored. Children were able to express their puzzlement, pursue the questions and issues that mattered to them, argue for their own point of view, and 'take on board' the arguments of their mothers, in notably supportive and varied contexts. Barbara Tizard and Martin Hughes emphasize five features of home life that are significant here. The first is the range of activities in which children are involved: the mundane daily activities of planning and cooking meals, shopping and trips, looking after pets, paying bills, doing laundry, watching neighbours out of the window engaged the children in the study in conversations that were rich in potential for expanding their understanding of people and the social world, for beginning to understand spelling, number, rhyme, and for discussing abstract concepts.

The second key feature is the *shared* history, experience and future life of child and mother. Parents are able, because of their shared lives, to help children to relate present to past experiences, and to build on and extend their knowledge base. The third feature is the opportunity for one-to-one attention and conversation in most homes – so different from the distracting and crowded experiences in most group settings. Perhaps most important of all, the fourth and fifth features of home life stressed by Tizard and Hughes are that the activities and talk at home are *'embedded in contexts of great meaning to the child'* (in contrast, inevitably, to much talk at school), and the close intense relationship between child and mother, their intimacy, their interest in, and concern for one another.

Tizard and Hughes give us a convincing argument for the potential of these experiences for children's intellectual progress. In the years since the pioneering work of *Young Children Learning*, have psychologists taken up the opportunity to examine further how these features of family life are linked to educational achievements? Have we learned more about the significance of early conversations within the family? There have been many studies of links between parental talk to children and their linguistic development, but what about other cognitive domains?

Since the publication of the book there have been some notable examples of research on children's experiences at home and their intellectual development. Peter Bryant's work has for instance established links between children's experience of nursery rhymes and their later reading ability;[1] Maureen Callahan's studies of children engaged with their mothers in cooking activity has related their conversations while cooking to their understanding of scientific concepts;[2] preschool literacy experiences have been linked to later reading skills.[3] And in the great burst of research over the past decade on children's understanding of mental states and of emotions[4] – their growing grasp of the connections between people's inner states and why they behave the way they do – there are consistent findings that link children's participation in discourse with family members about inner states to their later understanding of other people's mental states and feelings.[5] This research has recently expanded to include studies of parent–child conversations about shared past events to children's understanding of emotions and their grasp of the notion that memory of past events can influence current feelings and thoughts, and behaviour.[6]

There is also research that links children's participation in causal talk with their parents to their developing powers of reasoning and logic,[7] and their participation in family talk about feelings with their later moral sensibility and conscience development.[8] The consequences for children who because of deafness have limited experience of the kinds of conversations thought to play a part in the development of understanding of 'other minds' have also been documented.[9] However, the challenge raised by Tizard and Hughes' research for developmental psychologists – to document how far parent–child conversations may foster other aspects of intellectual growth, such as mathematical, biological or geographical concepts – remains to be taken up fully. Why should this be so? This kind of research, as the authors point out, is laborious to conduct, and does not provide quick answers to causal questions. But to re-read the book is to appreciate how rewarding such research will prove.

The puzzling mind of the four-year-old

A second message of the book which is of great relevance to those currently studying young children's thinking is that the conversations provide a remarkable window on the curiosity and intellectual energy of four-year-olds. In the context of their families, the children returned with great perseverance to intellectual issues that puzzled them, and pursued questions that interested or confused them. It is because the children were recorded for long periods of time and *with their mothers at home* that their 'thirst for understanding' is evident. Particularly striking is the analysis of 'episodes of persistent questioning', and the logical powers that the children showed in their pursuit of understanding. Tizard and Hughes show us the learning potential of children's 'passages of intellectual search', with notable illustrations. One is the conversation of Rosy with her mother that is triggered by the appearance of the window cleaner. Rosy's confusion about the links between money, work and consumer goods is exposed, but what is especially interesting is that she returns to the topic later in the observation, and appears to be aware that she has not fully grasped the relationships involved. Her questions are, it seems, motivated by her wish to clarify her misunderstanding.

A second illustration is an astonishing conversation between Beth, aged only three years and ten months, and her mother about sloping roofs, flat roofs, draining of water, snow – a conversation that demonstrates the potential of intellectual search *with her mother* as a way of learning about relatively abstract ideas. These are exactly the ideas that have been further explored since the 1980s by Barbara Rogoff and her colleagues in their studies of children's cognitive development within the framework of 'apprentices to learning'.[10] Tizard and Hughes argue that it was the child's curiosity *together with* the mother's desire to teach or clarify which created the enormous potential for learning in these family situations – a Vygotskian notion that has become much more widely appreciated at a theoretical level in the last decade or so.[11] This focus on the children's driving curiosity (what Susan Isaacs described as a thirst for understanding that in an intelligent child is 'a veritable passion') coupled with the mothers' interest in their children is surely what those concerned with cognitive development should include in their studies today.

Working-class children at home and at school

Tizard and Hughes suggested that this parental concern 'which converts the potential advantages of the home into actual advantages' might be affected (and diminished) if parents were stressed, or isolated, or were having to cope with large families. (There is indeed now research on children from 6 to 30 months that reports that parents in more crowded homes spoke in less sophisticated ways with their children and were less responsive – a difference that was evident when socioeconomic variables were controlled[12]). Among the working-class children in Tizard and

Hughes' admittedly limited sample of young girls, the features of home life that gave the home such a rich potential for learning were all present, as in the middle-class homes. There was not evidence for a 'language deficit' in the environment of these children. There were however differences in language style: for example, differences in the frequency of adults' complex use of language and adequacy of answers to why questions, in the frequency of children's 'why' questions and passages of persistent questioning, and in children's complex use of language. These may well have contributed to the striking differences evident when the children went to school.

This is clearly a theme that is relevant today, when social class differences in children's achievements at school are still all too clear. The analysis of social class differences in conversations and in language use has not been a 'fashionable' topic for psychologists to investigate over the last decade or so – but it surely deserves our attention. Recent analyses of children's understanding of mind in a sample of London children, for example, highlight major differences related to social class.[13] One particularly poignant theme running through the book is that in the school situation, the working-class children (many of whom were lively thinkers at home, asking questions, puzzling over problems) were subdued, passive and dependent – and already at four years old appeared to be at an educational disadvantage. The message for teachers from this and other recent books about ways of fostering conversations is clearly taken seriously today; the *Curriculum Guidance for the Foundation Stage*[14] sets out guidelines for helping to connect children's home and school lives. But we will only be able to understand how far the picture of disadvantage is still relevant today, and most importantly, why this should be, if we follow the strategy of Tizard and Hughes by studying children both at home and at school. It is clear that the 'mismatch' between the culture of home and of school is an issue that bears on the educational progress of children not only from different social classes but also from different ethnic and minority communities now in the UK, in the US and all over Europe (see for example Gregory's studies of Bangladeshi children in London,[15] as well as the classic study of Brice Heath[16] and for the implications of parental education levels on reading – see Greenhough and Hughes' research[17]). There can be no substitute for detailed studies of the same children in their classrooms and in their families, if we are to make progress in understanding how to help. Tizard and Hughes have shown us one way to address these issues, which we should surely take seriously.

Judy Dunn

Preface

This book is the account of an unusual research project. Some years ago, with the help of our colleagues Gill Pinkerton and Helen Carmichael, we made tape-recordings of the conversations of four-year-old girls at morning nursery school and at home with their mothers in the afternoon. A discussion of some of these conversations – which we have found a continual source of fascination – makes up the core of this book.

Our main motive for carrying out the study was to describe the ways in which young children learn from their mothers at home. It is nowadays widely assumed, almost without question, that professionals have a good deal to teach parents about how to educate and bring up children. The idea that professionals might learn from observing children talking to their parents at home has hardly been considered.

At the time we were planning our study we were beginning to question this assumption. We had both spent a lot of time observing and studying children in nursery schools, and had developed a strong appreciation of the value of nursery education for both parents and children. We were convinced – and still are convinced – that nursery schools and classes provide an important means of support for hard-pressed parents, and that they provide a secure and enjoyable environment in which young children can play, and explore the wider social world beyond the home. We were, however, uneasy about the claims being made about the value of nursery schools as a source of linguistic and intellectual stimulation. While nursery staff were undoubtedly spending a great deal of time talking to children, this time inevitably had to be shared among the large number of children in their care.

When we observed individual children, their conversations with nursery staff were surprisingly infrequent, and often restricted to a few brief exchanges. It seemed to us unlikely that the language environment of the nursery was richer than that of the home. However, we knew of no research which had attempted to make this comparison.

It soon became clear that the conversations in the working-class homes were just as prolific as those in the middle-class homes. There was no question of these children 'not being talked to at home', and few signs of the language deprivation that has so often been described. Although there were social class differences in the mothers' conversation and style of interaction, the working-class children were clearly growing up in a rich linguistic environment.

As we started to study and analyse the transcripts, we became increasingly aware of how rich this environment was for all the children. The conversations between the children and their mothers ranged freely over a variety of topics. The idea that children's interests were restricted to play and TV was clearly untenable. At home the children discussed topics like work, the family, birth, growing up, and death; they talked with their mothers about things they had done together in the past, and their plans for the future; they puzzled over such diverse topics as the shape of roofs and chairs, the nature of Father Christmas, and whether the Queen wears curlers in bed. Many of these conversations took place during recognizably educational contexts – such as during play or while reading books – but many did not. A large number of the more fruitful conversations simply cropped up as the children and their mothers went about their afternoon's business at home – having lunch, planning shopping expeditions, feeding the baby and so on.

Not only did we become increasingly impressed with the home as a learning environment, but we also became more and more impressed by the young child as a learner. We had the advantage, not available to a participant, of being able to study a whole afternoon of conversation in detail. It became clear that in many conversations the children were actively struggling to understand a new idea, or some information which didn't fit in with what they already knew, or the meaning of an unfamiliar word. When we looked more closely at these episodes – which we called 'passages of intellectual search' – we realized how much they revealed the young child as a persistent and logical thinker. These were not the illogical or whimsical characters suggested by, for example, the theories of Jean Piaget: they were powerful and determined thinkers in their own right. Their limitations seemed to be due far more to lack of knowledge and faulty assumptions than to any childish illogicality.

When we came to analyse the conversations between these same children and their nursery teachers, we could not avoid being disappointed. The children were certainly happy at school, for much of the time absorbed in play. However, their conversations with their teachers made a sharp contrast to those with their mothers. The richness, depth and variety which characterized the home conversations was sadly missing. So too was the sense of intellectual struggle, and of the real attempts to communicate being made on both sides. The questioning, puzzling child which we were so taken with at home was gone: in her place was a child who, when talking to staff, seemed subdued, and whose conversations with adults were mainly restricted to answering questions rather than asking them, or taking part in minimal exchanges about the whereabouts of other children and play materials.

These differences between the conversations with adults at home and nursery school were particularly pronounced for the working-class children. Compared to the middle-class children, they were more likely to be subdued, to play a passive role in the conversations, and to avoid asking questions of the nursery staff. The working-class children often took part in long and sustained discussions at home, but showed little evidence of this with the teachers. It was not hard to see how myths about working-class verbal deprivation might arise. Faced with an inarticulate child in the classroom, teachers might easily conclude that the child was just the same at home.

These observations of the same children with their mothers and their teachers left us troubled. On the one hand, they showed the power of the home as a learning environment, and the power of the young child's mind. At the same time, they showed how strongly young children could be affected by the move from one setting to another. The claim that children reserve their best thinking for outside school, with a resulting compartmentalizing of the knowledge that they acquire within school, has been made many times before. Our study suggests that this may well be true even at the nursery stage. Thus, although our study was concerned with the preschool period, the findings are relevant to wider educational issues.

We should make it clear that we use the term 'learn' in a loose sense. In order to find out whether children have learnt what has been taught them, a series of careful experiments would be required. In this sense we did not study learning. On the other hand, 'teaching' did not seem the right term, both because much that children appeared to be learning from their mothers was not the consequence of deliberate teaching, and because the children themselves often played an active part in initiating learning by their questions.

We hope that our findings will be taken in this wider context, and not used simply to criticize nursery schools. We do not believe that the problems we have identified are simply those of the nursery school; nor do we believe that they should provide a rationale for cutting back on valuable nursery school provision. As we have made clear many times, both here and elsewhere, there are many arguments for providing a comprehensive nursery service. Nor do we think that nursery teachers should feel personally criticized by our work. We have tremendous respect for their dedication and enthusiasm for carrying out a demanding job under difficult conditions. At the same time, as we point out in the last chapter, we believe that our study suggests some changes which might be made in nursery education.

This book could not have appeared without the help of many people. Above all, we must acknowledge the part played by Gill Pinkerton and Helen Carmichael in the original collection and analysis of the data, and the ESRC and DHSS for financial support for the project. Finally, of course, our greatest debt is to the children, their mothers and the nursery staff for allowing us to observe young children learning.

1

Why we studied children learning

'One of the most crucial ways in which a culture provides aid in intellectual growth is through a dialogue between the more experienced and the less experienced.'

J. S. Bruner, in *The Relevance of Education.*

The group of children who make up the main characters of this book can indeed be described, in Bruner's terms, as among the 'less experienced' members of our culture. At the time our study was carried out they were close to their fourth birthday, still a year short of the age when they would start compulsory schooling, and their experience of life was inevitably of a limited nature. This lack of experience could be seen in the often touchingly naive questions which they asked. It could also be seen in the large gaps which were frequently revealed in their knowledge, and in the many assumptions about the world, and the way people behave in it, which adults take for granted but which they were still in the process of discovering. And yet, despite their limited years, we found ourselves continually being surprised and impressed by these young children. As we studied their conversations we were forced to admire their curiosity, their open, questioning minds, and, above all, the persistent and logical manner in which they struggled to make sense of their world.

In the course of the book, we will see these children engage in two very different kinds of dialogue with the 'more experienced' members of our culture. First, we will be looking at them at home, as they talk to the person who is usually of central importance in their lives: their mother. Nowadays, about a third of mothers with children under five work outside the home, generally part-time, leaving their children in someone else's care. In addition, fathers are more involved than previously in their children's upbringing. Yet, despite these changes, it is still true that most preschool children, like those in this book, spend a large part of their waking hours at home with their mothers. Inevitably, mothers and children spend a good deal of their time talking to each other: about what each of them is doing, about events in the past or plans for the future, about the unexpected events that crop up during the day, or about the ideas and thoughts that occur to them in the course of whatever they are doing. Unplanned and frequently haphazard, these conversations between mother and child provide, as we shall see, a surprisingly rich source of 'aid for the child's intellectual growth'.

As well as looking at these children at home, we will also see them in a very different context, that of their nursery school. Like many British preschool children, the children in this book all attended a daily two-and-a-half-hour session at their local nursery class or school. These nurseries are happy and relaxed places, which provide children with a gentle introduction to the kinds of demands they will later experience in primary school. In particular, they encounter a relationship with an adult which is very different from the one they have experienced with their mothers. For the first time they will be interacting with someone who is trained and employed by our society for the sole purpose of 'aiding their intellectual growth'. Their conversations, as we will see, are of a very different nature from those taking place in the children's homes. Comparison between the home and nursery conversations reveals how differently children can behave in two settings – in some cases it is hard to believe it is the same child who is talking. In addition, the school conversations show how full of traps the deliberate process of aiding intellectual growth can actually be, and how this process can indeed even be counter-productive.

The conversations in which the children were involved provide a fascinating insight into their lives and concerns. They also provide material with which to answer some fundamental questions about the way in which young children think and learn, and the role which adults can play in this process. In the rest of this chapter we will outline the main questions which we asked, and explain why we thought these questions important. In the following chapters, we will present the (often unexpected) answers which we found, and show how these answers led us to question many prevailing assumptions, both about nursery education and about the way young children think.

What do young children learn at home?

The central interest of our study was to describe the educational contexts of the home. What do preschool children learn from their mothers, and how does this learning take place? An immense amount of learning certainly occurs in the early years. By the age of five many of the major intellectual competencies have been acquired – for example, an understanding of space and time dimensions, concepts of causality, of object constancy, and even a good knowledge of age and sex roles. On average, five-year-olds have a vocabulary of over two thousand words, and they can understand and use most types of complex sentence. But little is known about how this learning takes place, or the role that adults play in the process.

Psychologists currently advocate that parents should help their children learn by playing with them and reading to them. We wanted to see whether these were in fact the most fruitful learning contexts, or whether joint activity of other kinds, for example, doing housework together, or watching TV, or simply talking together at mealtimes, might be just as important. We also wanted to see if we could identify anything distinctive about the learning that takes place at home which might be different from the kind of learning that happens at school.

In view of the obvious interest and importance of these questions, it would be reasonable to assume that they had already been thoroughly investigated. But, in fact, the opposite is true. At the time that we started our study we could find little previous research on the topic. There was quite a body of research concerned with the way in which the language of very young children develops through interaction with their mothers. Most of this research involved intensive investigation of a few children, although one large-scale study of language development by Wells and his associates, which we shall refer to again, was already under way.[1] Little could be found, however, that was concerned with the broader educational questions in which we were interested.

Why has this topic been so neglected? We believe there are two likely explanations. The first is primarily practical. To discover what and how children are learning at home requires that the researcher must actually go into a child's home and observe what is happening there. This not only means an intrusion into the privacy of other people's home lives, but raises the question of whether the very presence of the researcher in the home will have a seriously distorting effect on what is going on. Added to this is the problem of accurately recording – and then analysing – all the unpredictable and sometimes chaotic events that occur. Tape-recorders and video cameras certainly make recording easier, but they also add to the unnaturalness of the situation. In addition, the subsequent analysis of these tapes is a laborious and time-consuming business, particularly if more than a small number of children is studied.

Faced with these problems, those psychologists who have been interested in how mothers teach have almost always brought them to a laboratory, and asked them to teach or explain some task to their children, or play with them using a 'standard' set of toys. The most famous of these studies was carried out by two American psychologists, Hess and Shipman.[2] They asked working-class and middle-class mothers to teach their child how to use a complex toy, such as 'Etchasketch', and compared the teaching strategies of the two social class groups. They found that the middle-class mothers taught their children more effectively, and used more explicit verbal instructions. However, one must inevitably have reservations about the interpretation of the results. Working-class mothers may well have felt less at ease in a laboratory setting than middle-class mothers. They may also have interpreted what was expected of them differently. More important is the fact that experiments of this kind cannot tell us what mothers choose to teach their children at home, or how they set about it, especially since teaching a specific task is a relatively rare event at home.

At the time that our study began a number of researchers, besides ourselves, were concluding that recording in private homes was the only way in which certain questions about the family could be answered.[3] The way in which we ourselves tried to overcome the difficulties we have outlined is described in Chapter 2.

A second reason why so little research has been done on what children learn at home is of a very different kind. The obstacle here is not so much the problem of obtaining information, but the belief in some quarters that there is not much to be gained from attempting to do so. In other words, the reluctance has been due to the general belief that mothers, as educators, have very little to offer.

This attitude may be partly due to the lowly, non-professional status which parenting is frequently given. Educational theorists, in fact, usually define education as a process entrusted by society to a specialist system involving teachers and schools. Hence what a teacher does in the classroom is, *ipso facto*, educational, while what a mother does is only 'upbringing' or childrearing. Parents themselves often accept this view, believing that education starts at primary school and is concerned with school 'subjects' This leads them to devalue their own contribution, even though it constitutes an essential underpinning of the school system.

It is true that upbringing in the early years, even if it has not been accorded the status of education, has recently attracted a good deal of professional attention. This attention has, however, almost all been critical, and has been concerned with improving, rather than studying, parenting. Psychologists in particular have argued that training for parenthood should begin in school, and be continued by adult education courses and by classes in antenatal and child health clinics. Hardly anyone has pointed out that this movement to educate parents has developed in the absence of any real knowledge on which it could be based. That is, there are remarkably few parental activities which we can predict with any confidence will lead to specific consequences for children.

We knew from our own previous research, and our experience in schools, that this tendency to disparage the parental contribution to education was shared by many teachers, and that teachers are often sceptical about how much children learn at home. One of us (BT), in a previous study, had asked nursery school teachers their opinion of the contribution that parents made to their child's education.[4] Nearly half the teachers, while stressing the parents' concern and affection for the children, thought that they made no positive contribution to their education at all. Typical comments were: 'In an enabling middle-class home, yes, but not round here'; 'To be frank, the children are better off in school'. In a current, as yet unpublished study, we asked reception class teachers in primary schools whether they would like to know more about their pupils' out-of-school lives and interests. Nearly half answered that such knowledge is not important, usually adding that there was very little to know. We suspected that the tendency to devalue, or even to write off, the children's home lives led teachers to underestimate the skills and interests that the children brought to school.

Do working-class children suffer from verbal deprivation?

As some of the above comments suggest, a tendency to devalue children's home lives is most evident in working-class areas. There is a widespread belief among educationalists that working-class parents do not stimulate their children adequately, and in particular do not develop their language. The most recent government report on the teaching of reading, A *Language for Life*, stated that 'an important contributory factor to reading difficulties is that many young children do not have the opportunity to develop at home the more complex forms of language which school demands'.[5] To remedy this situation, the report advocated that parents should be helped to understand the process of language development, and their role in it, while children should be encouraged to attend nursery school so that the nursery teacher can assist by 'measured attention to the child's language needs'. The parents, too, should be encouraged to spend time at school, watching the nursery teachers. This would lead to their altering the experiences they provide for their children at home and the kinds of conversation they hold with them. As one concerned teacher put it to us, 'If only parents understood what we are trying to do at school, it could be "nursery" for children all day at home.'

Surprisingly, these beliefs about the inadequate language used in working-class homes are not based on studies of how language is actually used at home. In general, psychologists have simply inferred from the poorer performance of working-class children on tests of spoken and written language that they have been linguistically deprived at home. Another aim of our study was therefore to observe in both middle- and working-class homes, to see whether there was evidence of working-class language deprivation, or whether this was an unsubstantiated myth. Again, our findings might alter teachers' expectations of children. They might also affect the nature of parent education offered in schools and clinics.

How competent are children as thinkers?

A further reason for observing young children at home was our suspicion that such observation might reveal them to be intellectually more competent than many psychologists and teachers have believed. Our suspicions were based on recent research within developmental psychology, which has cast a new light on young children's abilities. Much of this research, including work in which one of us (MH) was involved, has been critical of the ideas of the great Swiss psychologist, Piaget.

Piaget's theories have had a tremendous influence on primary education over the last thirty years. Some of his ideas have had a very liberalizing effect on schools. This is especially true of his theory that intelligence develops as a result of children's own actions on the physical world – they must discover for themselves, and explore, rather than be taught. However, Piaget also believed that young children think in a different way from adults. In particular, he claimed that until about the age of seven they are incapable of logical thought, and only able to see things from their own perspective.

It is certainly true that young children do not think as effectively as adults, and cannot solve problems which older children find easy. However, there is increasing evidence that their mistakes in reasoning may not be due to any essential illogicality. Recently, some developmental psychologists, notably Bryant[6] and Donaldson,[7] have devised experiments to show that children's apparent failures in thinking are due to failures of memory, or to misunderstanding what the adult wants them to do, especially in the social context of an experiment. Margaret Donaldson has pointed out that in everyday life one can see instances of children thinking in ways that do not fit easily into Piaget's theories.

Donaldson's own theories suggest that if one wants to see children at their most competent, one should not look at how they attempt tasks or questions set them by psychologists, but at how they attempt tasks which they have set themselves, in an environment which is meaningful and supportive to them. If Donaldson's views are correct, it seemed highly likely that by observing children going about their ordinary lives at home we would see examples of intellectual competence – such as logical reasoning or taking another's point of view – which might not be revealed elsewhere. At the same time, we would gain further insight into the kinds of topics which the children themselves were interested in. We might also shed light on how adults help children achieve their self-selected intellectual tasks.

How different are home and nursery school?

There were a number of reasons why we wanted to look at the children at nursery school as well as at home.

First, it seemed important to compare what children were learning from their mothers at home with what they were learning from their teachers at school. As we pointed out earlier, we thought it likely that mothers and teachers would be quite different in the ways in which they saw and approached the task of 'aiding children's intellectual growth'. The most widely held view within the educational world seems to be that such a comparison would demonstrate the superior techniques and skills of the trained nursery teacher. But it seemed to us possible that the mother might, in her own way, prove to be just as effective, if not more effective, as an educational agent.

We were also interested in seeing what effect the move from one context to another had on the children. Most people never see children in more than one context – parents have little idea of how their children behave at school, while teachers rarely see their pupils in an out-of-school setting. Often both teachers and parents suspect that the other knows a different child. Nevertheless, assessments of children's behaviour and abilides are made by psychologists on the basis of seeing children in the restricted setling of a classroom or test situation. It seemed to us important for both theoretical and practical reasons to see in what ways children's behaviour differed in the two very different settings of home and school. Were the abilities and interests they showed in one setting also revealed in the other? If this was not the case, psychologists would need to reconsider whether they were justified in assessing children in one setting only, while teachers or parents might have to consider how to tap the potential which children displayed in one setting, but not the other.

In addition to studying the effect of context on the children's behaviour, we were also interested in how far the children themselves made connections between their lives at home and at school. Did they link up what they were doing and experiencing in each location? Or did they appear to be moving between two distinct and unconnected worlds?

Our study: choices and decisions

We have outlined above the four main questions we were interested in: what the children were learning at home; what differences in learning at home were associated with social class differences; what skills and competencies they were displaying at home; and what the main differences were between the teaching of mothers and nursery teachers. In order to answer these questions, we decided to obtain a complete record of the children's interactions with adults during one afternoon at home, and two mornings at nursery school. We kept only a brief record of what the children did when they were alone or playing with other children – activities which occupied the majority of their time at school. The reader will note, therefore, that we did not make an overall comparison of the children's lives at home and at school. This was because the focus of our study was on the mother's – and, for comparison, the teacher's – educational role.

Any research project involves choices. By focusing on one issue, others are neglected. Some psychologists might argue with our decision to study adult–child conversations, on the grounds that the primary way in which young children learn is through exploring the physical world, and observing the effect of their actions on it. While we do not deny the importance of this form of learning, we were addressing a different question, one concerned with the role of the adult in giving meaning to the child's experiences.

From a different perspective, others might argue that by focusing on adult–child conversations we failed to take into account what children learn from other children. Again, we do not wish to deny the reality of such learning. Older children often deliberately teach their younger brothers and sisters, and younger children learn much from them by imitation. Some aspects of social understanding and social skills may indeed only be learned from interaction with other children.[8] However, there is a good deal of evidence to suggest that, at least in Western societies, parents are the major influence in the acquisition of knowledge and language. For example, we know that young children who spend most of their time with other children rather than adults – twins, children in large families, and children in institutions – are relatively slow in developing language, compared with first-born and only children. Further, we know that children's talk to adults tends to be made up of longer, more complex sentences, with a larger vocabulary, than their talk to other children.[9] Given limited resources, we therefore decided to focus on the person with primary educational responsibility for the young child, the mother. (We were well aware of the important role of the father in the child's life, but in most English families, including those we studied, mothers spend much more time with their children than do fathers.)

A further decision which we made was to study only girls. There would have been obvious advantages in studying both boys and girls, but in order to make statistically valid comparisons between them we would have needed a much larger number of children. Our main reason for choosing girls was that, in the preschool years, they are likely to talk more, and more clearly, than boys. In addition, we felt that in a society still dominated by men, there was some merit in focusing on girls, and on mother–daughter interactions.

Finally, then, we decided to observe thirty girls, fifteen from middle-class families and fifteen from working-class families, talking to their mothers at home and to their teachers at nursery school. In the next chapter we describe how we selected the children and how we carried out the study.

How we present our material

Our study was initially conceived in the traditional psychological format. That is, we made quantitative comparisons between different groups of children and mothers. We looked, for example, at how many questions of different kinds were asked, and at how many conversations on various topics were held. We also interviewed all the mothers after the observations were finished. This approach yielded very useful findings; the detailed results are presented in an appendix to this book, and have been published in scientific articles (listed in the appendix).

This format left us, however, dissatisfied. We felt a need to go beyond the tables, to look in detail at what was happening when individual children talked to their mothers and teachers. This was not simply a desire to give life to statistical tables by presenting illustrative examples. It was also because we thought that a study of specific conversations in depth would provide insights not obtainable from statistical analysis, and would generate new ideas about the issues with which we are concerned. This book, therefore, includes not only a discussion of our quantitative data, but also detailed discussions of individual conversations, and a study of one particular girl at home and at nursery school.

2

How we carried out this study

In this chapter we describe how we chose the children for the study, and how we recorded their conversations and prepared the transcripts. We also discuss the issues of whether our sample was representative, and how far the presence of recording equipment and an observer affected what we were trying to observe. Readers who are more interested in our results than our methods may wish to skim through or omit this chapter.

Selection of children

Because observing children, and analysing their conversation, is a very time-consuming process, we had to restrict our sample to only thirty children, fifteen in each of two social class groups. (Our criteria for social class are described in Chapter 6.) In order to make a valid comparison between the two groups, it was necessary for the children's circumstances to be as alike as possible in every way except social class. We have already explained our decision to study only girls. Young children develop very fast, so our next decision was to select girls within a fairly narrow age range, that is, within three months of their fourth birthday. At a younger age children's speech is sometimes hard for strangers to understand. By the age of four and a half, on the other hand, children in London often start at full-time primary school.

Since we wanted to observe children both at home and at nursery school, we included only children who went to a morning nursery school or class, and who were at home with their mothers in the afternoon. This was an easy requirement to fulfil, since the great majority of children only attend nursery schools and classes part-time. It did mean that families where the mother worked full-time were excluded from our study – but only 6 per cent of British women whose youngest child was under five worked full-time at that period. A third of the mothers in our study had part-time jobs in the mornings or evenings. We also excluded families where the father was likely to be at home in the afternoons, since this would have introduced a major variation into the home setting.

The next major requirement of the selection process was that the middle-class and working-class children should be drawn from the same schools. This was because we wanted to ensure that any differences between the children's behaviour at school, or the staff's behaviour towards them, were not caused by differences between teachers or schools which cater for one particular social class. All the children had been at the school for at least a term.

Our next decision was to exclude families that were in some ways atypical. Hence, we excluded families where the main language spoken was not English. We also excluded single-parent families and families with more than three children, on the grounds that they may function differently, and that less than 10 per cent of British children at that time lived in families of either of these types.[1]

Having decided on our criteria, we had now to find the children to fit them. In order to do this, we contacted all the nursery schools and classes in two local education authorities which we knew to contain sizeable proportions of children from both middle-class and working-class homes, and asked for the cooperation of the staff. No school declined to take part in the study. We then, with the help of the staff, drew up a list of children of the right age, sex and family size. The mothers of these children were contacted, and a short interview was held at the school with each mother. At this interview we asked the mothers for information not necessarily available to the staff, for example, what their educational qualifications were, what their husband's occupation was, and who looked after the child in the afternoons. We explained what the study would involve, and asked whether, if their child was selected, they would cooperate. Surprisingly, all agreed. Finally, we randomly selected two – or in some cases four – of the children who met our criteria from each school, with the proviso that equal numbers of working-class and middle-class children should be selected from each school. We aimed to involve as many schools as possible in the study so that our findings would not be distorted by any unusual features of a particular school or teacher. Eventually, we found our thirty children, fairly evenly distributed between nine different nursery schools and classes.

This selection process was lengthy, and the final sample very small, so the reader may reasonably wonder how representative it was. Certainly, our findings cannot be generalized to the groups we excluded, for example, large families and non-English-speaking families. A further consideration is that all our children attended a part-time nursery school. Nursery schools in Britain are free, but not compulsory, so it could be argued that families who use them, especially working-class families, are atypical. We had no evidence that this was the case – for example, when we asked the mothers why they were sending their children to school, none of the mothers gave 'educational' reasons. Usually, they said that the school was very near, and that their child got bored at home or needed company. However, the strongest reason for believing that our sample is not atypical is that many of our findings have been confirmed – in the much larger studies of three- and four-year-old boys and girls at home carried out by Wells in Bristol and Davie in Stoke.[2] The studies are not entirely comparable with ours, since Davie did not record conversation, and Wells only recorded ninety-second samples of talk, but where they overlap, the findings are similar.

Recording the conversations

The days of recording conversation by pen and paper are now over. Electronic audiorecording allows the researcher to listen to language that is hard to understand, many times if necessary. It also allows two or more independent observers to listen to the conversation and compare their interpretations.

We briefly considered the idea of using video or film, but soon dismissed this idea. Not only would the cameras and other equipment be obtrusive, but they would also be difficult to move around. We wanted the children to be free to move wherever they wanted, both at home and at nursery, and none of us relished the idea of running from one end of a playground to the other, carrying a heavy camera, and trying to keep an energetic four-year-old in the picture. Further, the analysis of video films is enormously time-consuming.

The audiorecording method we finally adopted, in order to allow the children freedom of movement, was to attach a radio-microphone to the child's clothing. This method had been used successfully by other researchers.[3] Radio-microphones are small microphones – like those used in TV interviews – which are connected by a lead to a small transmitter: this must also be worn by the child. The transmitter sends out a signal to a receiver which in turn feeds it into a tape-recorder.*

We experimented with different methods of attaching the radio-microphone to the child before reaching our final solution. This consisted of adapting an attractive sleeveless dress which could be worn by itself or as a tunic over a T-shirt or trousers. The manufacturer kindly provided us with a supply of eight of these dresses in different sizes and colours. The microphone was sewn into a padded pocket on the front of the dress, about fifteen to twenty centimetres from the child's mouth. The lead from the microphone was sewn into the lining of the dress, and ended up at the transmitter, which was in another padded pocket at the back of the dress. The transmitter was quite heavy at first, but we reduced its weight to 150 grammes by replacing its brass casing with a lighter aluminium casing. A short wire aerial hung loosely down from the transmitter inside the lining of the dress. The recording equipment was placed in the room in which the child spent the most time (usually the classroom at school, and the living room at home) so that the observer could easily check that it was working. Where possible, it was put out of the child's direct line of vision, for example, on top of a piano or behind a sofa.

There were inevitably some technical problems. Batteries would run out unexpectedly, leads would work loose, and the transmitter would sometimes fail to work at all. In addition, the recordings were generally of poorer quality if they were made near a main road – the receiver seemed to be particularly sensitive to taxi and lorry engines. On the whole, however, the arrangement worked surprisingly well, and we were able to obtain reasonably clear recordings.

What gave us most anxiety, though, was not whether the equipment would work, but whether the child would agree to wear the dress at all. Most four-year-olds have very definite ideas about what clothes they

* We used a speed of 1.7/8 inches per second on five-inch triple play reel-to-reel tape, giving a maximum recording period of three hours per tape. The transmitter was powered by a small nine-volt battery which had to be replaced every four hours. If the microphone is worn by the child, it can record everything the child says, as well as everything said to the child, within a radius of about fifteen feet. The radio-microphone works within a range of about one hundred yards of the tape-recorder; this means that the child could run freely about in the nursery playground, or in her garden, or on the pavement outside her home, and still be recorded.[4]

will wear, and we were seriously concerned that the child might refuse to put the dress on in the morning, or would take it off halfway through a recording session and refuse to wear it again. In the event, two children had to be excluded from the sample because they would not wear the dress. One or two children initially expressed dissatisfaction with it, but were persuaded by their teachers or mothers to carry on. Occasionally, if, for example, the child wanted to go in a paddling pool, the dress was taken off and for that period the observer recorded the conversation by pencil and paper. In fact, most of the children seemed to like the 'special dress', as it was usually called, perhaps because it made them feel a little bit special or important. We found it was best to ask the mothers to put the dress on the child first thing in the morning, rather than either attempt to do so ourselves, or ask the teachers to do so.

Presence of an observer

At the same time that we were developing our recording technique, we were also grappling with another problem; was it necessary for one of the research team to be present while the recordings were being made? We soon discovered that an observer was essential. When we tried making recordings without an observer present, we found it very difficult to work out what was happening. This was particularly so at nursery school. Young children's voices sound very similar when recorded, and from the tape alone it was very difficult to identify which child was speaking or being spoken to at any given time. In addition, much of what the child said – and what was said to the child – only made sense if one knew exactly what was going on. A remark such as 'I can't do this, because of this thing here . . .' is virtually incomprehensible without knowing the context.

The observer, then, had to follow the child fairly closely, in order to hear her conversation, and note exactly what she was doing. Only one child was observed at school each morning. Whenever possible, the observers tried to stay out of the line of vision of both adults and children, but nonetheless they must have seemed very intrusive.

The decision to use an observer brought us face-to-face with perhaps the biggest problem in observational research: how much does the presence of an observer affect what is being observed? In our case we were not only going to use an observer, but we also wanted the child to wear a special dress, fitted with a radio-microphone and a transmitter.

Was it not likely that this undoubtedly bizarre intervention into the lives of young children and their families would produce very unnatural and untypical conversations?

Most researchers who are experienced at doing observational work with young children believe that the effect of the observer is minimal. Our own previous experience in nurseries had suggested that, after an initial acclimatization period, young children, certainly under-fives, ignore the observer. However, it seemed unlikely that this would be the case for either children or parents in private homes, where a stranger is much more obtrusive. As parents ourselves, we found it hard to believe that we would behave normally with our children if a strange observer was sitting in the corner of the room noting down what was going on. The crucial question was whether the mothers would be so powerfully affected as to invalidate the results.

Given the importance of this question, it is surprising how little research has been addressed to finding out what effect an observer actually has. This is no doubt because observer effects are intrinsically difficult to measure. One approach which has been used is to compare a situation with or without an observer present. For example, two studies in America compared the data collected when an observer was present in a private house with data collected when a tape-recorder was left in the home.[5] In each case there were no significant differences between the two conditions. The problem with these studies is that there is no means of assessing what effect the tape-recorder by itself had on the families. Short of secretly concealing oneself in a cupboard, a true 'observer-absent' situation cannot be measured.

An alternative way of assessing an observer effect is to use a habituation technique. The researcher assumes that any effect due to the observer will diminish with time, and that this can be monitored by carrying out a number of successive observations. Of course, as long as the observer is present, one can never be sure that the observer effect has completely habituated and the family is behaving normally. Nevertheless, marked changes over a period of time would suggest that an initial observer effect is diminishing.

Previous research on this question suggested that some aspects of family behaviour might be affected differently from others. For example, those researchers who looked at the amount of behaviour directed towards the observer, or at the number of comments about the recording equipment, found that these kinds of behaviour rapidly diminish over the first few visits.[6] On the other hand, studies which looked at other aspects of the participants' behaviour found no significant changes over as many as six, seven or ten visits.[7]

In view of the inconclusiveness of previous research, we carried out a small pilot study to investigate for ourselves what effect our presence might have. In this pilot study we recorded nine children, both at home and at nursery school, over four successive days, using our special dress and with an observer present. As in the main study, all the observations at home were carried out by women: Helen Carmichael and Gill Pinkerton. We felt (perhaps incorrectly) that a male observer might add to the mothers' awkwardness, as well as possibly causing talk in the neighbourhood. However, some of the school observations were made by Martin Hughes.

As a first test of the effect of an observer, we measured the amount of conversation that was obviously related to the equipment and the observer's presence. This included talking about the observer or the equipment (e.g., 'Mum, when's that lady going away?'), as well as trying to engage the observer in conversation or get her to join in a game. As other researchers had found, this kind of behaviour was greatest on the first day of observation – both at home and at school – but rapidly diminished after the first day.

We then measured those aspects of talk which we thought might be affected if an adult tried to impress an observer. These included the total amount that the adult talked to the child, the amount of 'control' talk or discipline, and the amount of time spent playing with the child, teaching or explaining things to her, and giving her individual attention.

When we looked at how these categories changed over the four visits, we were somewhat surprised by what we found. We had expected that the observer's presence would be much more of a disruption at home than in a busy nursery school, and that, if there were any changes over time, these would occur at home rather than at school. In fact, we found the opposite. At home, there was no systematic variation at all from one visit to another on any of our measures. At school, however, a definite pattern emerged. The amount of staff talk to the child on the first day was significantly *lower* than on any of the other days. On the second day it doubled in amount, and on the third and fourth days gradually decreased. There were no significant changes in the *way* in which the staff talked. It seemed very much as if the staff were avoiding the child being observed on the first day, and subsequently gave her a good deal of attention, which gradually tailed off.

If this is so, then why did a similar process not occur at home? The answer may be that it is very much harder to vary the amount of attention you give to a child at home than in nursery. At home, the pattern of interaction between mother and child seemed to be firmly established, and based on deeply rooted habits. Indeed, most of the mothers told us that they had very definite patterns of how they spent their afternoons, and that during our visits they simply followed these routines as usual. It would hardly have been possible for them to avoid their child without eliciting protests, although it is possible that both teachers and mothers gave the children more attention than usual during the study.

It does not, of course, follow that because their behaviour did not change over four days the mothers were not in some way affected by the observer's presence. It seems more reasonable to conclude that this period was not long enough for them to habituate to the observer's presence. The important question for the study was whether the effect of the observer was such as to produce serious distortions in the way in which the mothers and children talked.

There are two sources of evidence with which we can try to answer this question. First, we asked the opinion of the mothers themselves. Some weeks after the recording one of the research team (Helen Carmichael) returned to interview them and, among other questions, asked them how they felt that they and their child had been affected by the recording. More than half of the mothers (eighteen out of thirty) said that they *had* been affected, in four cases on the first day only. None of them felt that they had been affected to such a degree that the recordings were unrepresentative; most would say only that they had felt 'a bit ill at ease, not quite natural'. Three said that they had been more patient than usual, but one said that she had shouted more than usual. Three said that they had tried to do more things with their children than they would normally have done. As to the children, nearly half the mothers (fourteen out of thirty) thought that they too had been affected by the recording, in three cases on the first day only. Three children were said to have been quieter than usual, while one 'talked twice as much as usual'. Two were said to have been better behaved than usual, but three 'showed off'.

This was undoubted evidence of an observer effect, but the observers themselves thought that the effect had been quite small. The mothers did not *seem* ill at ease; family behaviour seemed very 'normal' – tempers were lost, and children sometimes sworn at and slapped. Mothers got on with private activities, such as reading the paper, washing their hair, phoning their friends; children cried, sulked and shouted. To some extent, readers can make their own assessment from the conversations quoted in this book. Our own conclusion was that the mother's behaviour was probably modified in whatever direction she thought represented 'good mothering'. We doubted if it had been drastically altered – if only because of the important role played by the children's expectations and demands in shaping their mothers' behaviour.

On the strength of our pilot study, then, we decided not to use the data collected on the first visit to either school or home. We also decided that our recordings were sufficiently representative of 'normal' life to justify our proceeding with the main study.

When to record

Initially we tried various lengths of recording, up to six hours at a stretch. This was far too much of a strain on the observer – and probably the family – and we finally decided on a two-and-a-half-hour period. This meant that we could record a session without changing the tape, at a speed fast enough to get a good-quality recording.

In our pilot study we had made recordings of the children at three different times in the afternoon on different days – starting at 12.30, 2.30 and 4.30. We found that most talk happened in the first period, over lunch, and most play during the second period. From 4.30 onwards family life was much more chaotic, with fathers and sometimes older children returning home, and everybody's tempers becoming increasingly frayed as bedtime approached. We decided in the main study to record from whatever time lunch started – usually about one o'clock – for two and a half hours. This would give us both the lunchtime conversation and the afternoon play period, up till the time when some of the mothers set out to collect an older child from school. At school, we recorded the whole of the morning session (usually two and a half hours), from the time that our child arrived at school, except for periods when the whole class was brought together for a story or music.

Since there was not a great deal of adult–child talk at school, we recorded for three mornings at school, and two afternoons at home, in each case discarding the first day's recording.

Preparing the transcripts

When we had made the tape-recordings, we were faced with a major task: that of listening to the tapes and extracting and transcribing all conversations between the children and adults, both at home and at school.

For this purpose we employed a team of five transcribers who listened to the tapes on headphones and, using the observers' notes, located and typed out all the adult–child conversations. The transcripts were then checked over again by the observers, who corrected any mistakes or misinterpretations and added on the right-hand margin full notes, and where necessary drawings, about the context. The final product was a complete record of the conversation.

Researchers considering a similar study should note that this process of transcribing and editing is very time-consuming. One hour of a school tape took nine hours to transcribe, and a further three hours to check over and add context notes. One hour of a home tape took even longertwelve hours to transcribe and a further five hours to check and context. This adds up to approximately four thousand hours of work involved in collecting the data, transcribing it, checking it and adding context notes, before the analysis could even begin.

The nursery school setting

A brief description of the nursery schools and classes in the study may be helpful. All were run by the local authorities and, like the rest of the educational system, did not charge fees. Children aged from three to five years old attended for either the morning or the afternoon, each session lasting for two and a half or three hours. The class size varied from about twenty to twenty-five, and each class included both three- and four-year-olds, and was staffed by a trained teacher and a nursery assistant, sometimes helped by a student.

All the classes were plentifully supplied with a wide range of play materials. The children could choose their own play activities, and were usually free to go in and out of the adjacent outside playground when they wished. The staff's role was to suggest and stimulate play, to demonstrate craft or new play activities, and to talk to the children about what they were doing. Most schools had one or two group activities in the morning, which all the children were expected to join, usually a story and music session. We did not record these sessions, but we transcribed all the other staff–child conversations.

To simplify our analysis we did not differentiate between teachers, assistants and students, all of whom were considered 'school staff'. Although one might certainly expect differences between their conversational styles, the decision seemed legitimate, since, from the point of view of the children, all the adults present helped to provide the adult language environment of the school. However, when we quote conversations in this book, we refer to the grade of the staff.

What was left out of the transcripts

Since we were concerned with adult–child conversation, our study certainly does not give a complete picture of the child's day. Most of the time at school the children were not talking to the staff, but playing on their own or with other children. Quite often at home the children played in the garden or on the pavement or were in a different room from their mothers. Wherever the child went, the observer stayed reasonably close to her.

What we told the teachers, mothers and children

We told the teachers and mothers that we were studying language development in normal four-year-olds. We did not mention that we were also studying adults' talk to children, for fear of making them self-conscious, although from their remarks it was clear that they usually realized that their conversation, too, was picked up by the microphones. We asked both staff and mothers to try to behave as normally as possible, and explained that we would not be able to chat to them until the recording was over. We asked the mothers to explain to the children as much about the study as they thought they would understand. If the children tried to talk to the observers during the recording, they gave very minimal answers, and gently explained that they were busy. Staff and mothers were usually very friendly and welcoming. After we had finished both recordings at home, we often played back some of the tape to the mothers. At the end of the research project we held meetings in some of the schools for the staff and parents involved in which we described our main findings.

3

Learning at home:
play, games, stories
and 'lessons'

In this chapter and the next we discuss what children are learning from their mothers at home, and the contexts in which this learning takes place. As we pointed out in the first chapter, this question has rarely been studied. Some professionals believe that many children – particularly in working-class areas – learn little or nothing at home, and spend most of their time watching TV. In addition, parents are frequently urged by professionals to spend more time talking to, and playing with, their children, in order to help develop intellectual and linguistic skills. But these opinions and advice are offered in the absence of any real knowledge of how parents are currently educating their children.

One way to approach this question is to ask parents what they believe they are teaching their children at home. When we interviewed the mothers in our study we found that all of them had definite ideas about what they were teaching their children. Manners and obedience were usually mentioned first. Thereafter, twelve of the middle-class mothers, and four of the working-class mothers, indicated that a very wide curriculum was taught: 'We discuss everything'; 'She mainly learns through my answering all her questions'; 'Everything, how life is organized'. Eight of the working-class mothers, but only one middle-class mother, mentioned domestic and household knowledge: 'Housework'; 'Shopping'; 'Everything that goes on in the family'. Nine mothers in both social classes said that they were teaching their child to read, write or count. Only two mothers mentioned that they were teaching language, and no one referred to thinking skills or intellectual development.

We were able to compare these answers with our observations of what the mothers actually talked to the children about. Although we only analysed two and a half hours of recording, a great deal of talking occurred in this time. We began by dividing our transcripts into conversations, that is, episodes of talk on the same subject, ended by a change of subject, or by mother or child moving out of earshot. We then measured the length of the conversations by the number of 'turns' contributed by the participants. Thus the following conversation:

MOTHER: Come here, please
CHILD: In a minute
MOTHER: No, come right away

is a conversation of three turns.

On average, the children held twenty-seven conversations an hour with their mothers, and on average each of these conversations lasted for sixteen turns. There was a good deal of variation in these respects; at one extreme, one child held ninety-eight conversations with her mother during the afternoon, while another had only thirty. However, in all but the last mentioned home a great deal of talk occurred – these mothers did not require injunctions to talk more to their children.

The reader may wonder whether the presence of the observer led the mothers to talk more frequently than usual to their children. This issue was discussed in Chapter 2, but it is worth adding that the amount of talk was controlled as much by the children as the mothers – more than half the conversations were started by the children. In all the home recordings there were some quiet periods, when the children played in their rooms or in the garden.

In order to examine what the mothers were teaching, we scanned each of the mothers' turns of talk to see what information it conveyed. We looked at whether the information was about control (what the child should or shouldn't do) or about other kinds of knowledge. Information which was not about control was coded under one of twenty-seven headings, ranging from basic information about colour and size, through information about time relationships, family relationships, social interactions, to general knowledge and school-type subjects such as history, geography and science. Talk which conveyed only minimal information – for example, 'Yes', 'No', 'Thanks', 'That's nice' – was not coded. Questions, offers and suggestions were also excluded from this particular analysis, although questions were later analysed separately. A turn of talk which included a variety of information could be given more than one code.

On average, 28 of the mothers' 200 turns of talk per hour were concerned with control. The control issue that occurred most frequently in homes of both social classes was waste and damage: 'Don't spill it', 'Be careful not to break it', 'Mind where you put it' and so on. The issue of manners – such as correct table manners, or saying 'Please' and 'Thank you' – arose almost as frequently.

Much more of the mothers' talk was concerned with giving information that was not to do with control. On average, 150 turns an hour contained information on some topic – a vast amount for any child to be receiving. This information covered a wide range of topics. All but two mothers gave information from at least twenty-two of the twenty-seven categories of non-control information. The most frequently imparted category of information was concerned with the child's play, and the second largest category with information about members of the family, family relationships, baby care and development and domestic matters. Information about colour, size and number was also frequently given, as was general knowledge, including information about history and science. This information was usually given in very small snippets, and not in the form of 'lessons'. 'Science' mainly took the form of information about plants and animals. For example, Ruth was watching her mother weed when she saw something unfamiliar:

CHILD: There's a dead onion.
MOTHER: No, they're not dead onions, they're bulbs.
CHILD: Are they dead?
MOTHER: No, they'll come up again this year. They store all the food from the old leaves, they all rot down. It stores food, and the next year it comes up again.

Helen was watching a TV nature programme, when she saw something of interest:

CHILD: What's that, Mummy?
MOTHER: It's a chrysalis. After they've been caterpillars, when it's time for them to start being butterflies, they make a sort of shell for themselves and stay inside it for a while. They change into butterflies: That one's just come out of his chrysalis.

'Geography' usually took the form of information about where different places were. This was often in relation to holiday plans, but sometimes, as in the conversation quoted on page 28, in relation to play. 'History' was often prompted by pictures in a book:

MOTHER: And that's a knight. It's a man they called a knight, that used to fight, with a sword. And what's all this he's got on his body? [No answer] He's got armour on, like that man in the film.

In the rest of this chapter, and in the next chapter, we will consider in some detail the contexts in which this wide range of information was conveyed to the children. It was immediately obvious that some teaching occurred in recognizably 'educational' contexts, of the kinds mothers are urged to use, such as play and stories. Other teaching, however, occurred incidentally in the course of simply living and chatting together. In this chapter we will discuss how teaching occurred in four types of 'educational' context – play, games, stories and 'lessons'.

Learning through play

Play is generally considered the educational context *par excellence* of the preschool years. The value of learning through play was first put forward by the German educationalist Friedrich Froebel (1782–1852). The kindergarten and nursery school movement which developed from his writings freed young children from the tyranny of sitting in rows chanting and writing their ABC. Much later, Piaget provided a psychological justification for the doctrine, by arguing that the child's active exploration of a wide variety of objects is an essential precursor of later verbal and cognitive understanding. These ideas are now taken very much as axiomatic within the world of early childhood education.

But by no means all parents are familiar with this 'developmental' theory of play. Working-class parents in particular, and parents from other cultures, may regard play simply as a way in which children amuse and occupy themselves. One of us (BT) found in an earlier study that parents who take this view are often puzzled by, or even hostile to, the priority given to play by nursery school teachers.[1] Equally, professionals worry that these parents, by not playing with their children, may deny them educational opportunities.

In the present study we were able to see how much the mothers played with their children in the afternoon, and what the children seemed to be learning through this experience compared with what they seemed to be learning from their mothers in other contexts. When we interviewed the mothers after the recordings, we asked them for their views on play.

Our first question was whether they thought that play was important, and, if so, for what reasons. All the middle-class mothers, and eleven of the fifteen working-class mothers said that they thought play was important for their child. In giving their reasons, a few spoke of the child's need to express herself, but most talked about what the child learnt through play. Ten of the middle-class mothers and five of the working-class mothers singled out imaginative play as especially valuable. A few of them explained this value in the terms that most psychologists would use (i.e., extending the imagination, allowing for the working out or release of emotional tension or conflict). More often they mentioned its value in helping the child understand the adult world by acting out roles ('It's practice in life', 'She learns by copying adults'), or, in one case, 'It brings us closer together'. The working-class mothers were more likely to mention the value of play in teaching specific skills ('Snakes and ladders teaches her numbers', 'She learns how to draw and colour'). Four working-class mothers said that they thought play was not important, but just a way of occupying children.

But, although the majority of mothers thought their children learnt through play, fewer believed that it was important that they themselves played with their children. When we asked them, 'Do you think you ought to play with her?' most mothers in both social classes (twenty-one out of thirty) said no, arguing that children ought to be able to play on their own or with other children. This was no doubt partly because the majority of mothers did not especially enjoy playing with their child. Only seven gave an unqualified 'Yes' to the question, 'Do you enjoy playing with her?' Seven gave an unqualified 'No', and the rest gave such qualified answers as 'I prefer her to play with other children', 'If I'm in the mood', 'As long as she's a good loser'.

During the afternoon's observation we found that all but three working-class and two middle-class mothers played at some point, however briefly, with their child, and all the mothers talked to the children about their play. Most often, they would comment or make a suggestion while they got on with their housework or drank coffee. The average time spent in play by those mothers who did play with their child during the two-and-a-half-hour recording was thirty-five minutes.

The briefest time was twelve minutes, the longest was over two hours. There was no social class difference in this respect.

Learning through imaginative play

It was impossible to say how much imaginative play occurred at home. Unless the child talked about what she was doing, we had no means of knowing whether, if she played with a doll's house, for example, she was lost in fantasy or simply arranging the furniture. However, two-thirds of the children of both social classes talked to their mothers about an imaginative game at some point in the afternoon. Generally, they were playing on their own. Six middle-class mothers, but only one working-class mother, actually enacted a role in these games.

These mothers, whether intentionally or otherwise, usually turned the occasion to educational advantage. The games were almost always initiated and shaped by the children, but the mothers rapidly took on a major role. Presumably the children appreciated their mothers' participation enough not to resent this. If they had done so, they would surely have stopped playing. In fact, these games were usually very lengthy, and eventually terminated by the mother rather than the child.

Susan and her mother spent a good part of the afternoon sitting on the sofa going on a sequence of fantasy journeys. Throughout, Susan's mother, while joining in the game, ensured that the fantasy followed real-life geographical constraints, and provided a stream of geographical information. We quote a small part of this sequence:

CHILD: Do you want to go in the park?
MOTHER: Don't think so. Do you?
CHILD: Do you want to go to London?
MOTHER: Mm . . .
CHILD: I paid the London ticket.
MOTHER: What are we going on?
CHILD: We're going on . . . we got to go over the bridge. D'you want to go to a castle at Grandma's?
MOTHER: No, it's not in London. Where does Grandma live?
CHILD: In Shatham.
MOTHER: Chatham. Not London, though, is it?

After some negotiation they decide to go to London, and buy some 'tickets'.

> MOTHER: There's the tickets, don't lose them. Else you'll be turned off the bus. Why are we going to London by bus anyway? It's quicker by train.

Susan liked the idea of a train journey, and they set off to London on the train. Susan enlivened the journey by the introduction of a 'thief' who tried to steal their money and tickets. After a digression to discuss the nature of Father Christmas, she returned to the topic of journeys:

> CHILD: Where do you want to go now?
> MOTHER: Oh, um, some nice Greek island. I have to go by aeroplane though. Can you fly?
> CHILD: Not really . . . only pretend.
> MOTHER: All right, we'll go to Greece then.
> CHILD: Here! [Hands out a ticket]
> MOTHER: Thank you.
> CHILD: Where is Greece?
> MOTHER: [Laughs] Oh, now you've asked me! In the Mediterranean.
> CHILD: What?
> MOTHER: It's a long way. It's the name of a country. It's just along the coast by Shoreham [laughs]. That's what Helen [Susan's older sister] used to say. She used to think that Africa was next to Shoreham.

Susan made aeroplane noises for some time, and eventually they arrived in Greece:

> CHILD: Here!
> MOTHER: Oh, we're here already, are we? That's a very nice journey, thank you pilot. [She gets off the sofa, which is the aeroplane, and goes to the kitchen to get a cigarette]
> CHILD: Hey, you gone back to your home.
> MOTHER: I'm in Greece.
> CHILD: No, you're not. You walked back home, a long way away.
> MOTHER: Can't walk home from Greece, it's too far.
> CHILD: Why is it?
> MOTHER: It's a long way.

As the game continued, Susan was on the receiving end of a large amount of rather vague information about the whereabouts of places like London and Chatham, Africa, Shoreham and Greece. It is of course open to question as to how much of this she would retain; nevertheless, if this was her mother's habitual way of joining in fantasy play, then she would slowly accumulate some geographical concepts. It seems unlikely, if we examine these extracts, that Susan's mother joined in the fantasy game with any explicit intention of teaching her 'geography'. If she had, her information might have been more precise. Rather, it seems that she introduced geographical information into the conversation because she wanted to anchor the game to real life. This was not fantasy of an 'anything goes' nature, but rather an imaginative development based on underlying reality.

Susan's mother also insisted that the fantasy play should be logically consistent. This comes over particularly clearly later in the game, when Susan invited her mother to accompany her on a 'picnic':

MOTHER: Where are you going for your picnic?
CHILD: Out far in the red country.
MOTHER: In *what* country?
CHILD: The red country.
MOTHER: The red country? Where's that?
CHILD: The North.
MOTHER: The North? Oh. Is it hot or cold there 'cause I want to know if I got to take my shoes and socks [she is in reality sitting barefoot].
CHILD: Er . . . hot.
MOTHER: Oh, so I don't need my shoes and socks. What do I need?
CHILD: Mmm . . . going to sunbathe for a little? Then bring some clothes if it's cold.
MOTHER: You just said it was hot.
CHILD: Well it can get cold.
MOTHER: When?
CHILD: When it's North.
MOTHER: How do you know it's cold in the North?

Susan, not surprisingly, could not answer this question, and instead switched the conversation to the offer of lollipops (made from plasticine) for the picnic. She showed her mother that she'd made them with 'two things sticking down':

MOTHER: Down what?
CHILD: Some of these sticking down it.
MOTHER: Like ice cream running over the edge.
CHILD: Yes.
MOTHER: Mmm . . . but if we've gone North and it's cold, it won't melt.
CHILD: Oh, why?
MOTHER: Ice cream doesn't melt in the cold.

Susan's mother was not the only mother who imposed these kinds of constraints on her daughter's fantasy play. The following extract was from another long fantasy sequence involving a different child, Ann, and her mother. The fantasy was based around the theme of 'hospitals', but arose directly from an incident in real life. About halfway through the afternoon Ann's mother cut her finger on a tin of dog food. Ann was sent off to get cotton wool and Dettol while her mother washed the finger. After they had attended to the cut, Ann pretended that her doll had a cut finger, and that her mother was a nurse in the hospital:

MOTHER: What can I do for you?
CHILD: Her hand has got a cut.
MOTHER: Yes?
CHILD: She was fiddling about with some glass . . .
MOTHER: Yes?
CHILD: . . . and it broke. And she put her finger right in, and it got hurt.
MOTHER: And were you in the room? [Child nods] Then why didn't you stop her from fiddling with the glass?
CHILD: Well, you see, I was asleep, and she, and I couldn't hear her doing it.
MOTHER: Oh I see. Were you asleep in the same room?
CHILD: Yes.
MOTHER: Must have been very tired. Were you very tired? [Child nods] Why were you so tired?
CHILD: Because I was been to work.
MOTHER: Oh, you work, do you? [Child nods] What do you do?
CHILD: Nursing.
MOTHER: [Laughs] You're a nurse, are you?
CHILD: And I wear an overall that is white.
MOTHER: Yes?

CHILD: And it's got a white hat.
MOTHER: I see. So you're a nurse, well why couldn't you look after your own baby, then?
CHILD: But it's in a . . . in my work I ca . . . it's not allowed to take children.
MOTHER: Oh I see. Who d'you look after then in your work?
CHILD: Um . . . people, I have to, when I give them baths . . .
MOTHER: Yeah?
CHILD: They're fat.
MOTHER: Are they?
CHILD: And I have to lift them into their bath.
MOTHER: Good heavens! It must be very difficult . . . so you don't look after children then?
CHILD: No.
MOTHER: Are children people?
CHILD: No.

Ann's mother took a much more active role than Susan's mother in pushing along the fantasy, although it is hard to tell how much this was due to her assumed role as a 'nurse' in the play. The effect of her questioning was that Ann was forced to construct a logically consistent account of her 'child's' accident, her role in it, and her inability to cope with it herself. Indeed, her mother's questions resemble an interrogation of a suspect with a shaky alibi. These questions go way beyond what might be needed simply to act out the role of nurse; rather they seem to be part of a more general insistence on the part of her mother that Ann be logical and consistent in whatever she does.

The final sequence of questions, quoted below, is no longer part of the game, but seems to be an attempt on the mother's part to explore and clarify what Ann means by the words 'people' and 'children'. It followed Ann's statement, quoted above, that children are not people. It is a good example of the pressure often put on the middle-class girls by their mothers to be explicit and precise in their use of language.

MOTHER: What are children then?
CHILD: Well, they're children.
MOTHER: Then what are people?
CHILD: Women.
MOTHER: What about men?
CHILD: Men?

MOTHER: Yeah.
CHILD: Men are men. Women are women.
MOTHER: Yeah, well, who are people?
CHILD: People.
MOTHER: Aren't children people?
CHILD: No! They're childs . . .

These mothers, then, accepted their child's definition of the game, and the role assigned to them in it. At the same time, they exerted a strong influence on the game, particularly by ensuring that it closely resembled the real-life situation on which it was based. This behaviour is consistent with the kind of explanations the mothers gave of why they thought that imaginative play was valuable (page 26) – that is, that it helped the children to learn about the real-life situation on which the fantasy was based. These explanations were very different from those usually offered by psychologists, who tend to see fantasy play as important in helping to resolve emotional conflicts, or develop the imagination. In the course of playing with their children in these fantasy games, the mothers introduced a considerable amount of information. An equally important motive for some mothers seemed to be a desire to help their children to think logically and consistently. We are not advocating that this is the 'right' way for mothers to play with their children. Some may feel that it is best if mothers leave children to develop their own fantasies, and channel their educational efforts into other settings. Certainly this kind of play required concentrated attention from the adult, which many of the mothers were too busy to give or did not enjoy. Joyce's mother, for example, was particularly busy during the afternoon recording session, as she was preparing for the family to go away that weekend. She made only a minimal, though friendly, contribution to her daughter's fantasy game:

CHILD: Mum, I'm on holiday.
MOTHER: Are you?
CHILD: Yeah.
MOTHER: Where are you going?
CHILD: To the seaside where we went. [She goes off on her own, talking to herself, and returns later] Watch me, watch me swim, Mum. [She goes off again, then returns] I went right out in the deep.
MOTHER: Right out in the sea in the deep? You be careful.

CHILD: I went in deep.
MOTHER: Did you?
CHILD: Mm. Can I take some of that [food]?

At this point the conversation returns to the subject of the meal which Joyce's mother was preparing.

Other mothers, even when not busy, were content to initiate rather than take part in imaginative play. Cindy's mother was sunbathing in her garden, watching Cindy digging in the mud:

MOTHER: Why don't you make a cake?
CHILD: Cake?
MOTHER: Mm.
CHILD: All right, I'll make a chocolate cake. Of this? [Points to mud]
MOTHER: Mm.
CHILD: I just don't want to get my hands dirty.
MOTHER: Oh no, don't put your hands in it.

Later, Cindy's mother minimally participated by accepting a 'slice of cake'.

Wendy tried to involve her mother in a fantasy game like Susan's. Although her mother made a token effort, she was clearly rather bored:

CHILD: She's sick, Mummy [playing with her doll].
MOTHER: Sick? What's the matter, then?
CHILD: She can't go to school.
MOTHER: Oh, poor thing. I don't think she likes that dirty old cushion. Needs throwing away. [The conversation changed at this point]

Learning through games with rules

In terms of creativity, games with rules are at the opposite extreme of play to imaginative games. However, they, too, provide the adult with varied educational opportunities. During these games it was not always clear whether the mothers had explicit educational aims, or were primarily entertaining their children and themselves.

The educational potential of games with rules was demonstrated most strikingly by one child, June. During the course of the afternoon, June – whose father was an asphalter and who lived in a council flat – played a series of traditional games with her mother, including Hunt the Thimble, I Spy, and Knockout Whist. These games were clearly part of the family's repertoire of games, and the conversation was sprinkled with references to other occasions when they had been played, for example, with June's older brother and with her grandmother. It was also obvious that both mother and child enjoyed playing these games, and in fact June's mother was one of those who later told us that she enjoyed playing with her daughter.

Of the three games just mentioned, the skills which are acquired through playing Hunt the Thimble are the least recognizable as skills that schools might value, yet nonetheless they contribute to intellectual development. Working out whether an object is visible to another person, knowing whether a particular hiding place is easy or difficult, guiding the other person with remarks like 'cold', 'warmer', 'very hot' etc., and making use of such hints oneself, are all highly relevant to the process of the child overcoming what Piaget has called 'egocentrism'. This term is used by Piaget to refer, not to selfishness, but to the inability of the young child to see events and objects from the perspective of another. According to Piaget, egocentrism is not overcome until about the age of seven. Although in Chapter 5 we shall dispute this statement, there is no doubt that the ability to see another's point of view is a difficult skill, gradually acquired over a long period of time. For four-year-olds, Hunt the Thimble is an intellectually demanding game, which probably makes a valuable contribution to this process.

In I Spy the skills that are being learnt are obviously related to the acquisition of literacy. The main task in I Spy is to identify objects on the basis of their initial letter. There are signs that June was gradually achieving some competence in this area:

MOTHER: My go, right. I spy, with my little eye, something beginning with 'S'.
CHILD: Somethink beginning with 'S'.
MOTHER: And I'm looking at it [looks down at June's feet as she sits on the sofa].
CHILD: Socks?
MOTHER: No.
CHILD: Settee?
MOTHER: No.

CHILD: Table?
MOTHER: No.
CHILD: Shoes?
MOTHER: That's right! It's your go now, go on.
CHILD: I spy, with my little eye, somethink beginning with 'L', 'L', 'L', 'L' . . .
MOTHER: Light? [Child shakes head] Lamp? [Child shakes head] Lighter?
CHILD: [Shakes head] Clock!
MOTHER: Clock? That's 'C'.
CHILD: No . . . OK, I'll do that one agam. I spy, with my little eye, somethink beginning with 'C'.
MOTHER: 'C' . . . [pretends to think] . . . Ummm . . .
CHILD: And I'm looking at it [looks at the clock] . . . and it's up there . . . and it's black.
MOTHER: Ummm . . . [laughs]
CHILD: And it's a clock . . . a clock.
MOTHER: Curtains?
CHILD: No, clock. Like, clock, that's beginning with 'C'.
MOTHER: [Laughs] Clock!

June had obviously a long way to go before mastering basic literacy. But starting to think about words in terms of the letters which make them up is an essential element of literacy, and no mean achievement for her age.

What is of particular interest in the sequence just quoted is the way June's mother laughingly accepts her mistakes and deviations from 'correct' play. This light-hearted removal of tension from the situation may be of major help in the learning process.

June's most impressive performance was when she and her mother played two complete rounds of Knockout Whist. For those unfamiliar with this game, Knockout Whist is a simple card game in which each player starts with seven cards. Players lay down a card in turn, and the player with the higher card wins. Aces count high, but otherwise the cards follow the number sequence, in that a 'four' beats a 'three', and so on. One suit is 'trumps', and players must follow suit if they can. After all seven tricks have been played, the cards are redealt, but this time each player has six cards. The round continues until only one card is dealt to each player.

June seemed to have an understanding of the rules of the game.

However, the game was played at such high speed that it was impossible for the observer to get any reliable record of what cards were played, by whom, and in what order. Instead we have to rely on the recorded conversation between June and her mother which accompanied the game. The transcript of this conversation covered fifteen pages of typescript, and a short extract is given below:

MOTHER: [Deals out six cards each] You have to call. [Child won the previous round, so she decides trumps this time]
CHILD: Ooh, I got a good hand here again, but I can help it [arranges the cards in her hand]. I got two aces here.
MOTHER: You shouldn't tell me what you got, go on, call trumps.
CHILD: I call heart, I not putting a heart down.
MOTHER: Hearts [mother wins the first trick]. That's mine [child wins the second trick]. That's yours [child wins another trick].
CHILD: No, diamonds.
MOTHER: Oh, you've changed your mind. That's mine then [child wins the last trick: she has won four tricks to her mother's two].
MOTHER: So how many you got?
CHILD: Three.
MOTHER: You haven t, count. And I ve got . . .?
CHILD: Two. An' how many did I have?
MOTHER: Four. [Child says something unclear: mother deals five cards each for the next round] Five.
CHILD: Oh, I got a good hand here as well again . . . Ace of spaces.
MOTHER: What you gonna call?
CHILD: Diamonds.
MOTHER: [Looks at child's hand] You haven't got any diamonds.
CHILD: I have, I got one diamond.
MOTHER: You gotta have . . . call one with . . . the highest one. What you got an ace of?
CHILD: Spades.
MOTHER: Well call that then.
CHILD: Spades.

It would be difficult to think of an activity within the capacity of a young child that brings so many mathematical skills together. June, a child of forty-eight months, of average IQ, managed to recognize number symbols, count objects, know which numbers are bigger and smaller than others, as well as identify the suits, manage the cards, and grasp the rules of a whist-type card game.

Several mothers played traditional children's games such as Ludo and Lotto with their children. We do not know whether the games were played in order to teach number concepts, or to entertain the children, or, as seems most likely, for both reasons. Other mothers played avowedly educational games. Mary and her mother played a word-matching game, where a card with a word on it (e.g., 'tin') had to be matched with the appropriate picture. Mary found this game easy. In fact, it was obvious from the following conversation that she was interested in a more difficult aspect of reading, phonics. Her grasp of this skill was much better than June's:

CHILD: [Looking at a card with a picture a fish] How do you write 'kippers'?
MOTHER: How do you think you write kippers?
CHILD: 'Cuh' [pronounces 'C' phonetically].
MOTHER: Mm.
CHILD: 'Ih' [pronounces 'I' phonetically].
MOTHER: Mm.
CHILD: 'Puh' [pronounces 'P' phonetically].
MOTHER: Mm. Two of those. Two 'puhs'.
CHILD: 'Puh', 'puh'.
MOTHER: 'Eee', 'arr', 'ess', 'eee', 'arr', 'ess' [does not pronounce phonetically].

Later in the game, Mary again displayed her grasp of basic reading skills:

MOTHER: That's 'boy'. Can you think of another word with 'oy' in it?
CHILD: Toy.

Mary also played card games with her mother, and had acquired a good grasp of some basic number concepts. During lunch, apparently out of the blue, she held up her fingers and started to add:

CHILD: Does two and two make . . . four [holds up two fingers of each hand]?
MOTHER: Mm.

CHILD: Three and three makes . . . one, two, three, four, five, six
[holds up three fingers of each hand and counts them].
MOTHER: Mm.
CHILD: Count this . . . one, two, three, four, five, six, seven, eight
[holds up four fingers of each hand and counts].
MOTHER: Well done, yes that's right.

The use of the jargon word 'makes' suggests that Mary had not suddenly discovered addition, but was practising a skill her mother had previously taught her.

Teachers are often rightly concerned that parents should not force the pace of academic learning. Our observations suggested that the pace was often set by the children, who would also terminate the educational sessions, when they became too demanding. For example, Penny and her mother did a jigsaw puzzle in which number symbols (e.g., '3') were paired with the corresponding number of objects (e.g., three frogs). Before they started, Penny's mother wanted to remove the higher numbers from the puzzle, but Penny protested vociferously. 'No, not, no no no not no not the difficult ones out. No not put the difficult ones out.' Penny recognized quite a few of the number symbols, but because she could not count the objects on the cards accurately she could not match the pictures correctly with the symbols. Eventually she admitted defeat: 'Mummy, let's not do this one, 'cause this one's terribly difficult. I got to wait till I'm five.'

Beth's mother played a game with her, Stepping Stones, which was part of a commercial 'reading kit'. This kit was designed to help parents teach their children to read at home. It consisted of letters, simple reading books, puzzles and games. In Beth's house the reading lessons appeared to have a regular slot in the day, just after the early afternoon children's TV programmes. The Stepping Stones game is essentially a continuation of the reading activities. The 'stones' are large pieces of paper with words written on them, and these are laid out on the floor. Beth's mother called out sentences like 'I can see Mummy', and Beth jumped around from one stone to the next. She recognized the cards and their meaning well enough to introduce some flexibility into the game. When her mother called out, 'Look at my Mummy', Beth pointed out that the stone 'Mummy' was too far away from the 'my' stone, so she would jump to 'me' instead.

Stepping Stones is an uncompetitive game. The child did not gain anything from breaking the rules, and it was clear that Beth positively enjoyed following them. At one point, for example, she told her mother that she had seen her laying out the 'stones':

CHILD: [Laughs] I wasn't closing my eyes when you were starting.
MOTHER: Oh dear. You must close your eyes then.
CHILD: [Closes eyes] You call when I'm ready.
MOTHER: Ready!

Most board and card games, however, are competitive, and so are potentially fraught with tension. Four-year-olds are quite capable of following the rules of a simple game; their difficulties arise from the constraints of taking turns, not cheating, and winning or losing with good grace. Indeed, younger children often find it easier than four-year-olds to play, since they don't bother too much who wins or loses. By four, some children are starting to care so much about this aspect of playing games that it interferes with any enjoyment of them.

This point was well illustrated by Penny, whom we quoted (on page 38) playing a number-matching game. Penny in fact was unusually whiney on the afternoon we recorded, and the games in which she was involved were none too successful. While her younger brother, Sean, was amusing himself with some picture dominoes, Penny and her mother decided to have a game of Picture Snap. However, even before the game started, Penny made it clear that she was not prepared to follow the rules too closely. She announced that she wanted both the cards with engines on them, and when her mother said she wouldn't automatically get them, she got even more insistent. 'Well, lovey, that's sort of cheating, isn't it?' said her mother. Penny objected to her mother dividing the pack into two equal piles, and wanted more cards than her mother. Her mother then wanted to shuffle the pack so there would be more chance of getting 'snaps', but Penny refused. Eventually the game started, but Penny continued much as before. She was happy only as long as she was winning, and got upset when her mother said 'Snap' first: she even tried to prevent her from taking the cards she had won. Throughout the game her mother kept trying to get her to follow the rules. 'You can't win every time', 'You don't play if you're cheating', and 'People won't want to play with you if you cheat', but all this had little effect.

Most of the children who played competitive games with their mothers found it difficult not to cheat at times. However, some mothers seemed good-humouredly to accept a certain amount of cheating as inevitable, and this relaxed approach seemed more successful than a moralistic one. June, whose game of Knockout Whist we described earlier, was several times caught cheating by her mother. She responded by letting her mother win the next trick:

CHILD: I trump that [but she does not play a trump card].
MOTHER: Oh ho ho, that wasn't a trump.
CHILD: 'Cause I only got two of them, so I trump it.
MOTHER: All right then, go on.
CHILD: An' you can ... I'll let you have that one [she lets mother win the next trick].

In fact, June, perhaps believing that her mother must hate losing as much as she did, deliberately allowed her to win several times:

CHILD: I let you win, a little tiny easy one, you win that one [puts down a low card].

Games for fun

Psychologists place so much stress nowadays on what children learn through play that they often overlook the fact that some forms of play are primarily a source of fun and excitement. This is true of games like 'peep-bo' and chasing, and body-contact play like tickling and turning the child upside-down. Eight working-class mothers and two middle-class mothers in our study played games of this kind with their children during the afternoon, and they were obviously a source of great pleasure. They seemed to spring from, and to express, an affectionate intimacy.

This combination of fun and affectionate intimacy was sometimes expressed in words, rather than in bodily contact. Joyce and her mother played several word games. As we mentioned earlier, Joyce's mother was busy cooking, ironing and preparing for a weekend's caravanning. In any case, she was one of the mothers who later told us that she did not particularly enjoy playing with her daughter. For most of the afternoon Joyce was happily involved in helping her mother, and chatting to her, and at times these conversations became games. Here are two examples:

MOTHER: It's done, Joyce, it's done [looking at meat in the saucepan].

CHILD: Can I see, dear Liza, dear Liza [referring to a traditional popular song].
MOTHER: Dear Liza, dear Liza, there's a hole in my bucket, dear Liza.
CHILD: Oh yeah, dear Liza [looks at meat].
MOTHER: It's done, dear Liza.
CHILD: Dear Liza, dear Liza.
MOTHER: I'll give you, dear Liza, I'll give you, dear Liza, you saucy thing [cuddles child].
CHILD: Then I'll eat you, dear Liza [pats mother's bottom].
MOTHER: I'll eat you, dear Liza.

Later in the afternoon Joyce points out that there are some jam tarts in the rubbish bin:

MOTHER: You can chuck jam tarts away if they're old jam tarts.
CHILD: Yeah, but if they're not, you don't.

This exchange developed into a kind of chanted litany:

MOTHER: No, but if they are, you do.
CHILD: Yeah, but if they are not, you don't. If they are old, you do.
MOTHER: No, if they are, you do.
CHILD: If they're not old, you do.
MOTHER: If they are old, you do.
CHILD: If they're not old, you don't.
MOTHER: For the final and third time, you do.

But Joyce enjoyed this game so much that it continued for another six turns, until her mother wearied of it and changed the subject.

Word games of this kind are a great source of pleasure, but they also have educational value. An important part of the process of becoming literate is the ability to see words as objects which can be reflected upon and manipulated. One route to acquiring this ability is through games like these, in which the child plays with words rather than toys. It is most unlikely that the parents in our study had any notion that the games had any educational merit, and they may well have been less enjoyable if they had.

Games for fun and for excitement were the only kinds of games that some working-class mothers played with their children. It was possibly with these games in mind that these mothers answered, 'Play is mainly a way of amusing children.'

Learning through stories

Most professionals are convinced that it is important for parents to read to young children, in order to increase their vocabulary, stimulate their imagination, and develop a love of books. Our observations suggested that reading stories, or, more precisely, the questions that are asked about them, may have another important function, that of helping the child to clarify her ideas.

Unfortunately, we did not witness a large number of story sessions. Less than a third of the mothers read to the children during our recordings. This may have been because books and stories were linked with bedtime. Certainly, a number of the reading sessions that did occur were suggested by the mothers when the children became tired and fractious. Perhaps for this reason, story times were rarely the cosy, idyllic occasions traditionally portrayed in the media.

In more than half the sessions the children chose the book to be read. This often led to trouble: the children would choose a very difficult book, become bored and restless, but insist on their mothers reading it. A number of sessions ended abruptly when the mothers lost interest, because they thought the book silly, or because the children were not concentrating. In fact, only three story sessions were an unqualified success, in that the child retained interest and concentration throughout the story.

However, although the majority of story sessions were by no means idyllic, this did not mean that they were valueless.

Lynne's story session was a case in point. Like Penny, she was in a contrary mood throughout the afternoon, and her story session was no exception. Before it began, she had cheated all the way through a board game with her mother; she had also asked for puzzles and toys to be taken out and then lost interest in them. Finally, her mother asked in exasperation, 'What is it you *do* want, Lynne?' to which Lynne could only answer, crying, 'I don't know.' 'I think it's time I read you a story, 'cause you're tired, aren't you?' replied her mother. 'Come and give me a cuddle.'

Despite the cuddle, Lynne's contrariness persisted. She selected one of her older sister's library books, but the language was very difficult, and Lynne soon lost interest and interrupted to ask for a different book. 'Do you want me to read this or not?' asked her mother. Lynne nodded, but in a minute she turned several pages over and, pointing to another page, demanded, 'I want to do that one now.' 'No, you can't just flick the pages over,' replied her mother. 'It won't make sense.' However, Lynne persisted in her demands, and her mother, protesting throughout, started to read odd pages.

After several more abortive starts on unsuitable books, Lynne chose an illustrated volume of Bible stories. Despite misgivings – 'You won't understand some of the words' – her mother read it through. Lynne did not understand it very well and constantly interrupted with questions about the pictures and about half-understood passages in the book. In some senses, the story session was a disaster, with Lynne most of the time neither listening to, nor enjoying, the stories. Nevertheless, she did listen closely enough to focus on some aspects of the stories which puzzled her, and which led her to ask some penetrating questions. One episode of questions seemed to arise from her puzzlement over the various pictures of Jesus as baby, man and God in heaven. Her difficulty was increased by her mother's misunderstanding of her question in turn 4:

1. MOTHER: [Reading] 'Then they returned to Nazareth where the boy Jesus grew up.'
2. CHILD: Is that him growed up [pointing to picture of Jesus as a baby]?
3. MOTHER: That's baby Jesus.
4. CHILD: Is he growed up?
5. MOTHER: No, he's a baby.
6. CHILD: You say . . . is he . . . Mummy is he growed up?
7. MOTHER: What, now?
8. CHILD: Mm.
9. MOTHER: Oh, he's up, he's up, he's up in the sky.
10. CHILD: Who?
11. MOTHER: Jesus.
12. CHILD: Now?
13. MOTHER: Mm.
14. CHILD: Is that him a baby [points to picture in book]?
15. MOTHER: That was when he was a little baby, yes, but that was a long, long, long, long, long, long time ago.

Lynne then tried, in turn 16, to clarify what was puzzling her. It is uncertain whether she was still confused by the various manifestations of Jesus, or whether she was raising a general query about development. Her mother opts for the second alternative:

16. CHILD: Mum, why isn't he a baby any more?
17. MOTHER: Well, you were a baby once but you're not a baby now, are you? Mummy was a baby once, but she's not a baby any more, is she? She's a Mummy now.
18. CHILD: No, you're a little girl.
19. MOTHER: *I'm* not a little girl.
20. CHILD: You were.
21. MOTHER: I *was* once, a little girl, just like you, but I'm big now, and I'm a Mummy, I'm your Mummy.
22. CHILD: How did you get big?
23. MOTHER: You grow.
24. CHILD: How?
25. MOTHER: When you were a little baby, you were only about that big [mother holds hands apart], but look at you now . . . You couldn't speak, all you could do was cry.
26. CHILD: And I could say 'Ga-Ga'.

All the story sessions at home were punctuated by questions from the children, usually in large numbers. To a lesser extent, the mothers also asked questions. In this respect the story sessions formed a strong contrast to the TV sessions. When mother and child were watching TV together, we found that the children usually sat quietly, and generally asked very few questions. Their mothers, on the other hand, did a lot of talking, pointing out anything that interested them, including links with the child's own experience. They also fed in a lot of relevant general knowledge by their comments.

During the story sessions, the children's comments were nearly as numerous as the mothers', and many of their mothers' contributions were in answer to the children's questions. Thus, apart from the extension of general knowledge and vocabulary which might come from the story itself, the mothers almost always added information of their own. They often linked the story with the child's own experiences; the children themselves sometimes made this link.

In the example that follows, Rosy's mother had finished washing up and offered to read her a story. Rosy chose a book about a puffin, and her mother commented that she had not read this book for a long time. The story started smoothly, with much general knowledge about puffins being transmitted, both in the story and in Rosy's mother's comments. At one point Rosy seemed puzzled by her mother's unusual speech construction:

MOTHER: Spotter puffins are the ones who go out and find out where all the fish are to be had.
CHILD: What do fish be had?

Her mother interpreted her question as asking where the puffins went, and explained this to her. The story continued, but Rosy became very uneasy when the puffins see a boat being shipwrecked:

CHILD: Do, um boats, when they're on, right on the sea, break like that?
MOTHER: Well, not very often, but sometimes they do. If the weather's very bad, and they get thrown against the rocks, they do break up.

Since the family were planning a summer holiday in France, Rosy found this answer unsettling:

CHILD: I, I, I don't want to. I'm not going, but we won't go on, if there's too many people on the boat we won't go on it, will we?
MOTHER: Are you thinking of us going to France? [Laughs]
CHILD: Yeah.
MOTHER: Those boats don't break up.

Rosy was not prepared to be reassured so easily, and contested her mother's less than consistent explanations:

CHILD: Why don't they?
MOTHER: Well, it a only big boats that go out in very stormy weather.
CHILD: But why won't they when we go to France?
MOTHER: Well, we're only going to be on the, in the boat for quite a short time.
CHILD: But it's quite a long way.
MOTHER: It's not very far really, to go from home to France.

The story continued with a helicopter rescue, but the puffin hero was caught in an oil slick. Rosy became very anxious and nervously shook the box she was holding:

> CHILD: That's her son [pointing to another puffin] who looked after her, and she cried.

The puffin is rescued from the slick by a fisherman and taken to his home, where two other puffins come to visit him. Rosy pointed out that a step in the story was missing:

> CHILD: But why did, how did, Puffred and Freebie know where they were?
> MOTHER: I don't know, I suppose they must have seen him.

When Puff recovers, he becomes a spotter puffin and goes fishing with the fishermen, but this left Rosy with fresh anxieties:

> CHILD: But when's his mother coming to collect him?
> MOTHER: Oh well, I expect he sees his mother, quite a lot of his mother.

The story ended, and Rosy announced, 'I don't like it.'

The book had certainly involved her emotionally, in that she 'took on another's sorrows'. All the misfortunes which overtook the puffin Rosy saw as potentially threatening to herself. Not only did she make a clear link between the puffin's shipwreck and her own projected sea journey, but her distress at the puffin's separation from its family seemed to be linked in her mind with her anxiety about the possibility of being separated from her mother. A story which involved the dual trauma of being shipwrecked and of being separated was almost too distressing. Nevertheless, Rosy was able to verbalize these anxieties and obtain some reassurance, even if this reassurance did not match the intensity of her anxiety.

These two examples of story-reading at home serve to illustrate some of the potential educational advantages mothers have in this context. Because of the one-to-one situation, the mother can allow the child to pursue a line of questioning as long as she wishes, without having to cope with the competing demands of other children. The close relationship between mother and child means that the child feels able to express any anxieties that may be aroused by the story. As a result of the mother's intimate knowledge of her child, she is able to interpret indirect references to these anxieties (as in the last conversation, 'Are you thinking of us going to France?'); she can also link what happens in the story to the child's own past experiences and future plans.

'Lessons': writing

In the educational contexts so far discussed the child learns in the course of an enjoyable game or story. Sitting a child down for a lesson is a practice long abandoned by teachers of under-fives, but we discovered it flourishing in a few families.

We observed several working-class mothers teaching their children to write their names, as an exercise in itself, unrelated to other activities. This was sometimes a quick, almost casual, occupation. At other times it was undertaken very seriously.

Samantha was colouring in her colouring book, and drew what looked like a letter 'h'. She showed it to her mother, who suggested she copy the words at the bottom of each page in the colouring book. Samantha did not seem interested in this idea, so her mother made another suggestion:

MOTHER: I'll do your name and you copy it.

CHILD: Yeah.

MOTHER: All right [writes 'Samantha' at the top of the page]. There's your name up there. You try and copy that. Underneath . . . you do it underneath. [Samantha starts to trace over mother's letters, having been taught tracing at school] Not over the top of it. Not like you do at school. You do it by yourself underneath. You try and copy it.

CHILD: Can't [makes a scribble that doesn't look like a letter].

MOTHER: That's not like it, is it?

CHILD: I can do one of these ones [points to letter 'a'].

MOTHER: Do one, then. [Child draws an approximation to an 'a'] Nearly right. Not quite, nearly. You can do one of these, can't you [points to an 'h']? Do one of them.

CHILD: I don't know how to do it. Oh yeah.

MOTHER: Put a bit on the end, going over.

CHILD: [Writes an 'h'] Going over, over a little bump.

MOTHER: That's right. And what about this one [points to the 'm']? That's got two.
CHILD: I can't do . . .
MOTHER: That's 'm' it is, got two humps.

Samantha had difficulty with the 'm' and asked her mother for help:

MOTHER: Yeah, but you'll never learn to do it if I do it for you, will you? Right, look [draws an 'm' under the original 'Samantha'].
CHILD: Yeah.
MOTHER: Two . . .
CHILD: Umps.
MOTHER: Two humps. Right?
CHILD: Yeah. I'll copy that now. Two umps.

Samantha continued to copy the letters:

MOTHER: Now this one with the hump next [points to the 'h'].
CHILD: Oh yeah, I doned it. [Child had done an 'h' earlier]
MOTHER: Yeah I know, but you can't just do them all over the place. You gotta do them next to one another. Next to that one [points to where the 'h' should go].
CHILD: Put a little bump [draws an 'n'].
MOTHER: No, that's not right. You've got to have a bit up here. What about this bit? The tail? [Mother means the upward stroke to convert 'n' into 'h']
CHILD: Oh yeah. [But Samantha draws an 'l' instead, below the level of the writing]
MOTHER: No, there.
CHILD: That doesn't matter.
MOTHER: It does matter. How's someone gonna know what your name is if you write it all over the place?

The lesson continued for some time in a similar vein. Samantha's mother clearly regarded what she was doing as a serious matter, something it was important to get right. She sternly and instantly drew attention to Samantha's errors. She did not allow her to escape from the task, nor was she willing to accept a low standard of achievement. In fact, Samantha's efforts received no praise at all. This approach to teaching is very different from that currently in use in schools, and it is understandable that mothers like Samantha's are distrustful of what they regard as 'soft' progressive methods. Samantha's mother, in fact, seemed to be critical of the school for teaching the children to trace.

It should be noted that Samantha's mother's methods had their merits. She had developed a rich vocabulary ('tails' and 'humps') for teaching, and she seemed to be fairly successful at getting this across. She also managed to get across something of the meaning of the task – for example, when she asked how someone is 'going to know what your name is' if Samantha did not do it correctly. Most important, she succeeded in holding Samantha's attention for quite a long period of time.

In Chapter 7 we quote similar conversations in which Donna's mother teaches her child to count and to spell. Like Samantha's mother, she seemed aware that schools currently use a rather different approach.

As we have seen, it was not only working-class mothers who were teaching their children basic literacy and numeracy, although it was mainly working-class mothers who sat their children down for 'lessons'. One middle-class mother was teaching her child to read through a commercial reading scheme, the game component of which has already been described (page 38). The lessons took place at a regular time each day. A number of other mothers taught reading, writing and number, either in the context of games (see above), or incidentally, during everyday activities (Chapter 4). In none of these cases did we get the impression that the children were being pressured into doing something they disliked, or were not ready for. On the contrary, they were interested in what they were learning and seemed to enjoy, and often initiated, their lessons. Tina, for example, brought some pencils to her mother:

MOTHER: All right, what are you going to do?

CHILD: I'm going to do my name. What are you going to do?

MOTHER: Watch you.

CHILD: No, you must do something. [But mother doesn't]

MOTHER: What's that? [Child does 'O']

CHILD: Orange. Is it like an orange? Now what shall I do? Down up [tries to write 'n']. Oh, what shall I do? Up. That's not the way, is it?

MOTHER: No, this is the way you do it [writes 'Tina'].

Tina tried to copy the letters in her name, but, discouraged by her lack of success, switched to drawing a house.

'Lessons': survival skills

A second area of knowledge which some mothers tried to teach their children in 'lesson' style was how to cope in potentially dangerous situations – for example, crossing the road, being lost, or going into deep water at the seaside. It was clear that the mothers were deeply concerned for their children's safety, and anxious to teach them survival skills. Unfortunately, teaching of this kind, done out of context, is difficult for young children to understand. This may be because it involves hypothetical situations beyond the child's experience, or because it involves the use of concepts, for example, 'left' and 'right', which are somewhat beyond the grasp of a four-year-old. In their attempts to transmit this information mothers tended to resort to techniques they must have remembered from their schooldays – asking questions, and trying to elicit a particular answer. In every case it was doubtful what the child had learned.

Pauline's mother, for example, was helping her to write her name when she asked:

MOTHER: What do you say to a policeman?
CHILD: Ah . . . [Hesitates]
MOTHER: If you're lost.
CHILD: If you lost.
MOTHER: You tell him your . . .? [Leaves sentence hanging for child to fill in]
CHILD: Tell him your name.
MOTHER: You tell him your name [in tone of agreement].
CHILD: Yeah.
MOTHER: And what do you tell him?
CHILD: Do your name.

It was clear that Pauline had no idea of the answer she was supposed to give at this point. Her mother then prompted her:

MOTHER: No you don't do your name. What do you say to him? Policeman? 'Mr Policeman, I'm lost.' [Child laughs]
CHILD: Yeah.
MOTHER: And he'll say to you, 'Where do you live?'
CHILD: I says . . .

MOTHER: What do you say?

CHILD: What did he say? [Both laugh]

MOTHER: No! No, be serious, Pauline. Wh-What do you say?

CHILD: Um ...

MOTHER: When you ... When he asks you, 'Pauline, where do you live?'

CHILD: I said, 'I live down by the grass.' [There is grass outside the flats]

This reply is a nice example of what Piaget called 'egocentrism', that is, the child failing to realize that another person may not share her assumptions and knowledge. Her mother points out the inadequacy of her reply:

MOTHER: Down by the grass! [Repeats this in a derogatory manner] You know the address?

Pauline did not seem to know what an 'address' was, but she did not admit to her ignorance:

CHILD: Eh?

MOTHER: Do you know the address?

CHILD: Yeah.

MOTHER: Yeah and what do you say to him?

CHILD: Um? I've I said ... [Hesitates]

MOTHER: What number house?

CHILD: Um ... number six.

MOTHER: No you don't live at number six.

CHILD: What?

MOTHER: You say, 'My name is Pauline Robinson.'

CHILD: Yeah.

MOTHER: 'And I live at seventeen ...'

CHILD: Yeah.

MOTHER: '... Fleet Flats.

CHILD: Yeah.

MOTHER: You say it.

CHILD: Seventeen.

MOTHER: Sally does. She says it. [Sally is older daughter]

CHILD: Seventeen.

MOTHER: No, you tell him your name.

CHILD: Yeah. I say, 'Seventeen Fleet Flats.

MOTHER: Seventeen Fleet Flats.

CHILD: Yeah.

MOTHER: So when you're lost you tell him that.

CHILD: Yeah [laughs].

MOTHER: He'll say, 'Now we'll take you home to see your Mum.'

CHILD: He don't [laughs].

MOTHER: If he knows where you live he will.

CHILD: He won't. He say, 'Where you live?' I say, 'I live down Fleet Flats.'

MOTHER: Yeah but you gotta give him the number.

CHILD: Look! Number six.

MOTHER: He'll take you to the wrong house. If you tell him number six. You have to tell him the proper number.

CHILD: What?

MOTHER: You say, 'Seventeen.'

CHILD: Yes.

MOTHER: Don't you?

Not only had Pauline forgotten her flat number, but she now seemed worried by the idea of being lost, and by the possible appearance of a policeman. She found it difficult to grasp the idea that she needed to be told what to say *if* she got lost, and *if* she met a policeman. This confusion seemed to be made worse by her mother's use of 'when', rather than 'if', and it was never finally resolved:

CHILD: He don't come today.

MOTHER: Oh no, this is when you're lost. When you get lost.

CHILD: Where?

MOTHER: Well, you never know. 'Cause you're going down the beach in the summer, aren't you?

CHILD: Yeah.

MOTHER: Irene and all. [Irene is a neighbour who sometimes takes Pauline to the beach]

CHILD: Yeah.

MOTHER: And if you lose her.

CHILD: Yeah.

MOTHER: And you see a policeman.

CHILD: Yeah.

MOTHER: And the policeman comes up to you 'cause someone's bound to pick you up on the beach, aren't they? [Mother's tone is sarcastic]

CHILD: Um. I'm gonna see a policeman on the beach tomorrow.

This last remark illustrates clearly that Pauline is still confused by the lesson. At this point she saw a book under the sofa, and changed the subject. Her mother admitted defeat and abandoned the lesson.

Overview

We started this chapter by describing the wide range of topics which the mothers in this study discussed with their daughters. (In Chapter 8 we will show that these topics differed in some respects from those discussed at school.) We then considered the contexts in which the topics were presented, and went on to discuss the recognizably 'educational' contexts of play, games, stories and lessons.

We saw that most of the mothers thought play was important, and spent at least a brief period in the afternoon playing with their children. Imaginative play was a vehicle for giving large amounts of general knowledge, and for an insistence on logical and coherent thinking. Games with rules tended to be more overtly linked with the beginnings of literacy and numeracy. Stories, and the questions they gave rise to, introduced much general knowledge, gave the child an opportunity to clarify what was puzzling her, and allowed her to express her anxieties and to obtain reassurance. Some mothers introduced their children to writing in a formal way.

In this chapter we have quoted conversations from fourteen different homes. Of course, none of the mothers introduced topics to the children in *all* the contexts we have described. In two and a half hours we saw only a brief glimpse of their total time with their children. Nevertheless, it seems likely that these examples give a good representation of the range of topics and learning contexts found in most of the homes.

4

Learning at home:
living and talking together

In Chapter 3 we showed how some mothers turned play, games and stories to educational advantage, while a few gave their children formal 'lessons'. But in most families these occasions were relatively rare. A few mothers devoted most of the afternoon to the child, but generally they had housework to do or younger children to care for. In their free moments they often preferred to drink coffee and smoke, while chatting to their child, rather than play with her.

This did not mean that the children were missing out on learning opportunities. One of our strongest impressions from this study was of the amount which children learnt from simply being around with their mothers: discussing what each was doing, or had done, what they would do next, arguing with each other, and, above all, endlessly asking and answering questions. In this chapter we will describe some of these contexts of everyday life, and discuss what the children were learning in them.

An everyday learning context:
making a shopping list

Making a shopping list is a good illustration of the learning potentialities of an ordinary household event. In the example we quote below, Pauline and her mother had been drinking coffee, and intermittently discussing what shopping was needed. Pauline's mother picked up her shopping list, and started to alter it and add it up. She certainly did not embark on this activity for educational reasons, but she did use the occasion to try to get over to Pauline the message that the contents of a shopping list have to be related to the amount of money available. Pauline was initially curious about what her mother was writing, and assumed it was a note to their friend and neighbour, Irene, who lived upstairs:

CHILD: What you gonna write? Irene?
MOTHER: No.
CHILD: Who?
MOTHER: Adding up.
CHILD: Padding up?
MOTHER: To see how much my shopping comes to.
CHILD: Packing up?
MOTHER: Adding up.
CHILD: I think you said 'padding up'.

Later Irene called round and offered to do some shopping for her in the local 'Vivo's'. The offer was accepted. Irene left, and Pauline's mother started to cross off from her shopping list the items Irene was going to buy for them:

MOTHER: We've only got that little bit of shopping to get now [shows Pauline the list].
CHILD: Mummy? Can I have one of them drinks? Can I?
MOTHER: Get some more drink?
CHILD: Yeah. Can write it down on there [points to where she wants it written on the list]. Up here.
MOTHER: I'll get you some when I go tomorrow.
CHILD: Aw! [Disappointed]
MOTHER: All right? 'Cause I'm not getting it today.
CHILD: No . . . In in the 'Vivo's'?
MOTHER: Haven't got Daddy's money yet.
CHILD: *I've* got no money.

Pauline seems to have misheard her mother at this point. Her mother corrects her:

MOTHER: No, I haven't got enough to get my shopping. All of it.
CHILD: Not all of it?
MOTHER: Irene's just taken five pounds. She'll bring some change

back. If she's got some, she'll bring some change back. It's not enough to get all that. Is it? [Points to the shopping list]

CHILD: No.

MOTHER: See? So when Daddy gets paid I'll get some more money and then I'll go and get the rest.

CHILD: Yeah. That's nice, isn't it, Mum?

MOTHER: Mm . . . I got one, two, three, four, five, six, seven, eight, nine, ten, eleven, twelve [counts items on list].

CHILD: [Joins in counting] Nine, ten, eleven.

MOTHER: Fourteen, fifteen, sixteen, seventeen, eighteen bits.

CHILD: Mum, let's have a look! [Mother shows child the list] Do it again.

MOTHER: We gotta get rice, tea, braising steak, cheese, pickle, carrots, fish, chicken, bread, eggs, bacon, beefburgers, beans . . . Oh, Irene's gone to get them [crosses off beans] . . . peas, ham, corned beef.

CHILD: And what's that [points to a word on the list]?

MOTHER: That's lemon drink [crosses off 'lemon drink']. She's just gone down to get that one. See?

What might Pauline have learned from this conversation? If asked, her mother would probably have singled out the counting activity; when interviewed later, she mentioned that she was teaching Pauline to count. But a great deal more information than this was transmitted. Pauline was learning some basic facts about shopping – for example, that planning and foresight is involved and that making a written list is a useful way of organizing this. She was learning that the number of items that can be bought has to be balanced against the money available, and that this in turn may depend upon whether the wage-earner in the family has been paid yet that week. She might even have acquired some idea of what can be bought for a sum like five pounds. In a wider sense, she was learning how women often support each other, and that she and her mother were financially dependent on her father.

What may be less obvious is that Pauline was also acquiring some important knowledge about the nature of written language. It is often suggested that working-class children do not have much experience of their parents engaging in 'literate' activities; yet a shopping list provides an extremely vivid demonstration of the way in which written language may be used within a meaningful human activity. The power of the written word lies in its ability to link up different contexts in space or tune, and here it is doing precisely that – forming a link between the home, where the decisions and choices are made, and the shop, where they are carried out. The list can also cope with sudden changes of plan – a friend offering to do some of the shopping leads to some items being crossed off the list. The activity is thus not only emotionally but intellectually more powerful than the labelling of pictures, which is likely to be Pauline's introduction to writing when she starts at infant school. It is not clear from the conversation how much Pauline understood about the nature of written language, but her comments suggest she had a good idea of the basic properties and functions of a list.

Looking out of the window

Seeing something novel out of the window was a situation which often created an educational exchange. It was not simply that the child was given some new information about what she saw, but that her intellectual horizons were at times extended in unexpected ways. In the next chapter we discuss at length a conversation which arose from seeing a window-cleaner, in the course of which the child's understanding of the relationship between work and money was extended. The following, much briefer, conversation illustrates how a casual conversation about a neighbour could affect the child's thinking.

Susan and her mother were looking out of the window when they saw a man arriving at the house next door:

CHILD: What has he got a bag on his back for?
MOTHER: He drives a motorbike. He can't carry it. Needs two hands to steer the bike. [Child laughs]
CHILD: Is he gonna do it?
MOTHER: He's just come home from work. It's Dick's lodger. [Dick is the next door neighbour]
CHILD: What?
MOTHER: The man who lives upstairs in Dick's house. The one that you woke up in the middle of the night when you made a noise.
CHILD: What?
MOTHER: The one that lives in the room next door to your bedroom.
CHILD: Does he wake up?
MOTHER: He can hear you when you make a lot of noise.

CHILD: What did he say?
MOTHER: Should think he gets a bit angry.
CHILD: Not gonna scream.
MOTHER: You're not gonna scream. I should hope not.

During this conversation Susan has been told, and appears to have assimilated, not simply information about who lives next door, but also that the neighbour's room is in fact adjacent to hers, and that her activities impinge on, and annoy, him. Information of this kind helps the child to understand her social environment. It may also have more far-reaching implications for her intellectual development. By explaining the way in which the child's activity affects someone of whose existence she had not even known, the mother is helping the child to overcome her 'egocentrism'. As we mentioned earlier when discussing June's game of Hunt the Thimble, we found a number of examples of children not yet four who could undoubtedly take another's point of view. Conversations like the one above were probably an important factor in helping this ability to develop.

Living with babies

Nearly half the girls in our study had a younger brother or sister. Often the baby was awake and active for part of the afternoon's recording. The learning situations that this afforded varied from one family to another.

Pauline's mother spent a good deal of time looking after and entertaining the baby. Pauline seemed very fond of her little sister, Ruthie, and was quite happy to spend a lot of time helping her mother. As a result, she was exposed in the course of the afternoon to a rich stream of information and advice about looking after a baby.

Much of this information took the form of a running commentary on the baby's needs and how to meet them. At the very start of the session Pauline's mother was unable to feed the baby because she was crying: 'She's crying so much she don't want any.' Pauline was sent off to get the baby's bottle, and this instantly stopped her crying: 'See how she stopped? Thirsty.' Ruthie finished the bottle and this was pointed out to Pauline: 'Look at that. She's drunk all that now. She *was* thirsty.' Pauline was then shown how to hold the baby, and how to give her a biscuit, and her mother explained how biscuits help teething. Later

Pauline helped her mother when the baby's nappy was changed. She fetched a clean nappy, and cream for the baby's bottom, and she was allowed to put cream and then powder on the baby. Finally, she was allowed to give the baby another bottle as she was settled down.

Although not yet four, Pauline was given more information about baby care, and more responsibility for helping with the baby, than many professionals would consider giving to much older children.

None of the other children with babies was so closely involved in their care. Some mothers encouraged the girls to give maternal care to their dolls while they looked after the baby. Others tried to divide their own attention between the older child and the baby. Nevertheless, the presence of the baby inevitably widened the children's horizons. Beth, for example, learned that doctors not only appear when you are ill, but also give babies developmental health check-ups. While at lunch, her mother told her:

MOTHER: I saw Dr Jones this morning. I took Naomi to see him now that she is one, if she was all right. If she's a nice healthy baby.

CHILD: And what did the doc, and what did Dr Jones say?

MOTHER: He said that she was *very* well. Except that she's still got her funny snuffly breathing. He said that would just disappear after a while.

CHILD: But what, what did you say to him?

MOTHER: I said I thought she was . . . she seemed very well.

Several mothers used the baby's presence to bring home to the children an understanding that they had once been babies, too. Erica laughed as her baby brother ate with his fingers, and her mother said, 'You used to eat like that when you were a baby. You used to eat chocolate blancmange with your fingers.' Their mothers often interpreted the baby's behaviour – 'I think he wants to get down' – and the children themselves projected into the baby's mind: 'Mummy, I think she wants to go into the garden', 'I don't think he wants any more to eat'.

With the exception of Pauline, who seemed to have entirely taken on a maternal role, the children were ambivalent in their attitude to the babies. At times they played and talked to them lovingly, while at other times they snatched their food and toys, teased and expressed resentment. Mina was the most intensely jealous of the children. At one point in the afternoon, when asked what she would like for her birthday, she replied, 'I'd like Tessa [the baby] put back inside your tummy.' She frequently made fun of Tessa, and although she did not attack her, she did express a death-wish towards another baby:

> MOTHER: You know Phil and Nora? That came round? And she had a baby in her tummy?
> CHILD: Mm.
> MOTHER: Well, it came out yesterday, and she had a little boy!
> CHILD: Oh! Are they gonna come round?
> MOTHER: No, not for a little while yet, I shouldn't think.
> CHILD: Why? Is it gonna die?
> MOTHER: Why should it die?
> CHILD: 'Cause I want it to die. I do.

Mina's mother naturally got very upset by this remark:

> MOTHER: Don't be horrible! What a nasty thing to say! Supposing someone said to you that they'd like Tessa to die, you'd be really sad, wouldn't you? Phil and Nora love their new baby and they'd be ever so sad if they thought you were saying that. Don't really mean it, do you? [Mina shakes her head and changes the subject]

Her mother's comments suggest that she did not realize, or was unwilling to acknowledge, the full force of Mina's angry feelings towards Tessa. Mina herself clearly thought that the baby must reciprocate them. On one occasion Tessa reached out towards Mina:

> MOTHER: She's saying, 'Let me feel your face.'
> CHILD: 'Let me scratch your chin,' she's saying.

Mina's mother tried to foster a more friendly attitude in Mina by explaining about the vulnerability of babies and encouraging Mina to put herself in the baby's place. For example, Mina laughed when the baby cried, and her mother said, 'I really don't like to see children laugh when someone is sad, that's not nice. If I were to laugh at you when you were sad you'd be *really* annoyed. And little Tessa can't say, "Don't laugh at me Mina."' Another strategy of Mina's mother was to point out aspects of the baby's behaviour which might interest her, especially developmental trends ('Have you noticed she's beginning to pick things up?'). What she did *not* do was to involve Mina in the care of the baby.

Thus the mere presence of a baby in the house did not mean that children would have similar learning experiences. While Pauline was virtually serving an apprenticeship in motherhood, for Mina the presence of the baby involved many discussions about kindness and about other people's points of view. We cannot, of course, tell whether Pauline's more loving relationship with her sister was the cause or the result of her involvement in baby care. However, Judy Dunn, in a study of relationships between siblings, found that those children who were encouraged to take a real and practical part in caring for their baby brothers and sisters from the first weeks of their life were particularly interested in, and affectionate towards, them. She also found that this early good relationship tended to persist over a six-year period.[1]

Discussing past and future events

One particularly important feature of the home as a learning environment is the fact that mother and child have a wealth of shared experience to draw on in their conversation. For the most part, this is concerned with events which they have shared together in the past. Often, however, it extended into planned trips or outings in the future – as in Rosy's family holiday in France (page 45).

The next conversation that we discuss is of particular interest because of the sensitive way in which the mother responds to the child's puzzling over a past event. Joyce is having a sandwich for her lunch, while her mother makes a cup of tea and then starts to prepare the evening meal. The conversation was complex, and after quoting it, we will analyse it in some detail:

1. CHILD: Mum, it was good to have something to eat while you was at the seaside, wasn't it? [Mother cuts sandwich]
2. MOTHER: Was good, I agree.
3. CHILD: Well some people don't have something to eat at the seaside.
4. MOTHER: What do they do then? Go without?
5. CHILD: Mm.

6.   MOTHER: I think you'd have to have something to eat. [Kettle boils and mother makes tea]

7.   CHILD: Yeah, otherwise you'd be [unclear] won't you?

8.   MOTHER: Mmmm. When we go to David's school we'll have to take something to eat. We go on the coach that time. [Joyce and her mother are going on an outing with older child's school]

9.   CHILD: Mmm. To the seaside?

10.   MOTHER: Mmm. Probably go for a little stroll to the seaside.

11.   CHILD: Mmm? Yes, I still hungry.

12.   MOTHER: When?

13.   CHILD: When we was at the seaside wasn't I?

14.   MOTHER: We weren't. We had sandwiches, we had apples.

15.   CHILD: But we, but when we was there we were still hungry wasn't we?

16.   MOTHER: No, you had breakfast didn't you?

17.   CHILD: But, we were thirsty when we got there.

18.   MOTHER: Yes, suppose so, yeah we were.

19.   CHILD: What happened? We wasn't thirsty or hungry.

20.   MOTHER: Why weren't we? What happened?

21.   CHILD: Well, all that thirsty went away.

22.   MOTHER: Did it?

23.   SCHILD: Mmmm.

This conversation illustrates both the limitation of Joyce's ability to express herself, and the way in which she struggles to express complex ideas despite these limitations. In this she has varying degrees of success. In the first part of the conversation (turns 1–7) she is able to bring out and contrast two separate but related facts: (1) that it was good to have something to eat at the seaside, and (2) that other people didn't have something to eat. These two statements can even be seen as the premises of a logical argument, with the implication being (3) so what do other people do? We will never know if Joyce would have made this step by herself, for her mother makes it for her (turn 4). Later on in the conversation, however, Joyce is less successful in conveying her meaning, despite her mother's attempts to help her (turns 11–23). All the same, one can only admire Joyce's persistence as she struggles to express herself, culminating in the delightful creation in turn 21: 'all that thirsty went away'.

We do not know what prompted this conversation, although it is likely that eating a sandwich in the kitchen reminded Joyce of eating sandwiches at the seaside. For whatever reason the puzzlement arose, the situation allowed her to express it. Joyce and her mother were together in the kitchen, both engaged in their different activities, with time and space for Joyce's musings to be expressed and allowed to develop.

Her mother plays an important role in the conversation. By her support and responsiveness she helps Joyce express her meaning, and follow through some of the implications of what she is saying. Throughout, the mother is sensitive to what Joyce is trying to say: indeed, at one point (turn 12) she shows considerable insight into her daughter's meaning. On the previous turn Joyce has said, 'I still hungry', a remark which would seem ostensibly to refer to the present situation in the kitchen: Joyce is, after all, eating her lunch. Yet there is an alternative possibility – that she is still referring to the picnic – and her mother somehow picks up this ambiguity and attempts to clarify it in turn 12. As it turns out, the child was still thinking about the picnic, and for the next few turns Joyce's mother tries, albeit unsuccessfully, to discover what is still puzzling the child.

The mother's role, however, is not just a responsive one. In turns 8 and 10 she introduces some new material into the conversation, telling Joyce about a planned trip to the seaside with her brother's school. This information is not of immediate relevance to the child's concern, and it is possible that she sees it as an unwelcome intrusion. The point about this new information, however, is the way it is linked to what has gone before. Through the common elements of 'picnics' and 'seaside' the mother and child are able to link a past event with a future event, thus enabling the shared world of common experience to act as a backcloth to their conversations. The creation of and referral to a shared world is a typical feature of many conversations between mother and child, and we believe that it is of fundamental importance. As we show later, the lack of a shared world between staff and child at school constitutes a considerable barrier to communication.

In the following conversation, Cathie, a much more articulate child, relives a shared past experience with her mother. Cathie is not struggling with an intellectual problem, as Joyce was: the conversation serves rather as an emotional link between mother and daughter, and it also allows Cathie to talk through again what was clearly a frightening experience. The conversation occurs when a trailer comes on TV for the Walt Disney film *The Treasures of Mate Cumbe*. This happened to be a film that Cathie and her mother had already seen at the cinema:

CHILD: Look, it's *The Treasure of Acka Coombie* [sic].

MOTHER: Oh, I remember, do you remember it? When they're just about to find the treasure?

CHILD: Yes . . . but we went with Harriet and Irene.

MOTHER: That's right. Do you remember this bloke in the storm?

CHILD: Yes . . . and you thought he was dead, he was drowned, didn't we?

MOTHER: We thought he was drowned, didn't we?

CHILD: Mmmm.

MOTHER: And then he comes back at the end. Do you remember?

CHILD: Mm . . . he had blood on his arms and all over his face, didn't he?

MOTHER: Not as much as that, did he? He just had some bruises and a few scratches . . . do you remember? Then he was all right and they all got home safely.

CHILD: Mm.

MOTHER: That was a very frightening scene, wasn't it?

CHILD: Mm.

MOTHER: Very scary.

CHILD: And they're only people dressed up with masks and arrows.

MOTHER: Yes, they were, weren't they?

CHILD: Pretend arrows.

MOTHER: Yes.

CHILD: And bows, arrows and bows, bows and arrows. That one's called Davy, isn't it?

MOTHER: Yes it is, that's Davy, and he suddenly falls down the pit, doesn't he?

CHILD: Mm.

MOTHER: That was exciting, wasn't it?

The excerpt from the film ends, but Cathie and her mother carry on discussing what had obviously been a disturbing experience:

CHILD: We went with Harriet and Irene.

MOTHER: Yes.

CHILD: But Irene was a bit frightened.

MOTHER: She was very frightened, wasn't she?

CHILD: Mm.

MOTHER: You and Erica [Cathie's sister] weren't nearly so frightened.

CHILD: Not as frightened as Irene and Harriet.
MOTHER: No you weren't.

Reliving the experience of seeing an exciting and, at times, frightening, film seems to have established a closeness between Cathie and her mother, which is reflected in the structure of this conversation. Neither adult nor child is dominating the conversation, but both are equally and independently bringing up their own memories of the event. At the same time, they are both paying careful attention to each other's contributions, and they acknowledge and respond to what the other person says. Through their conversation, and the closeness it established, Cathie re-experienced the fear of the original outing in a secure setting, and perhaps had her anxiety allayed.

Discussion of past and future events could serve another function, that of helping the child to reach a clearer understanding of what had happened, or was going to happen to her. In the following conversation, for example, Samantha's mother tells her about an impending trip to see a speech therapist. Samantha is naturally apprehensive, and wants to know what will happen. Her mother attempts to reassure her:

1. MOTHER: Oh Samantha, you've got to go and see another lady on Tuesday.
2. CHILD: What lady?
3. MOTHER: Another lady wants to hear you.
4. CHILD: What lady?
5. MOTHER: The lady at the clinic wants to hear you speaking on Tuesday.
6. CHILD: [unclear] where [unclear] goes?
7. MOTHER: No, where you got your ears tested. She's going to learn you how to say your words properly.
8. CHILD: I don't know all the words.
9. MOTHER: Yeah. But she's going to learn you. She's going to teach them to you.
10. CHILD: What's her name?
11. MOTHER: Em . . . Miss Patrick.
12. CHILD: And . . . that's where I got my ears tested?
13. MOTHER: Where you got your ears tested then.
14. CHILD: That's where I'm going?
15. MOTHER: Mm-mm.

16. CHILD: Kevin mustn't make a noise. [Kevin is Samantha's younger brother, who was presumably told to be quiet when Samantha was having her hearing tested]

17. MOTHER: That was when you were getting your ears tested, he mustn't make a noise.

18. CHILD: No.

In this conversation both Samantha and her mother link the planned visit to the speech therapist with a previous trip to the clinic. In turn 7 Samantha's mother tells her that she's going back to the same clinic where she got her ears tested, and Samantha herself checks this again in turns 12 and 14. In turn 16 she recalls something that happened on a previous visit – her younger brother was asked to be quiet during the test. Some of the anxiety is thus taken out of this unknown future experience by these links to the shared past.

Watching TV

There is a widespread belief that young children nowadays spend much or most of their time at home in unproductive TV-viewing. However, Davie, who observed three- and four-year-olds in Stoke on Trent throughout the day, found that they were actually watching the screen on average only sixty-five minutes a day.[2] This was, admittedly, longer than they spent on other activities, such as listening to stories, but it by no means amounted to 'most of their time'. She found that middle-class and working-class children watched for the same amount of time, although the TV sets were switched on for much longer periods in the working-class homes. There was also no social class difference in the amount of time that mothers watched and discussed TV *with* their children – on average, only seven minutes a day.

In our study, too, we found no evidence of massive TV-watching. Seven middle-class and five working-class children watched TV during our two and a half hours of observation, usually the special early afternoon programme for young children. In half of these cases, the mothers watched with the children for at least part of the time. On average, those children who watched TV spent eleven minutes watching. This compared with the overall average of sixty-two minutes spent in play during the afternoon, and nine minutes spent listening to stories by those children who were read stories.

What might the children have learned from watching TV? TV-watching with their mothers provided the same kind of educational opportunities as listening to stories. The children asked questions about what puzzled them: 'What's the matter with him?' 'Is she going to be cross?' 'Why is he talking so quickly?' Often, as in these examples, the children's questions were concerned with people's motivations. Less frequently, they asked about puzzling objects or events. Helen's question about a chrysalis was quoted on page 40; Lynne asked a series of questions about a TV puppet:

CHILD: How do they make him talk?
MOTHER: They just talk . . . the man talks in a funny voice.
CHILD: Is he inside him?
MOTHER: No, he puts his hand inside, and then makes the puppet move, and then he talks.
CHILD: What?
MOTHER: He talks, and it sounds as though the puppet's talking.

However, the children tended to ask fewer questions while watching TV than when listening to a story. Their mothers, on the other hand, tended to ask more. They pointed out things of interest, named letters, asked the children what they could see, or reminded them of parallels in their own experience: 'We saw horses like that in the park with Daddy, remember?' The middle-class mothers, in particular, fed a lot of relevant general knowledge to the children when they watched TV with them, either amplifying the programme or in response to a child's question. Beth was puzzled by a reference to the celebrations for the Queen's birthday:

CHILD: But it's not our Queen's birthday, because she's had hers, hasn't she?
MOTHER: Well, this is her official birthday, remember, Daddy was telling you about it. When they have things like this.

Most of the time, though, the children watched on their own. Without a special study, it is impossible to know what the children learned at these times. Sometimes their mothers tried to find out, but even the most articulate children gave unsatisfactory answers. This may have been because the narrative task was difficult for them, or they did not choose to tackle it, but often they seemed not to have understood what they saw. Mary watched TV while her mother prepared dinner, and over dinner her mother asked her:

MOTHER: What did they do on *Pipkin* [the programme]?
CHILD: They, they did music and – and Hartley did . . .
MOTHER: They were singing?
CHILD: Mm-mm.
MOTHER: What was the tortoise called?
CHILD: He's just called tortoise.
MOTHER: Mm-mm. I saw him singing the last few minutes. What about Granny Pipkin, what did they do there?
CHILD: I don't know, I think they made a pie.
MOTHER: I think it was broth, did they make a stew or soup or something?
CHILD: I don't know, I just don't know.
MOTHER: What did they put in it?
CHILD: Things.
MOTHER: Oh did they?
CHILD: I don't know what else.

Whether or not their mothers watched TV with them, it seemed likely that the regular occurrence of the programmes helped children to gain some idea of clock time, and of the days of the week. These are concepts which four-year-olds find difficult, but are beginning to grapple with. The children often asked when a favourite programme would come on. The following conversation with Beth illustrates that the most verbally advanced girls had already developed some concepts in this area, admittedly still somewhat confused:

MOTHER: What day is it today? [Referring to which children's TV programme is shown today]
CHILD: On Thursday, it's *In the Town*.
MOTHER: Ah, but it's Wednesday today, isn't it?
CHILD: It's *Mary, Mungo and Midge* on Thursday.
MOTHER: Yes, but it's not Thursday, it's Wednesday, I think, isn't it? Yes.
CHILD: I can hear, I can hear, *Mary, Mungo and Midge*.

The regularity of children's TV programmes also helped to structure the children's lives into a routine. A number of them watched the children's programmes while their mothers prepared or cleared up lunch; Mary was always sent to play in her room on her own after lunch, and called down for the 1.30 programme; Ruth's reading lesson was scheduled for the end of this programme. Routines of this kind probably helped the children by making it easier for them to predict their days, and may have been consciously used by some mothers as a managerial device.

Disputes

Professionals who are dubious about how much working-class children learn at home often point to the endless disputes that they believe are characteristic of these families. In our study we found a tendency for working-class families to have either large numbers of disputes or hardly any.

We defined a dispute as occurring when either mother or child made a demand which was refused by the other, and a 'comeback' was then made by the original demander. That is, a dispute must last for at least three turns. In the four most disputatious families, between 30 and 50 per cent of mother–child conversations included at least one dispute. On the other hand, in five of the working-class families less than 5 per cent of conversations included a dispute. By contrast, the great majority of middle-class families (twelve out of fifteen) had a dispute rate of between 10 per cent and 15 per cent, and no middle-class family had a dispute rate of more than 19 per cent.

How did some mothers avoid disputes? It was our impression that in most families where disputes were few the mothers took the initiative in structuring the child's afternoon. These mothers tended to announce their intentions and suggest activities for the child ahead of time, so that one followed another without a hiatus. But not all dispute-free families were of this type. Some mothers were much more passive, and seemed to avoid disputes by good-naturedly acceding to their children's requests. In the disputing families, they generally refused their child's requests, and rarely suggested activities for them, or announced their intentions ahead of time. Their children had long unoccupied periods when they did little but argue.

However, we were very struck by the extent to which disputes provided a learning context. In 68 per cent of the disputes in our middle-class families, and 57 per cent of the disputes in our working-class families, the mothers sooner or later gave an explanation for their demand or refusal. *All* the mothers, except those who had very few or no disputes, gave some justifications. In Chapter 7 we illustrate the learning potential of one very disputatious home. Another example is given in Chapter 5 of a mother giving her child a considerable amount of general information during a dispute about rosehip syrup.

In the following dispute, Kelly, who constantly wrangled with her mother, was on the receiving end of a variety of information. This ranged from a discussion of relative sizes to insights into the relationship between her parents and advice as to how to approach her father for help. Kelly's bicycle had stabilizers. She had lent it to bigger boys in the block of flats, and as a result it was now broken, and would not stay upright by itself:

CHILD: It's not fixed. It's still tipping over. Fix it.
MOTHER: [Annoyed] Well, you let the big boys ride it, don't you?
CHILD: It's broken. [Moans]
MOTHER: [Angry] Go on, it won't hurt you. Oh God you drive me nuts. You let them ride it. So what do you expect? It gets broken and Daddy says he's not going to mend it again. I'm not going to keep paying the price for you, Kelly. I tell you not to let the big boys ride it, and what do you do?
CHILD: Joan [a friend] did.
MOTHER: Joan's not too big. Colin and David are. Colin and David are far too long for your bike and they break the stabilizers on it. Now you've got to ask your Daddy to mend it tonight. I bet you he moans. You ask him, I'm not asking him. I did yesterday. You'll have to be good for him tonight and he might do it.
CHILD: [Seeing younger sister on another bike] Mummy, let me have a go. [The wrangling continues]

We are not suggesting that family disputes should be encouraged; the most disputatious mothers were irritable and may have been somewhat depressed. Our point is rather that disputes are one of the many everyday family situations where the mother has an educational intent – she wants to justify herself, or make clear to the child the implications of the child's actions. The potential of disputes for learning, especially social learning, is therefore considerable.

Writing to Granny, and other 'embedded context' tasks

In Chapter 3 we saw that some mothers taught writing as a lesson. However, other mothers encouraged their children to write as a way of communicating. To use a term which has recently become prominent in developmental psychology, they 'embedded' writing in a meaningful activity, rather than teaching it out of context. Thus, some children were encouraged to make and write birthday cards, others to write letters.

Over lunch, Cathie's mother suggested, 'We'll write a letter to Grandma after lunch, shall we? She'd like that.' Later in the meal, she said, 'Let's think what we're going to say to Grandma.' Lunch finished, she fetched some writing paper:

MOTHER: Now, I'll write, what are you going to say to Grandma?
CHILD: Dear Grandma, I hope you are right, em . . . love from Cathie.
MOTHER: I hope [writes 'I hope'].
CHILD: I hope.
MOTHER: You [writes 'you'].
CHILD: You.
MOTHER: Are [writes 'are']. All [writes 'all'].
CHILD: Right.
MOTHER: Love to Grandpa.
CHILD: Love from Cathie . . . kiss, kiss, kiss.

Cathie's familiarity with letter-writing was evident from the conventional message which she dictated. Her next remarks show that she had a good knowledge of the whole routine:

CHILD: Mummy, don't you have to, don't you have to put the address, Mummy?
MOTHER: Mm.
CHILD: I've got an envelope.
MOTHER: You've got an envelope, OK.

It was clearly not infrequent for Cathie's mother to write to dictation and then get Cathie to copy her writing, because without any explicit reference to this step, her mother said:

MOTHER: Shall we write in the garden, or shall we write in here?
CHILD: Write out in the tent.

They both went into the garden, carrying notepads, and Cathie crawled into her tent. Then she asked:

CHILD: But what can I press on?
MOTHER: There . . . [Giving her a book]

Her mother then gave Cathie her notepad to copy from:

MOTHER: Copy that, and press on there, OK?
CHILD: Copy what?
MOTHER: Copy 'Dear Grandma and Grandpa'.
CHILD: Yes . . . thank you.

Her mother sat in the garden, reading a newspaper, while Cathie copied 'Dear Grandma':

CHILD: Mummy, look.
MOTHER: 'Dear Grandma', lovely, 'and', very good, are you putting in 'Grandpa' now?
CHILD: No, you do Grandpa.
MOTHER: You make a Grandpa and then I'll show you how to write the next bit.
CHILD: 'D' is for Grandpa? [She pronounces it 'dee' rather then 'duh']
MOTHER: 'G for Grandpa. [Gee]
CHILD: What is 'G'?
MOTHER: 'G' for Grandpa like the big 'G' you put for Grandma.
CHILD: You mean one of these [points to 'G']?
MOTHER: Yes . . . a nice big 'G' . . . and then you needn't put Grand, you can just put G'pa- so put a big 'G' and then put a 'p'.

The discussion continued, with the whole letter-writing episode in the tent lasting for over ten minutes. It is clear that Cathie, who had just celebrated her fourth birthday, had a good understanding of some fundamentals of literacy – that the written text conveys a message, that it is made up of separate words corresponding to spoken words, that these words are made up of individual letters, and that the written text reads from left to right.

A good deal of '3R' teaching occurred in a much more incidental manner. Counting was the most common number activity. The contexts of the home provided many natural settings for counting. The mothers counted knives as they set the table, counted the items on their shopping list, asked the children to count the number of people coming to tea, or the number of sausages they had put on each plate. The children obviously enjoyed counting and often initiated it themselves. Again, this counting was usually in a very meaningful context, for example, counting the coins in their money box. Their skills were still rudimentary. One of the most elementary number skills is to know by rote the number series, but a good many of the children made errors early on, e.g., 'one, two, three, four, five, sixteen'. Their major problem, however, was in one-to-one correspondence, that is, counting objects correctly, without double-counting or missing one out.

Some of the mothers taught more advanced number skills. Susan's mother saw a traditional children's number song as a good context in which to teach subtraction. She and Susan were singing nursery rhymes together. Partway through the song, which describes a progressive reduction in the number of buns in a baker's shop as they are sold, she stopped singing to teach subtraction in a more explicit way:

MOTHER: If you've got three currant buns in the baker's shop [holds up three fingers], look, and I take one away [folds one finger down], how many are left?

CHILD: [Sings] 'Three currant buns in the baker's shop'

MOTHER: How many's left if I take one away from three [holds up three fingers and folds one down]?

CHILD: Two.

MOTHER: That's right.

CHILD: 'Three . . .' [Starts to sing]

MOTHER: No. *Two* currant buns in the shop.

At this point Susan, who seems to have grasped the principle, takes on the role of teacher and begins to instruct her mother:

CHILD: 'Two currant buns in the baker's shop, round and fat with sugar on the top. Come a boy with a penny one day' [stops singing]. Put your hand up with two fingers. [Mother does so]

'Along come a boy with a penny one day' [folds one of mother's fingers down].

MOTHER: How many's left now?

CHILD: [Sings] 'One currant bun in the baker' [stops singing]. Put your finger out ... [Mother holds up one finger] 'Along come a boy ... and took it away.' None left.

MOTHER: None left now!

Susan obviously enjoyed her mastery of this task, and suggested:

CHILD: Shall we play, shall we play, shall we play three currant buns in the baker's shop again?

MOTHER: If you want to.

CHILD: You put your three fingers up [lifting up all five of her own fingers].

MOTHER: That's more than three. How many's that?

CHILD: Don't know.

MOTHER: Count them.

CHILD: One, two, three, four, five, six, seven, eight [she starts to count her fingers correctly, but goes wrong and screeches with laughter].

MOTHER: Don't be silly.

At this point it became clear that Susan had not yet an adequate enough grasp of number to master the lesson fully, and she reverted simply to singing the song. We found that other children besides Susan protected themselves from any tendency by their mothers to exert excess pressure, by changing the subject or becoming 'silly' when too difficult demands were placed on them.

In the next chapter we show how Donna's mother tried to teach her addition in relation to the number of cakes needed for tea.

Size and shape concepts (e.g., big/little, more/less, bigger than/smaller than, square/round) were used frequently and casually by all the mothers. Conversations about relative size were also quite common. June, for example, tried on an old coat, and her mother pointed out that it was too small, she had grown too fat. Erica and her mother discussed at length which toys would fit into her toy pushchair:

MOTHER: Jane's legs are too long, aren't they, what about Tommy? He fits in quite well, doesn't he?

CHILD: And Teddy. And the other teddy.
MOTHER: I don't know if they will all three fit in.
CHILD: I see.

A similar conversation is quoted in Chapter 6, page 119. Occasionally, mathematical words were deliberately taught. Susan's mother was getting spoons out for a dolls' tea-party:

CHILD: Get a bit more 'poons out.
MOTHER: A *bit* more?
CHILD: Yes.
MOTHER: A *few* more.

Sex-role teaching

It was often hard to determine how much of the teaching in the home was the result of a deliberate intention on the part of the mother. Values and attitudes were sometimes transmitted explicitly, at other times implicitly. We did not make any systematic analysis of the teaching of sex roles, but there were many conversations when the mother's views on this topic were implicitly or explicitly transmitted to her child. Donna's mother's priorities with her time, for example, were a frequent subject for discussion. It was usually made clear, as in the following conversation with Donna, that housework had to come before playing with the child:

MOTHER: I got washing to do, ironing to do, hoovering . . .
CHILD: Yes?
MOTHER: Well, it all takes time.
CHILD: And then you're finished?
MOTHER: Yes.
CHILD: I don't want you to do hoovering and washing.
MOTHER: I'm sorry, but I've got to.

The way in which roles are shared between mothers and fathers was conveyed in many subtle forms. Fathers were implicitly depicted as powerful people. This power was usually seen as benefiting the family. The children learned that mothers and children are dependent on fathers for ferrying (few mothers could drive, or had access to a car), for money, and for mechanical skills ('Oh, you've broken that. Daddy'll have to mend it'). They also learned that an important role for women is to provide household services for men ('Nanny's going shopping. To get Granddad some dinner'; 'I've got to see Daddy has a clean shirt').

The fathers' power was sometimes depicted as potentially threatening as well as positive. As we saw earlier (page 70), when Kelly's bicycle got broken, she was told, 'Now you've got to ask your Daddy to mend it tonight. I bet you he moans. You ask him, I'm not asking him. I did yesterday. You'll have to be good for him tonight and he might do it.' Ann's mother tore a page out of a notebook for her to write on, and commented, 'You'd better not tell Daddy I gave you a piece of paper out of his book.' These mothers were conveying to their daughters a realistic understanding of relationships and sex-role divisions within their families. In some cases the mothers had internalized these attitudes to such a degree that they became uneasy if even a pretend sex-role change was suggested; as in the case of Elaine's mother:

CHILD: You be Mummy, I'll be Daddy.
MOTHER: You be Daddy? OK . . . No, little girls should be Mummies, not Daddies. You be Mummy, I'll be Auntie.
CHILD: Mm?
MOTHER: Let's pretend Daddy's at work. OK?

Although we have no quantitative evidence on this, our impression was that sex-role teaching was much more intense in the home, especially in some working-class homes, than at nursery school.

Special characteristics of home learning

Our study suggests that learning at home occurs in a wide variety of contexts, and that there is no good reason to single out any one context, such as mother–child play, as especially valuable. At the start of the study we had suspected that joint activity of any kind between mother and child might provide the most important learning experiences, but we found no evidence to support this idea. In fact, as we shall show in the next chapter, the most intellectually challenging conversations tended to occur at mealtimes, or when mother and child were doing nothing in particular, or when the child was watching her mother at work.

What seemed to be important, in fact, was not the particular context, but the mother's desire for the child to learn, coupled with the child's curiosity and wish to learn. Educational considerations, in the broadest sense, were often at the forefront of the mothers' minds. They were dedicated teachers, intent on teaching their child what they thought was important for her to learn. The topics varied, of course, from family to family. However, almost every trivial event could be an occasion for teaching.

This does not mean that home life *automatically* provides rich learning experiences. Some mothers, perhaps if very depressed, or some childminders caring for a child in their home, may have little commitment to education. Equally, in some situations, children may not turn to adults for companionship or to satisfy their curiosity. In Chapter 8 we show that this tends to be the case at nursery school.

A notable feature of learning at home was the large amount of general knowledge that the children were given, especially in relation to the ordinary everyday events of living in a family. The children were particularly interested in people, their motivations and activities, and much of the knowledge that their mothers gave them was concerned with the social world.

Giving young children information and general knowledge is not currently seen as a priority by psychologists. Instead, the central educational task in the preschool years is seen to be the fostering of basic language and thinking skills. In our view, this is mistaken. The major communication and thinking problems of young children arise, not from inability to reason or compare, but from misinformation, lack of information, and from the lack of a coherent conceptual framework in which to fit their experiences. This argument will be developed in the next chapter.

Further, possession of relevant information can increase children's security and confidence. We have already quoted several conversations in which the children's anxiety seemed to some extent allayed by being helped to an increased understanding of events. Beth had an amazing amount of general knowledge for a child aged three years and ten months. On one occasion she interrupted a fantasy game with her teacher to announce:

CHILD: Do you know, my baby's one now.
STAFF: Your baby's coming here when she's older.
CHILD: She'll go to playgroup when she's two, though.
STAFF: Will she?

CHILD: Yeah. Because when you're two you go to . . . When I was
two I went to a playgroup.
OTHER CHILD: So did I.
CHILD: That shows you, that people go to playgroup when they're
two.
STAFF: Why do they go to a playgroup?
CHILD: Because they're not old enough to go to school.
STAFF: I see. And how old were you when you came here, then?
CHILD: Three or four.
STAFF: Three or four. Then what happens when you're five?
CHILD: You go . . . When I'm five I'll only . . . I'll go to a . . . I
expect I won't come to here any more.
STAFF: Where will you be, then?
CHILD: Be? In a different school, of course.
STAFF: Do you know which school you're going to?
CHILD: Cross Road [her local primary school].

Beth's knowledge of the various stages of early education, and the ages
at which transfers between them occur, was better than that of most
adults. It seems likely that being able to situate her past and future
within the educational system in this way gave her extra confidence in
moving through life.

As we have seen, another special characteristic of teaching at home is
that it usually occurs in a context of great meaning to the child. While
this seems likely to facilitate learning, it also represents a limitation
which the child must eventually overcome. Number, for example, must
be separated at school from the context of card games or rock cakes if
the child is to advance in mathematics. This point will be taken up again
in Chapter 8, when we discuss home–school differences.

Overview

In this chapter we showed that many everyday events in family life – for
example, making a shopping list, looking out of the window, and even
irritable wrangling – can involve important learning experiences for
children. Mothers are particularly well placed to play an important
teaching role because they share the child's world, extending from the
past into the future. No single context seemed particularly valuable for
learning; it was the mother's desire to teach or clarify, and the child's

curiosity, which created the learning potential. We argue that the large amount of information and general knowledge conveyed in the home is important both for intellectual growth and for increasing children's security and confidence.

5

The puzzling mind
of the four-year-old

'The thirst for understanding springs from the child's deepest emotional needs, and with an intelligent child it is a veritable passion.'

Susan Isaacs, in *The Children We Teach*.

In the last two chapters we were primarily concerned with what the children were learning at home, and the contexts in which this learning took place. In this chapter we focus much more on children's thinking, the way in which they attempt to make sense of their world, and the difficulties they encounter. These issues are not only of great intrinsic interest, but also have considerable bearing on how adults can best help children to learn. We shall argue that the learning model currently held by many psychologists and teachers leads them to underestimate not only the capacities of young children, but also the potential of adults to assist in intellectual growth.

The thirst for understanding of which Susan Isaacs wrote emerges very clearly from our transcripts. In children a good deal younger than those we studied this thirst is mainly satisfied by exploring the physical environment and handling new objects; their mothers complain that they are 'into everything'. By the age of three or four, however, much of the child's exploration is through words. The child has become essentially a puzzler, eager to extend her understanding through dialogue with adults. Parents now complain that their children 'never stop asking questions'. Asking questions is the most obvious manifestation of the puzzling mind, and we will begin our discussion by considering the questions which the children asked.

Children's questions

Children's questions, especially their 'Why' questions, have interested many psychologists and educationalists. According to Piaget, children's questions reveal their intellectual limitations. He believed that before the age of seven or eight children have no real understanding of causation or logic. They have a 'precausal' model of the world, in which everything happens because of someone's intentions, or because 'it must be so'.[1] Other psychologists, notably Susan and Nathan Isaacs, have disputed this view.[2] They saw children's questions as an indication of an active intelligence trying to make sense of the world, a forerunner of scientific curiosity. Parents, maddened by apparently incessant questions, may be inclined to take them less seriously. It can often seem that children's questions are mainly a form of attention-seeking, or a way of keeping the conversation going, especially since, as several studies have shown, young children rarely ask 'Why' questions of other children.[3]

In our study, we certainly found that the children asked their mothers a very large number of questions, on average twenty-six an hour. Individual children varied greatly in this respect. During the two and a half hours at home, one child asked only eight questions, while another asked 145. Questions formed a slightly higher proportion of the talk of middle-class than working-class children.

Since asking questions was such a striking feature of the children's behaviour, it seemed important to determine their significance. Did they really play an important part in the children's intellectual lives, or were those parents who experienced them as irritating demands nearer the truth?

The children's questions seemed to arise in three fairly distinct contexts. In the first context, which we called 'business', the questions were prompted by the need to carry out some activity. Many of these were 'Where' questions: 'Where are the scissors?' About a quarter of all the questions at home arose in this context. Although obviously fulfilling a useful function, these questions appeared to make little contribution to intellectual growth.

In the second context, which we called 'challenges', the questions arose in the course of a dispute about what the mother or the child should or shouldn't do. They usually started with 'Why?' or 'Why should I?' and amounted to 10 per cent of all questions at home. It may be thought that questions of this type are not real questions, but rather a device for challenging adult control. Although this often appeared to be partially or wholly true, nevertheless, whatever the child's motivation, these questions had the same educational potential as genuine questions. This is because it was very unusual for mothers to reply to them by simply saying, 'Because I say so' – only seven out of 139 'challenges' at home were given this response. In the majority of cases, if the mother answered the question at all, she eventually offered some kind of justification or explanation.

Sometimes, as in the following conversation with Mina, the child extracted a considerable amount of information from her mother by a series of challenges:

1. MOTHER: What do you want a drink of?
2. CHILD: Rosehip. [By this she meant 'rosehip syrup']
3. MOTHER: Oh, you've just had a drink [of that].
4. CHILD: Rosehip [firmly].
5. MOTHER: Right, one more drink of rosehip, and then we've got to keep the rest for Tessa, all right? [Tessa is Mina's baby sister]
6. CHILD: Why?
7. MOTHER: Because Tessa can't drink orange squash, and things like you can.
8. CHILD: Why can't she?
9. MOTHER: Because it's all too sweet for her. Not good for babies, that sort of thing. It's not good for anybody really, but we still drink it. When we go to Sainsbury's we'll get you a drink of your own.
10. CHILD: Why?
11. MOTHER: Well, then you won't have to keep drinking the rosehip, will you?
12. CHILD: I will [defiantly].
13. MOTHER: *No*, Mina [firmly].
14. CHILD: Why?
15. MOTHER: Because the rosehip costs a lot of money.
16. CHILD: Is Tessa going to drink it all?
17. MOTHER: Tessa only drinks a little weeny bit, so it lasts quite a long time, but if you drink it, you drink about a whole bottle a day.

This conversation illustrates the type of explanations that a challenge may elicit. It also shows that 'Why' questions which are challenges may also contain an element of genuine curiosity. Certainly Mina starts the series of questions by challenging her mother's ruling on what she can drink, and her remarks in turns 12 and 16 show that she is still feeling resentment towards her little sister over the rosehip syrup. However, the possibility that she is curious about her mother's justifications cannot be ruled out. The main point we want to make, though, is that, whatever her motive, Mina is being given, and appears to be taking in, a large amount of information about babies' feeding and drinking habits, the expense of rosehip syrup, and so on.

Mina's mother had trained to be a teacher, and her willingness to justify her decisions at length may be considered predictable. The following conversation of Donna's, however, was typical of those heard in working-class homes:

CHILD: [Challenging her mother's statement that she had no time to play with her] Why? Why do you have to do your washing?
MOTHER: Well, I didn't do none yesterday. We went out, didn't we, up to Nanny's yesterday.

In two brief sentences Donna's mother implicitly conveys that washing must be done at least every other day (there is a baby in the family) and that she must give it priority over play. In addition, she is reminding the child about what happened the day before, and pointing out that this event had implications for today's activities.

In both these conversations the children's no doubt irritating refusal to be fobbed off by their mother's initial ruling led to an extension of their understanding. For this reason, 'challenges' may be of much greater educational importance than some of those asked in the third context which we considered, those which seemed to be primarily prompted by curiosity. About two-thirds of all the questions at home were of this kind, for example, 'Where's the baby?' 'What's that?' 'How do you do that?' 'Why are you going upstairs?' 'Why is she going home?' 'Why is it a home for old ladies?' Some curiosity questions, like the first of these examples, are straightforward requests for information on familiar topics, where the answer is likely to be one of several known alternatives. This type of curiosity question has a very similar status to the 'business' question, and is probably of less significance to development than challenging questions. Others, like the second question – 'What's that?'

– may be asked about something novel, and could lead to the child learning a new label, with perhaps additional information. ('Binoculars. We can look at the birds in the garden with them, they'll look much bigger.')

'How' and 'Why' questions, like our third and fourth examples, are potentially important because they may lead to enhancing the child's understanding of mechanisms, processes and motivations. In fact, very few of our girls asked 'How' questions. As Piaget pointed out, young children are much more likely to ask 'Why' questions about motives and intentions. In our study, many of their questions to their mothers centred around such issues (e.g., Child: 'Why are you going upstairs?' Mother: 'It's time to wake the baby').

While curiosity questions often enhanced the child's knowledge, we attached particular importance to a special kind of curiosity questions, which we called 'puzzled questions'. These were questions prompted by the child's puzzlement when faced by facts or events which seemed discordant with her previous knowledge and experience. 'Why is she going home?' 'Why is it a home for old ladies?' were questions of this type. The first question was prompted by the unusual departure of a teacher in the middle of the morning, the second by the mother's remark that an old lady they knew had gone to live in a home for old people. This second question suggests that the child was aware that people usually live in family groups, and that she was puzzled by the anomaly now presented to her. As Nathan Isaacs pointed out, it is the clash between a familiar rule and a contrary fact which has led scientists to their major discoveries. Most educators would like to encourage and stimulate questions of this kind from children.

'Why' questions formed about a quarter of all the questions asked at home. Half of them were asked in the context of curiosity, and half during arguments. We attempted to analyse separately those 'Why' questions which were apparently prompted by puzzling over an anomaly from the intellectually less interesting ones, but the task proved impossible. Often there was considerable uncertainty about what prompted the question, and unambiguously 'puzzled' questions were rare. Moreover, not all 'puzzled' questions began with 'Why'. Later in this chapter we will see conversations in which the child is certainly puzzled, but does not express her puzzlement by 'Why'. In fact, the tendency, which we originally shared, to think of 'Why' questions as especially important to intellectual development seems mistaken. It is the intention behind the question, not the words with which it is expressed, that is crucial.

Some of the questions which we classified as arising in the contexts of curiosity and argument could be regarded as primarily conversation fillers or attention-seeking devices. In any particular case it was often impossible to decide. From an educational point of view, the motivation may not have mattered; provided that the mother answered the question, the child's understanding was likely to have been advanced. In Chapter 6 we discuss how frequent and how adequate the mothers' answers were.

Why did the children ask so many questions? After reading the transcripts, we doubted whether attention-seeking played a major role. We also doubted Piaget's theory that many young children's questions are of the 'Why is the tree there?' type, that is, questions which arise because children do not realize that many things happen by chance. It seemed to us rather that the children asked questions because there was a great deal that they did not know about the world, and many occasions when they were conscious of ignorance, misunderstanding and confusion. Often, the questions which we categorized as 'curiosity' questions occurred during conversations in which the child was deeply involved in struggling to understand her world.

Episodes of persistent questioning

Our analysis of children's questions left us dissatisfied. We suspected that by focusing on individual questions – rather than on passages of sustained questioning – we were missing some of the most crucial characteristics of the children's thinking: that is, their persistence, their desire to understand, and their logical power. It also seemed likely that the focus on individual questions had misled earlier psychologists, including Piaget. Electronic recording equipment, by enabling research-ers to study long conversations, as well as intermittent conversations over a long period of time, makes a different approach possible. In the rest of this chapter, we discuss some of the issues that arose from an analysis of passages of persistent questioning.

Misunderstandings not detected

Some of these passages arose because of a misunderstanding between mother and child, which the mother did not detect. In the following conversation, the child became very distressed by her mother's failure to understand. The central problem was caused by the child's difficulty in holding in mind the two meanings of the word 'letter'. The conversation arose when Carol's mother was helping her erect a 'play-house' in their living room. The door of this play-house was made of cloth, and had the words 'Wendy House' written on it: it also had a letter-box on which was written the word 'Letters'. Carol's mother told her what the words 'Wendy House' meant, and then pointed to the word 'Letters':

MOTHER: What does it say down there?
CHILD: What does it say down there?
MOTHER: It says . . .?
CHILD: Wendy.
MOTHER: No. That word doesn't look the same as that, does it? [Compares 'Letters' with 'Wendy'] it says 'Letters'. That's a letter-box. Where the postman puts the letters.

Carol, however, was confused. She wanted her mother to say what word those letters constituted. She had not grasped the uniqueness of the situation: that the letters in fact made up the word 'Letters':

CHILD: No . . . Wha . . . What is that? What are those numbers called?
MOTHER: They're letters, not numbers.
CHILD: No . . .
MOTHER: 'L'.
CHILD: No. What are . . . What is . . . What is the name there?
MOTHER: That's 'Letters'.
CHILD: No, what's the name there?
MOTHER: 'L'.
CHILD: No. What are . . . What is . . . What is the name there? [Getting upset]
MOTHER: That's 'Letters'.
CHILD: No, what's the name there?
MOTHER: 'Letters' you mean? Like 'C' for Carol?
CHILD: [Sob] . . . I mean the name. [Carol is by now quite distressed]
MOTHER: Come on, it's 'Letters'. That's where the postman posts the letters. Like our postman . . .

Carol's mother distracted her attention from this source of distress, and they continued to erect the house. However, the confusion in Carol's mind did not appear to have been resolved, nor did the mother seem to have realized what the problem was. Indeed, it seems likely that misunderstandings of this kind – where adult and child become locked on to different meanings of the same word – are particularly difficult for the adult to detect, since this would require a substantial shift in their perception of the situation to encompass the child's meaning.

A variant of this type of misunderstanding occurred in the following conversation. Here, Lynne's mother failed to detect that in referring to 'Nanny's Daddy' Lynne was talking about her grandfather, not her great-grandfather. Lynne was drawing a picture of her grandmother ('Nanny'), when she asked:

CHILD: Where's Nanny's Daddy?
MOTHER: Nanny's Daddy? He's up in heaven.
CHILD: Oh, he's not up, not really up . . .?
MOTHER: Yes, he died.
CHILD: No, not Nanny's . . . He's not . . .
MOTHER: He is, he got very, very old, and he just died.
CHILD: Is Nanny up in heaven?
MOTHER: No, she came up here the other day, didn't she?

Lynne broke the tip of her felt tip pen at this point, and the topic of conversation changed.

This short conversation illustrates very nicely the bewilderment a four-year-old can easily fall into. Many children of this age have difficulty with the relative nature of terms such as 'father' or 'husband', and this can often create misunderstandings. The confusion is confounded by Lynne's inexperience. An older child would probably have realized that she would have been told if her grandfather had died in the past few days, and his death would not have been referred to so casually. Lynne lacked the experience that might have helped her realize that there was a misunderstanding, and instead tries to make sense of what her mother is saying. In her last question – 'Is Nanny up in heaven?' – she seems to be making an inference in an attempt to clarify the situation; her reasoning seems to be that if her grandfather who was alive and well a few days ago, is now up in heaven, then maybe her grandmother is there too. Lynne's mother puts her right on this one, but fails to spot the underlying misunderstanding.

Misunderstandings detected but not resolved

Birth and death, growth and development were topics in which most children were intensely interested, but confused. They were the source of several conversations in which the children expressed puzzlement. We have already discussed one such conversation in Chapter 3, when Lynne asked why Jesus wasn't a baby any more. While most children seemed aware that they themselves had been babies, and that they would one day grow up into adults, many of them still seemed puzzled by the idea that substantial adults – like their parents or teachers – had once been babies or little children, or by the fact that age and size were not automatically correlated. Since these issues involve very complex ideas, it is not surprising that the children were often left with their puzzlements.

In the following conversation, it emerged that Erica believed that size and age go together. In response, her mother launched into an explanation of the genetic basis of height differences, which left Erica more confused than before. The conversation arose out of the blue while Erica watched her mother putting nappies on her teddy bears:

CHILD: Mummy, I shall grow up before Maria, won't I? [Maria is a friend of Erica's]

MOTHER: Not much, darling, she's about the same age as you.

CHILD: Oh, 'cause I'm bigger than her.

MOTHER: Yes, but Maria will probably always be a bit shorter than you 'cause her mummy and daddy are shorter than me and Daddy. So Maria will probably never be as tall as you, even when she's grown up.

CHILD: Why?

MOTHER: It doesn't mean to say she won't be as grown up as you, she just won't be as tall as you.

CHILD: Why, because I'm a mummy?

At this point Erica's mother finished with the teddies, and started to talk about them.

The difficulties of explaining complex issues are also illustrated in the next episode. The conversation arose when Ruth was cutting out some pictures which her mother had drawn on cards:

MOTHER: It a difficult for you, 'cause you're left-handed, isn't it? You're doing very well.

CHILD: It's not difficult.

MOTHER: No, doesn't seem to be, anyway.

CHILD: P'raps one day you'll grow up into a left-handing ... people ...

MOTHER: No, I don't think so, 'cause when you have a left hand it means you were born like that, you don't usually change.

CHILD: But I'm holding a piece of paper right-handed.

MOTHER: Yes, yes, but you, the main thing you're doing is with your left hand. 'Cause your left hand's the stronger hand, the one that does everything, isn't it?

Ruth then reverted to talking about her cutting-out activity.

This conversation reveals some interesting misconceptions on the child's part. She seemed to believe that her mother might still grow up, or perhaps that 'grow up' means the same as 'grow older. She also seemed to believe that left-handedness might develop in an adult. The conversation shows how easy it is to give confusing explanations. The mother's final remark ('the one that does everything') seems to contradict precisely what she is trying to say: namely that being left-handed doesn't mean that the left hand does everything, as Ruth seemed to think.

Even when less complex issues were raised, the mothers' explanations were often not sufficiently clear or explicit to resolve the confusion. This was the case in the following conversation, which took place while mother and child were having lunch together, with the baby on the floor. Apparently out of the blue, Mina started to talk about tigers:

CHILD: Do you like tigers? Do you?

MOTHER: Tigers?

CHILD: Mm.

MOTHER: I like to look at tigers, yeah, they're lovely.

CHILD: Tigers!

MOTHER: Yeah, they're lovely to look at, they're really lovely. See them running. Nice to watch them in the zoo.

CHILD: No, real ones.

MOTHER: Mm. I don't like to go too near them though in case they try and eat me.

At this point Mina became puzzled. Her puzzlement was probably related to a remark of her mother's a little earlier that the baby
couldn't swallow her rattle, since it was too big to go in her mouth.
Hence, Mina seemed to be reasoning, a tiger couldn't dispose of her
mother.

> CHILD: They won't.
> MOTHER: They might.
> CHILD: Do they . . . do they eat you? [Puzzled]
> MOTHER: No, if they were hungry they might try.
> CHILD: Have they got mouths – small mouths?
> MOTHER: No, they ve got great big mouths.
> CHILD: Your size?

Mina's question is ambiguous. 'Your size?' could mean either that tigers'
mouths are as big as her mother's mouth, or as big as her mother's
body. Her mother interprets the question in the former sense:

> MOTHER: Pardon?
> CHILD: Your size?
> MOTHER: What, you think I've got a great big mouth?
> CHILD: No, the tigers.

Mina's reply indicates that there has been a misunderstanding, which
her mother, by then asking 'What do you mean?', expects her to clarify.
Whether or not Mina was up to this task we shall never know, because
her mother makes an imaginative leap to the other possible meaning.
Having made this leap, one might have expected Mina's mother to
follow up the child's questions, but in fact she allows the conversation
to fizzle out:

> MOTHER: What do you mean?
> CHILD: Got a big . . .
> MOTHER: Oh, their mouths the same size as me? [Holds her
>   arms to show the size of the whole body rather than just her
>   mouth]
> CHILD: Oh uh um.
> MOTHER: No, not that big.
> CHILD: Why?
> MOTHER: They're just not.

As was often the case, no explicit clarification occurred, and the conversation lapsed. The child's final 'Why?' suggests that she still failed to understand how her mother could fit into the tiger's mouth.

The concept of intellectual search

Mina's conversation about the tiger is an example of what we decided to call a *passage of intellectual search*. This is a conversation in which the child is actively seeking new information or explanations, or puzzling over something she does not understand, or trying to make sense of an apparent anomaly in her limited knowledge of the world. Such episodes are characterized by a sequence of persistent questioning on the part of the child, in which she considers the adult's answers and relates them to her existing knowledge; this in turn may lead to further questions on the same topic. 'Passages of intellectual search' reveal both the strengths of the child – her persistence, her logic, and her ability to assimilate complex ideas – and the frailty of her knowledge, or the naivety of her misconceptions. They were particularly frequent in the transcripts of the middle-class children (see Chapter 6).

The concept of Father Christmas gave rise to several passages of intellectual search. At this age, children are beginning to puzzle over the multiple inconsistencies in the Father Christmas myth. At the same time, they do not have a firm grasp of some of the basic aspects of the story – for example, that Father Christmas only visits at Christmas time. In the following conversation Penny is mainly concerned to establish what steps are required in order to get the Christmas present she wants. The conversation arose apparently out of the blue, when Penny was making a card for a friend's birthday, and her mother was looking at a catalogue. Penny's mother had promised to buy her a doll's ballerina outfit for her next birthday, and Penny was thinking through the implications of this promise. Presumably she knew from her own experience of getting and giving presents that she would be unlikely to accompany her mother when she bought the ballerina outfit. In this case, she reasoned, someone would have to look after her:

CHILD: Mummy, who will look after me when you get the 'dancellina' for my birthday?
MOTHER: Your birthday's not till next year, love.
CHILD: No, I know, I don't . . . I mean that . . .

MOTHER: Who will look after you? I expect we'll probably get it when you're at school or something.
CHILD: Oh . . .
MOTHER: Might have it from Father Christmas.
CHILD: No . . . oh yeah! [Excited]
MOTHER: You'd have it much sooner.
CHILD: I'll have to go in his house and ask him.
MOTHER: You often see Father Christmases in the shops around Christmas time. You could ask him for a ballerina outfit for your little doll.

There is a short digression while Penny and her mother discuss Penny's dressing up as a ballerina at nursery that morning. Penny, however, is still thinking about Father Christmas and the ballerina outfit, and she spontaneously returns to the topic:

CHILD: Does Father Christmas . . . give me . . . does Father Christmas say 'No' if he hasn't got a . . . hasn't got a . . . dancellina one?
MOTHER: Well, he usually does have those things.
CHILD: Will *you* ask him?
MOTHER: We'll do what you did last year, and you can write a letter to him. Remember?
CHILD: And what will he say if I write a letter to him?
MOTHER: He'll say, 'This looks a nice letter, I'll see what I can get. She wants a dancer's outfit.'
CHILD: He won't know my name.
MOTHER: He will if you put your name on the bottom.

Penny then asks her mother to write to Father Christmas, and her mother explains that it is much too early in the year to do so.

As well as demonstrating Penny's ability to work out what Father Christmas might or might not know, this conversation contains several features which characterize intellectual search in four-year-olds. First, there is the way in which Penny returns to the topic that is puzzling her, even though the conversation has moved on. We saw several instances of children repeatedly returning to a topic that was preoccupying their thoughts in the course of an afternoon, so that a topic that apparently arose out of the blue might be a throwback to an earlier conversation over which the child had been brooding. Secondly, there is the difficulty which Penny has on more than one occasion in expressing herself. This was not so much a characteristic of Penny – who was normally an articulate child – but more a general feature of intellectual effort. There were a number of occasions when a normally articulate child would become hesitant and inarticulate, and these were usually occasions when she was struggling to express a particularly difficult or novel idea. Finally, there is the logic and consistency which Penny brings to her projection into the future. Clearly she does not subscribe to the idea that Father Christmas is an omniscient figure who knows exactly what every child wants. Rather, she treats him as an ordinary mortal who is constrained by normal human limitations – he might run out of ballerina outfits, he will have to be told by Penny what she wants, and he will not know her name unless he is also given this bit of information.

Susan, also, was confused about several aspects of the Father Christmas story. The following conversation arose when she was playing with a toy handbag, and her mother remarked how pretty it was:

CHILD: Did Father Christmas give it to me?

MOTHER: Ah, I think he did. Not this Christmas though . . . nor last Christmas.

CHILD: Did he give it to me for my birthday?

MOTHER: What, Father Christmas? He doesn't come on your birthday.

CHILD: When does he come?

MOTHER: Christmas. That's why he's called Father Christmas. Did you see him last Christmas?

CHILD: No! Did you?

MOTHER: No. I didn't see him. I was asleep.

CHILD: We wasn't. We was thinking if Father Christmas was out of window.

MOTHER: And was he?

CHILD: We didn't have a look out of the window. We only thought.

The conversation moves on to discuss who had been staying with Susan the previous Christmas, and the games they had all played together. But, as with Penny, Susan is still thinking about Father Christmas:

CHILD: Mummy?

MOTHER: Mm.

CHILD: Did you think if Father Christmas was coming here?

MOTHER: I knew he was going to come, yeah.

CHILD: Did you think he was coming down the chimney?
MOTHER: No, I didn't think he was coming down the chimney.
'Cause we haven't got a fireplace.
CHILD: Why haven't we?
MOTHER: Well, we've blocked them all in . . . we left the basement
door open, didn't we, so that Father Christmas could come in.
CHILD: Last year?
MOTHER: Mm.
CHILD: Must have been windy.

For some reason, Susan's mother failed to grasp what she meant by this
inference, and asked, 'Why must it have been windy?', although it seems
clear to us that she was referring to the effect of leaving the basement
door open. Susan ignored the question, and returned again to the puzzle
of Father Christmas's visit:

CHILD: Why did you let Father Christmas in?
MOTHER: Well, he had to bring your presents in.
CHILD: I didn't know he was coming in here.
MOTHER: Well, where did you think he was going to take them?
CHILD: Did he, did he, didn't he, know if he, if he know like our
house was?
MOTHER: Oh, he knows where all the children's houses are.
CHILD: I mean, doesn't he know what, what, what like it is?
MOTHER: What it looks like? [Child nods] I expect he does. He's
been here before, hasn't he?
CHILD: Had he?
MOTHER: Mm, he came the year before.

The conversation continued with further questions from Susan about
what Father Christmas brought the presents in (a sack, she was told)
and whether the sack was too heavy for him.
    This episode illustrates again many of the features of intellectual
search we saw in Penny's conversation – the way in which the child
returns to the topic that is puzzling her, her occasional lapses from
articulateness when she is struggling to express a difficult idea, and the
logical and persistent manner in which she pursues the topic. Yet there
are differences between the two conversations, particularly in the way in
which the child's conceptions of Father Christmas are exposed.
    The conversation involving Penny gave us little insight into her con-

ception of Father Christmas, apart from her treatment of him as a fairly human figure. In contrast, Susan's conversation reveals much more of her beliefs. At the start of the conversation she seems to think that Father Christmas gives her birthday presents as well as Christmas presents. Later she wonders if her mother thought he came down the chimney, apparently not having assimilated the fact that the fireplaces are blocked up. She goes on to express surprise that he came into the house at all, and then starts to wonder how Father Christmas knows what her house looks like. She also does not realize that he is supposed to pay annual visits. Her last questions are indeed very similar to Penny's, and suggest that young children start from a more human idea of Father Christmas and work outwards, rather than starting from a more omniscient view of him and then discovering his more human limitations.

Clearly the concept of Father Christmas is not an easy one for children to grasp, given the haziness with which he is surrounded and the lack of logical consistency within the concept itself. It is not at all surprising that they should have misconceptions about the myth, which can only be clarified by the kind of conversations we have quoted. These two conversations also demonstrate the ability of the young child to project imaginatively into another person's perspective, and make realistic assumptions about what that person might or might not be expected to know. We were impressed with how frequently they did this, and by their ready interest in exploring other people's motivations, knowledge, and points of view.

Intellectual search:
struggling with several complex ideas

The learning potential of what we have called 'passages of intellectual search' is well illustrated in the following long episode, in which the child's confusion about the relationship between money, work and consumer goods was exposed, and to some extent clarified. The conversation started while Rosy and her mother were having lunch, and was triggered off by the appearance of the window-cleaner in the garden. Rosy's mother went off to the kitchen to get him some water, and called out to her neighbour, Pamela.

CHILD: What did Pamela say?
MOTHER: She's having to pay everybody else's bills for the window-cleaner, 'cause they're all out.

CHILD: Why they all out?

MOTHER: 'Cause they're working or something.

CHILD: Aren't they silly!

MOTHER: Well, you have to work to earn money, don't you?

CHILD: Yeah ... If they know what day the window-cleaner come they should stay here.

MOTHER: They should stay at home? Well, I don't know, they can't always ...

At this point the window-cleaner appeared at the dining-room window, and cleaned the window while Rosy and her mother carried on with lunch. The conversation switched to what they might have for pudding, and what they might do that afternoon. Rosy, however, was still thinking about the window-cleaner ...

1. Child: Mummy?
2. MOTHER: Mmm.
3. CHILD: Umm ... she can't pay everybody's, er ... all the bills to the window-cleaner, can she?
4. MOTHER: No, she can't pay everybody's bills ... she sometimes pays mine if I'm out.
5. CHILD: 'Cause it's fair.
6. MOTHER: Mm, it is.
7. CHILD: Umm, but where does she leave the money?
8. MOTHER: She doesn't leave it anywhere, she hands it to the window-cleaner, after he's finished.
9. CHILD: And then she gives it to us?
10. MOTHER: No, no, she doesn't have to pay us.
11. CHILD: Then the window-cleaner gives it to us?
12. MOTHER: No, we give the window-cleaner money, he does work for us, and we have to give him money.
13. CHILD: Why?
14. MOTHER: Well, because he's been working for us cleaning our windows. He doesn't do it for nothing.
15. CHILD: Why do you have money if you have ... if people clean your windows?
16. MOTHER: Well, the window-cleaner needs money, doesn't he?
17. CHILD: Why?
18. MOTHER: To buy clothes for his children and food for them to eat.

19. CHILD: Well, sometimes window-cleaners don't have children.
20. MOTHER: Quite often they do.
21. CHILD: And something on his own to eat, and for curtains?
22. MOTHER: And for paying his gas bills and electricity bill. And for paying for his petrol for his car. All sorts of things you have to pay for, you see. You have to earn money somehow, and he earns it by cleaning other people's windows, and big shop windows and things.
23. CHILD: And then the person who got the money gives it to people . . .

It seems until turn 11 Rosy was under the impression that the window-cleaner pays the housewives, and not the other way round. In the course of the conversation the relationship between work, money and goods is slowly outlined for her, but it is still unclear from her last remark whether she has really grasped all that has been said. The conversation in fact continues later on, after Rosy has watched her mother actually hand over the money to the window-cleaner:

1. MOTHER: I expect the window-cleaner's going to have his lunch now.
2. CHILD: He would have all *that* much lunch [stretches arms out wide] because he's been working all the time.
3. MOTHER: Mm . . . I expect he gets very hungry, doesn't he? I expect he goes to the pub and has some beer and sandwiches.
4. CHILD: He has to pay for that.
5. MOTHER: Yes, he does.
6. CHILD: Not always, though.
7. MOTHER: Mm, always.
8. CHILD: Why not?
9. MOTHER: They won't give him any beer and sandwiches if he doesn't have any money.

At this point Rosy clearly wonders why he cannot do without money to go to a pub:

10. CHILD: But why doesn't he use his own food?
11. MOTHER: Well, he might do, I don't know, perhaps he brings his own sandwiches, do you think?
12. CHILD: He go to a pub and he has his lunch some *and* he has it at his home.

13. MOTHER: Oh, he wouldn't do both, no.
14. CHILD: He would do all of those a few times. But he usually go
to a pub.

Rosy's mother ends the conversation, with an example of the 'planning
ahead' child management we discussed in Chapter 4:

15. MOTHER: Mm. Come on, sit up. Now I'm going to do the
washing up, then I'll read you a story, and then I'm going to read
the newspaper a bit.

Rosy's remarks in this third conversation (especially turn 6, 'Not
always, though') suggest that she has only hazily grasped what she has
been told, and her understanding of money transactions still seems
shaky. This is not because she lacked the intellectual capacity, nor
because her mother's explanations were too complex. Rather it seems
likely that this conversation reveals something which is characteristic of
the slow and gradual way in which a child's understanding of an abstract
or complex topic is built up. It may take a considerable time, as well as
several more conversations like the one above, before Rosy has grasped
the complexities of the relationships involved, and she may have to
return to the same topic again and again before she achieves full
understanding.

It is interesting to consider why Rosy keeps asking questions on this
topic. Clearly, her initial questions were asked out of curiosity aroused
by the unusual event in the daily routine – the arrival of the window-
cleaner and the subsequent conversation between her mother and the
neighbour. But her later return to the topic suggests something beyond
this initial curiosity. Indeed, it suggests that Rosy is at some level aware
that she has not grasped the relationships involved, and that her
questions are motivated by her desire to clarify her misconceptions. Why
she should be aware of her own lack of understanding is not clear – she
could perfectly well have stayed with the idea that the neighbour did
receive money from the window-cleaner, and got on with her lunch. The
fact that she did not suggests that she was at some level dissatisfied with
her own grasp of the situation, perhaps because it didn't fit with other
facts that she knew, and wanted it sorted out.

Confusion about the relationship between work, money and goods
seemed to be less common among the working-class children. Perhaps
because their fathers' work was more clearly related to money, rather

than to the interest of the job, or because with a more limited income the arrival of the weekly pay packet was a more important event, the relationship between money and work was more often discussed in working-class families. In Chapter 7 we quote a conversation of one working class child, Donna, who had a much better grasp of this relationship than Rosy.

Intellectual search: the power of a puzzling mind

It should be clear by now that mothers often gave answers to the children's questions that were less than full, or that failed to meet the central point of the question. Advances in children's understanding seemed to depend as much on their own efforts to achieve greater clarity as on the quality of their mothers' initial explanations. This point is very clearly exemplified in the following conversation. Beth, aged three years and ten months, and her mother were having lunch together. The conversation was preceded and succeeded by silence:

CHILD: Is our roof a sloping roof?

MOTHER: Mmm. We've got two sloping roofs, and they sort of meet in the middle.

CHILD: Why have we?

MOTHER: Oh, it's just the way our house is built. Most people have sloping roofs, so that the rain can run off them. Otherwise, if you have a flat roof, the rain would sit in the middle of the roof and make a big puddle, and then it would start coming through.

CHILD: Our school has a flat roof, you know.

MOTHER: Yes it does actually, doesn't it?

CHILD: And the rain sits there and goes through?

MOTHER: Well, it doesn't go through. It's probably built with drains so that the water runs away. You have big blocks of flats with rather flat sort of roofs. But houses that were built at the time this house was built usually had sloping roofs.

CHILD: Does Lara have a sloping roof? [Lara is Beth's friend]

MOTHER: Mmm. Lara's house is very like ours. In countries where they have a lot of snow, they have even more sloping roofs. So that when they've got a lot of snow, the snow can just fall off.

CHILD: Whereas, if you have a flat roof, what would it do? Would it just have a drain?

MOTHER: No, then it would sit on the roof, and when it melted it would make a big puddle.

This episode represents a remarkable attempt by a child not yet four to explore an abstract topic. We do not know why she was thinking about sloping roofs in the first instance, as there was nothing in the earlier conversations (which were concerned with how she should eat her lunch and a planned visit to the doctor later that day) which even hinted at this topic. Nevertheless, once the topic was raised, Beth pursues it with a penetrating, remorseless logic. Her mother explains that sloping roofs allow the water to drain off and so prevent rain coming through the roof. However, Beth can think of a counter-example: she knows that her school has a flat roof but rain does not come through the roof there. Beth's mother meets this objection by introducing the idea of a drain, and in the next turn extends the topic by pointing out that countries with a lot of snow need even more sloping roofs. Beth then wonders what happens about snow if you have a flat roof, and reintroduces the idea of a drain: an idea she has assimilated with unusual speed in the short space of time since it was brought up. (Note here her appropriate use of the logical connective 'whereas'.) Her mother explains that the snow melts into a big puddle, although she is perhaps misleading in suggesting that a drain would not be needed to take the melted snow away.

Beth was an exceptionally intelligent and thoughtful child, and it would be wrong to suggest that all the children took part in conversations of this quality. However, the conversation certainly illustrates the potential of intellectual search as a method of learning, as well as demonstrating the power of a very young mind in pursuit of relatively abstract knowledge.

A new perspective on the young child's mind

Our study of four-year-old children at home and at nursery school led us to doubt some widely held beliefs and assumptions about the nature of the young child's mind. Most of these beliefs derive from the work of Jean Piaget.[4] Piaget's theories are complex, and difficult to present briefly without distortion. Perhaps his major contribution, which is fully supported by our evidence, is that learning is an active process, not a matter of passive absorption. The reader familiar with Piaget's theories will note that the process of intellectual search which we describe, in which the child thinks about the adult's answers to her questions, incorporates them into her thinking and then asks further questions arising from them, strongly resembles Piaget's notion of learning by assimilation and accommodation.

A second major component of Piaget's theory is that the intellectual structures of the child's mind are different from those of an adult. Children think differently from adults, and young children from older children. It is only after innumerable experiences, and reflection on these experiences, that mature forms of thinking develop. Again, we would not dispute this theory. Although in some of the conversations we have quoted the children are thinking as capably as their mothers, if not more so, in others (sometimes involving the same children) their intellectual limitations are obvious.

However, there are other aspects of Piaget's theory which we, along with a number of other contemporary psychologists, would contest. Piaget held that the active process of learning in childhood is largely dependent on experiencing and responding to innumerable acts of exploration. The process is long and essentially solitary. It follows from Piagetian theory that until the child is six or seven adults can play only a minor part in her intellectual development. This notion of the 'exploring' child, learning about the physical world by acting on it, seems to us to capture much of the essence of the very young child. But by the age of three or four, we would argue that dialogue is as important as physical exploration. At this stage the child explores by means of words, as much as through action. And as we have shown, adults can therefore play an important role in advancing the child's understanding through conversation.

Nor do we accept that the young child is as intellectually limited as Piaget believed. According to Piaget, children between the ages of two and six or seven are at a 'preoperational' stage. They are egocentric, by which he did not mean selfish, but able to see things only from their own perspective. Hence they cannot argue in any real sense, because they do not realize that others may see things differently. They also cannot think logically, because they cannot keep apart statements that exclude or contradict each other. Commonly, they reverse the relation of cause and effect. They have no real understanding of causation, but believe that everything happens because of someone's motivation, or because 'it must be so'.

Our transcripts suggest that young children are much less egocentric and illogical than Piaget believed. We found many examples (as in the 'Father Christmas' conversations) of their awareness of, and interest in, other people's viewpoints. Perhaps the most straightforward example occurred when Ruth had been to the lavatory. She was bending over so that her mother could wipe her bottom. In this position, her mother could not see her head:

CHILD: Mummy, you lost me.
MOTHER: I have lost you, yeah.
CHILD: Can you only see my bottom and legs?
MOTHER: That's right.
CHILD: And shoes and pants.
MOTHER: That's right. Stand up straight.
CHILD: Here I am.
MOTHER: That's nice. There she is, back again. Off you go!

This conversation not only revealed Ruth's ability to work out what her mother could see of her, but also showed her expressing this knowledge in a kind of game – 'You lost me' – which her mother readily echoed – 'There she is, back again!' Of course, neither Ruth nor her mother really believed that Ruth had been 'lost', or gone away: rather, the game provided a convenient framework for exploring the situation. There are many parallels here with a task which one of us (MH) devised for studying precisely this ability in preschool children. In this task, the child has to 'hide' a small boy figure from one or more policemen figures who are 'looking for him'. As with Ruth and her bottom, the children in the policemen task found little difficulty in constructing other points of view in the game-like situation.[5]

As well as working out what other people can see, the children frequently demonstrated the ability to calculate or infer what another person might know – or what they might need to know in order to carry out a particular action. Some children are less capable of this than others: we do not want to suggest that these four-year-olds were as able as adults to look at things or events from another's point of view. In particular, their ability to judge what information must be given to other people so that they could interpret their remarks was not always very well developed. Several of the conversations at school quoted in Chapters 9 and 10 illustrate this limitation. However, this skill is not always deployed by adults: most of us are egocentric from time to time. Our point is that these very young children did not totally lack the ability, but rather seemed to need a good deal more experience in its use.

Moreover, the children seemed extremely interested in other people's viewpoints, and in the way in which they are similar to, and different from, their own. Interest in other people – both children and adults – was a characteristic feature of most of the children in the study, and manifested itself in many different topics: their friends, other members of the family, growing up, birth, illness and death, what people did for their living, and so on. Indeed, it is worth remarking on the breadth of the children's interests, and the complexity of the issues which they raised. It is sometimes supposed that children of this age have special, childish interests, mainly to do with mothers, babies, dolls, teddies and animals, and such a view would be reinforced by most of the picture books published for children of this age. The conversations in our study suggest that, on the contrary, all human experience was grist to their intellectual mill.

Nor can we accept that young children are illogical, or incapable of making reasonable inferences from the information at their disposal. The transcripts – and particularly the episodes of intellectual search – contained many examples of children pursuing a topic that puzzled them with a painstaking and rigorous logic. While we agree with Piaget that young children's thinking is not the same as adult thinking, we do not believe that the essential difference lies in their illogicality. Instead, we would argue that their two major handicaps are their enormous ignorance and the limited conceptual framework within which their experience and thought is organized.

Although it may seem obvious that young children are very ignorant, this aspect of their functioning is rarely discussed by professionals. An imaginative leap is needed to understand their situation, in which almost everything that adults take for granted has yet to be learned. Because they are such active thinkers, children usually construct their own theories to fill the gaps in their knowledge. These theories surface and can be observed when a misunderstanding is apparent. Rosy's belief that tradespeople supply their customers with money, which emerged in the 'window-cleaner' conversation, is widely held by young children, although parents are not always aware of it. One child in our study, Sandra, made it clear by a request to her mother that she believed that the street lights were controlled from a switch in her living room. Another child, Pauline, appeared to believe that people with the same first name also have the same surname:

NEW TEACHER: What's your other name, Pauline who?
CHILD: Pauline Robinson. I've got two Pauline Robinsons.
TEACHER: Two Pauline Robinsons? Who's the other one?
CHILD: Pauline there [pointing to other child called Pauline].
TEACHER: We've got another Pauline? Yes, I don't think she's Pauline Robinson. Got Pauline, the same name as you. I think she has another name that's different from you.

Vida, possibly confused by a well-known children's TV programme, thought that clocks told the day of the week. She was playing with a toy clock, and the day was Wednesday:

CHILD: Where's Wednesday?
MOTHER: Where's Wednesday?
CHILD: Mm.
MOTHER: Today.
CHILD: Where is it? Which number?
MOTHER: It's here.
CHILD: Where?
MOTHER: Where? Oh, no, don't have it on the clock, you have it on a calendar.
CHILD: Oh.

Samantha asked for some cream to put on her face because she felt hot. Her mother spotted the cause of her error and corrected her very clearly: 'You don't put cream on when you're hot. You put cream on when you're sunbathing.'

The apparent illogicality of young children is thus often due, in our view, not to faulty logic, but to the fact that somewhere along the route they have taken on board false assumptions, or lack the experience to reject an implausible implication of a particular line of argument. The conversation on page 87, in which Lynne was puzzled about 'Nanny's Daddy' is a good example of this. So too is the following conversation, involving a four-year-old who was not in the study. Her older sister announced that she was going off to help 'get ready for the party':

CHILD: Whose party is it?
SISTER: Franny's Mum and Dad's party.
CHILD: Were Franny's Mum and Dad born on the same day?

The child's conclusion is a valid deduction from her limited knowledge. People have parties on their birthdays, and so if two people are having a party on the same day, they must have been born on the same day. The child did not lack logic, but rather lacked the knowledge that adults hold parties for reasons other than birthdays. For this reason we doubt the current theory that it is children's illogicality that makes them willing to believe in the truth of fairy stories. It seems more likely that they accept the reality of Father Christmas, the recovery of Red Riding Hood from the wolf's stomach, or the world that can be found at the bottom of a well, because they lack the knowledge to rule these events out as impossible.

The children's problem in thinking is not just that they lack useful items of information, as, for example, an older child might not know the name of the prime minister. It is rather that they have an imperfect grasp of a vast range of concepts which an older child or adult takes for granted. Thus, in this chapter, we have seen children believing that size and age are associated, that adults can 'grow up', that tradespeople pay their customers, that goods don't necessarily have to be paid for. These ideas are not foolish, but stem from their own experience – for example, of seeing shopkeepers giving change to their mothers. A good deal more experience, together with discussion with adults, will be needed to clarify these issues.

The impression we gained was that the mind of the four-year-old contains a large number of half-assembled scaffoldings which have yet to be integrated into a more coherent framework. At the same time, this lack of completeness allows the young child a certain degree of mental fluidity, in a way that may characteristically differentiate her from older children or adults. Particular objects or events are not necessarily viewed from a single viewpoint – as they might be by an older child or an adult – but may be seen from a number of different viewpoints, some appropriate, some less so. Thus Ruth, seeing bulbs in the garden, called them 'dead onions'. When her mother corrected her, she still persisted in asking, 'Are they dead?' This is not a question for adults, whose conceptual framework is much more fixed: alive and dead are not categories they would normally apply to either onions or bulbs.

This lack of knowledge, and the mental fluidity associated with it, may explain why questions are so prominent in the nursery years. The children in this study seemed in some sense aware that their conceptual framework was not yet substantial enough to cope with their experiences, and engaged themselves actively in the process of improving their intellectual scaffolding. The passages of intellectual search seemed particularly useful in this process, and indicated that the children were at some level aware that protracted dialogue with adults was a useful way of developing their conceptual knowledge. As we shall see in Chapter 11, these issues are not only of interest to psychologists, but have a direct bearing on nursery education, and on the kind of advice that is given to parents.

Overview

In this chapter we have argued that children of three or four have an intense need to understand their world, reflected in the large number of questions they ask. Analysis of entire conversations, especially 'passages of intellectual search', rather than individual questions, reveals the persistent and logical way in which they try to extend their understanding. It also reveals extensive areas of ignorance, misinformation and misunderstandings. The Piagetian model of children's minds, in our view, underestimates their thinking capacities, and fails to appreciate the way in which adults can help them to clarify their ideas.

6

Working-class verbal deprivation: myth or reality?

Up to this point we have not placed particular emphasis on the children's social background. We have, it is true, mentioned that some learning contexts (such as the mothers' use of imaginative play) were more common in the middle-class homes, while other contexts (such as formal 'lessons') were more common in the working-class homes, but we have not reported any systematic comparisons of the two social class groups. In this chapter we describe the analyses which we carried out to compare the learning environment of the middle-class and working-class homes.

Why study social class?

As we pointed out in Chapter 1, there are many psychologists, teachers and playgroup leaders who believe that working-class children are linguistically deprived, and in this chapter we will examine these beliefs in the light of our findings. However, there are also many who argue that social class is not a relevant factor for people working with young children. We will begin, therefore, by explaining why we included social class as a major variable in our study.

By social class we refer to the occupation of the children's fathers, which is the usual basis for social class classification. In the British Registrar General's classification, occupations are ranked from I to V, according to their supposed prestige. The major divide in this classification is between middle-class or white-collar workers (classes I, II and III non-manual) and working-class or manual workers (classes III manual, IV and V).

This classification of social class is one of the most powerful descriptive tools in the social scientist's armoury. The basic framework of a child's life – from her chance of surviving her first year of life to the age at which she is likely to marry, the number of children she is likely to have, and her chance of dying from various diseases – is strongly related to her social class.[1] Further, studies of childrearing carried out in Nottingham by John and Elizabeth Newson show that every aspect of childrearing, from the likelihood of children sucking their thumbs to the kind of punishment they receive, is related to social class.[2]

Social class influences are particularly strong in education. A major longitudinal study of British children – the National Child Development Study[3] – found that children from social class V are six times as likely to be poor readers at age seven as those from social class I, and fifteen times as likely to be non-readers. Of course, these are all statements of probabilities; plenty of middle-class children are poor readers, and working-class children are sometimes very successful at school. But the most powerful factor in explaining many aspects of children's lives remains the social class of their fathers.

How a man's occupation comes to have such a marked impact on his children's lives is an intriguing question. Occupation must be a 'proxy' variable, standing for a whole range of variables usually associated with it, including income, housing, educational status, values and beliefs. Many social class differences clearly stem from inequalities in wealth, but this cannot be the whole story. Economic factors alone cannot explain, for example, why fewer middle-class women than working-class women smoke, but more breastfeed their children, encourage their imaginative play and read them bedtime stories. It seems likely that these behaviours are determined by the kind of knowledge available to a person, including the kind of newspapers, magazines and TV programmes they select, and by a whole range of attitudes and values. But why should people in different occupations have different values? Both educational level and differing life experiences may be intervening factors. Thus someone who has been to a college or university, or whose livelihood depends on her skill with written language is likely to be much more concerned about the kind of books her children read than someone who relies primarily on her manual skills.

Because there is so much evidence that social class is related to many aspects of childrearing, any study of learning at home is bound to take this variable into account. This is especially true, as we show in the next section, if language is the focus of interest.

Social class and language development

For fifty years American and British studies have consistently shown that, on average, working-class children score lower than middle-class children on IQ tests and tests of language development.[4] While some psychologists argue that these differences in test scores are due to genetic differences in intelligence, it is more common to explain them in terms of differences in children's home environments. In particular, it is frequently argued that the underlying cause of working-class children's low test scares is the 'verbal deprivation' of their homes. In consequence, the children are said to lack the language skills needed to handle the demands of the classroom, and this, it is argued, is the underlying cause of their relative underachievement in school.

The precise nature of this verbal deprivation at home has been variously described. The crudest version is that working-class children are barely talked to by their parents. This belief leads to the following kind of injunction to parents, quoted approvingly in the Bullock Report: 'When you give your child a bath, bathe him in language.'[5] A more sophisticated theory holds that in 'disadvantaged' homes language is only used for simple purposes – for example, to describe events, or to control children. In another passage, the Bullock Report states: 'If a child does not encounter situations in which he has to explore, recall, predict, explain . . . he cannot bring to school a readymade familiarity with such uses.' Other widely held beliefs are that working-class mothers never play with their children, and that they fail to answer their questions.

Common to all versions of the 'verbal deprivation' theory is the following argument: that working-class children have deficient language skills; that these are due to deficiencies in the language environment of their homes; and that their inadequate language skills are the main cause of their poor performance at school. All three steps in this argument have been challenged by the American linguist, William Labov. In 1969 Labov wrote a famous paper about the language of black ghetto children, called 'The logic of non-standard English', in which he argued that 'the notion of verbal deprivation is part of the modern mythology of educational psychology'.[6] Labov contended that, far from receiving inadequate language stimulation at home, ghetto children grow up in a highly verbal culture, and that their dialect has the same potentiality for logical thinking as does standard English. Hence he concluded that it cannot be the language deficiencies of the child which are responsible for poor school performance. Language compensatory programmes are therefore unnecessary and misleading. The cause of the children's low educational achievement must be sought, not in their homes, but in the schools – for example, in the low expectations or low standards of the teachers.

Why, then, Labov asked, has the myth developed? His explanation was that lower-class children tend to become monosyllabic in conversation with authority figures. This apparent verbal deficit, he argued, is in reality a response to a social situation which they perceive as threatening. He illustrated his point by quoting from an interview transcript in which a black child answered questions briefly, almost monosyllabically. When the same interviewer transformed the social situation by sitting on the floor, sharing around potato crisps, bringing along another child, introducing taboo words and topics, and turning the interview into something more in the nature of a party, the previously non-verbal child began to talk freely. Labov concluded that the social situation is the most important determinant of verbal behaviour, and that an adult must enter into the right social relationship with a child if he wants to assess his language capacity.

It should be noted that Labov did not claim that there were *no* social class differences in children's language. He suggested that lower-class children might need help in learning to be explicit, and in extending their vocabulary, but not in conceptual and logical thinking. Some psychologists, however, have taken the view that there is no real social class difference in language ability. Deficits, they argue, appear only in test situations, where working-class children may be less at ease or less well motivated than middle-class children.

Most of the theories we have outlined are based on remarkably little evidence. First, no one has shown exactly how working-class children's verbal deficits result in difficulties in the classroom. What precisely are the language demands which they cannot meet? Secondly, there have been very few first-hand studies of whether language usage does in fact differ in families of different social class. The evidence usually cited relates either to very artificial situations, for example, mothers teaching their child a task or playing with them in a university laboratory, or to interviews in which mothers were asked what they talk about to their children. Thirdly, those psychologists who argue that test scores underestimate working-class children's language skills have not demonstrated their case by showing that in more natural situations there is no social class difference in these skills.

Our own study allowed us to make a new contribution to this issue. By observing mothers and children at home we were able to see whether or not there was any evidence for the generalizations that are so often made about language in homes of different social class. By following the children from school to home we were able to see whether, as Labov claimed, the way in which working-class children talk is adversely affected by the school setting. Finally, by testing the children on a standard verbal intelligence test we were able to see whether their test scores bore any relation to our measures of their spontaneous talk at home.

How we selected our social class groups

To ensure contrasting social class backgrounds, we selected children from two distinct groups. In the middle-class group the fathers came from social class I and II; in the working-class group from social class III manual, IV and V. In all our middle-class families the father was in a professional occupation, for example, journalism, social work or teaching. In the working-class group, nine of the fifteen fathers were in skilled manual occupations, for example, an engine fitter, electrician and heavy goods driver. The other six were in semi-skilled or unskilled occupations, for example, an asphalter, building labourer and milkman.

To allow for the influence of the mothers, we included her level of education in our selection criteria. That is, the middle-class group was selected from those whose fathers were in social class I and II, *and* whose mothers had either attended college or university, or had qualified to do so. The working-class group was selected from those whose fathers were manual workers, and whose mothers had left school at the minimal school-leaving age, with no public examination successes. The working-class mothers were thus educationally at the opposite extreme to the middle-class mothers. Because we used both educational and occupational criteria, the differences between the families were likely to be greater than in most British studies which have used only occupational criteria.

A third of the mothers in both groups worked part-time. In the case of the middle-class mothers, they generally worked as teachers, play-leaders or students; in the case of the working-class mothers, generally as cleaners. As would be expected, the middle-class families lived in superior housing. All but one lived in a house rather than a flat, and all had a garden. Of the fifteen working-class families, six lived in council flats without gardens, and the rest in terraced houses which had a small back yard or garden. All the children had a reasonable quantity of toys and books, although the middle-class girls were more likely to own toys similar to those of the nursery school.

Is there a social class difference in the amount of mother–child talk?

We began our analysis by seeing whether we could confirm one of the most widely held beliefs about social class and language, that 'no one talks to children in working-class homes'. We found no evidence to support this belief. There was no significant social class difference in the number of conversations, the length of conversations, or of the number of words in either mothers' or daughters' 'turns' of talk. In all but one working-class family a considerable amount of talk occurred. There was thus no support for the simplistic notion that the working-class children suffered from a lack of exposure to spoken language.

Is there a social class difference in the use of language?

The second belief that we attempted to investigate was that language is used for different purposes in middle-class and working-class homes. In Britain, this view has been put forward most forcefully by Joan Tough.[7] She argued that young working-class children rarely use language for such complex purposes as making comparisons, recalling the past, offering explanations or looking for differences. Most of their talk is concerned with controlling others ('Stop that'), expressing needs and wants ('I want my milk'), self-protection ('You're hurting me') and labelling ('That's a car'). According to Tough, working-class children have little experience of having their questions answered, or of hearing explanations, reasoning, predictions and projections into the experience of others. The model of language usage presented to these children is therefore very limited.

Based on these views, Tough devised a training programme for teachers which would enable them to appraise and foster children's complex use of language. Thousands of nursery and infant school teachers have taken this course.

We examined our transcripts to see if they offered support for Tough's views. Each turn of both mothers' and children's talk was scrutinized to see whether it involved using language in one of the more complex ways described by Tough:

1. Making comparisons, similarities and differences, e.g., 'You're too big for that lorry.'
2. Recalling events, e.g., 'Last week we went to Granny's, didn't we?'
3. Making future plans, e.g., 'We'll go swimming tomorrow.'
4. Linking at least two events in time, by the use of such words as 'while', 'when', 'until' and 'then', e.g., 'We can't go shopping till Daddy gets home.'
5. Describing purposes of objects, e.g., 'The elastic is for making a mask.'
6. Giving reasons, explanations, purposes or results of actions, e.g., 'The cat's run away 'cause you pulled her tail.' (Explanations which took the form of assertions, authority statements or the expression of wishes – e.g., because it is/I want to/I say so – were excluded.)
7. Using conditionals concerned with hypothetical events, e.g., 'If it stops raining we can go in the garden.'
8. Making generalizations and definitions, e.g., 'Pigs don't fly, birds do.'
9. Reasoning and inferring, e.g., 'If you eat your sweets, you can't save them.'
10. Projecting into self or other's thoughts or feelings, e.g., 'I expect Kate is feeling very sad now.'
11. Problem-solving, i.e., creative insight into the situation, e.g.,

CHILD: We haven't enough lolly sticks to make it. MOTHER: Well, we'll break them in two, then.

It should be noted that in our analysis the use of language was only scored if it was explicit. Thus a conditional statement ('If . . . then') was only scored if both parts of the statement were expressed. Similarly, an explanation was only scored if cause and effect were explicitly linked by the speaker. This decision was made because implicit uses proved so hard to spot that we did not feel confident that we could measure them reliably.

Of course, a great deal of routine conversation does not involve these usages of language. The following brief conversation, for example, did not include any complex use of language.

CHILD: Mum!
MOTHER: Yes.
CHILD: Let me play out?
MOTHER: You want to play out? Well, you're not to go away.
CHILD: OK.

Contrast the following equally brief, but linguistically more complex exchange between Joyce and her mother, which, like the first, took place in a working-class home:

CHILD: Mum! Watch this come down like a helicopter. [Joyce twists the chain of her swing]
MOTHER: Yes, but I did ask you to use the end swing, the rope one, in case that one bashes into someone.

We found that the middle-class mothers used language for complex purposes significantly more often than the working-class mothers – on average, adding the different usages together, fifty-one times an hour compared with thirty-eight times an hour for working-class mothers. The proportion, as well as the rate, of these uses of language was higher in the talk of the middle-class mothers. The averages conceal wide variations and there was a good deal of overlap between the social classes. However, five of the working-class mothers had lower scores than any middle-class mother.

This social class difference was present in all our categories of complex usage, with one exception, linking events in time. For each category the difference was relatively small – for example, on average the middle-class mothers gave explanations, or explained the purpose of objects, twenty times an hour, the working-class mothers fifteen times an hour:

Although there were social class and individual differences between mothers, *all* the mothers made comparisons, offered explanations, used 'If . . . then' constructions, and linked events in time, and all but one used language for recall and to discuss the future.

Here, one of the mothers who made the least use of language for these purposes is looking out of the window with Sandra:

MOTHER: Look. There's that bird.
CHILD: Where?
MOTHER: On the path. Eating some bread.
CHILD: Yeah.
MOTHER: Till Kitty [the family cat] sees him.
CHILD: Yeah, he run away. And Kitty would eat him.
MOTHER: She would if she could catch him.
CHILD: Yeah. I like birds.
MOTHER: Do you like birds?
CHILD: Yup.

In this brief conversation the mother introduces a future perspective and qualifies the child's prediction by introducing a conditional. The frequency of such remarks in every recording makes it very hard for us to believe in the reality of homes where intentions, possibilities, alternatives and consequences are not discussed.

Often, the mother's attempts to control the child involved her in using language for complex purposes. Samantha was scribbling in a colouring book when her mother intervened:

MOTHER: You colour in the pictures. Look, like that [points to one that Samantha had already done correctly. She goes on scribbling]. Samantha, they're not for drawing on, they're for colouring in.

At this point the cat came in the room and lay on the colouring book. Samantha stroked him.

MOTHER: Don't pick him up, because he's not very well. D'you know why he's lying on your book?
CHILD: That's why he wants, I think he wants to do some.
MOTHER: No – 'Cause it's nice and cool. Paper's nice and cool. [It was a very hot day]
CHILD: I want him to get off [tries to pull cat off].
MOTHER: You're making his tail wagging. Don't do that, Samantha.

A social class difference was also present in the frequency with which the *children* used language for complex purposes. This difference – on average twenty uses an hour in middle-class children compared to seventeen in working-class children – was considerably smaller than the difference between their mothers, but it was present in all the major categories of language usage. As with the mothers, it is important to note that the working-class girls did not lack these important verbal skills, but rather on average they used them less often. During the course of two and a half hours at home, all gave explanations, all but one made comparisons, recalled past events and discussed future plans, and all but two linked events in time and used 'If . . . then' constructions.

It must also be borne in mind that, in the case of both mothers and daughters, our analysis referred only to explicit uses. We do not know how the inclusion of implicit uses would have altered our findings.

Is there a social class difference in explicitness?

We have already noted Labov's suggestion that lower-class speakers may be less explicit in their use of language than middle-class speakers. The notion that implicitness characterizes working-class speech is also involved in Bernstein's theory that working-class speakers are oriented to a restricted language code, and middle-class speakers to an elaborated code.[8] (Bernstein's theory of codes contains many other elements, developed and refined over a long period of time.)

In an implicit use of language, the meaning of the statement is not fully spelled out, since the speaker assumes that the listener understands the unspoken component of the message. Most conversation contains a proportion of implicit talk. For example, one might say, 'I can't go for a holiday this summer, I had the outside of my house painted', or 'I'm not turning the central heating on, it's June'. It would be tedious and unnecessary to spell out the connections which are left implicit in these remarks. Yet the remarks can only make sense to people with enough experience of our culture to understand what is left unspoken. Another kind of implicit communication occurs when one person understands what another wishes and carries it out without being explicitly asked to do so. In Chapter 4 we cited the example of Cathie, who as part of what was clearly a familiar routine, copied her mother's writing without any explicit instructions.

To assess the extent of implicitness in communication would be a difficult and time-consuming process, and we did not attempt it. Generally, implicit communication is entirely successful, in the case of both adults and children, especially among people who know each other well. However, because of their relative lack of experience, children sometimes have particular difficulties in understanding explanations which are not spelled out explicitly.

The following exchange, for example, can have done little to clarify Kelly's belief that her mother could make candles:

CHILD: Where you make the candles [on the cake for her fourth birthday]?
MOTHER: Where did I make the candles? I had the candles.
CHILD: Had the candles?
MOTHER: Four.

Pauline's mother, worried that the baby might choke on the biscuit she had been given, issued a mysterious warning:

MOTHER: Don't play with her while she's eating it, just in case she gets a lump in there.
CHILD: Lump?
MOTHER: Mm.
CHILD: Why?
MOTHER: [No answer]

Because of the difficulty of measuring the extent of implicitness in a communication, we did not examine overall social class differences in this aspect of language. However, we did have some evidence that the middle-class mothers put more demands on their children to be explicit. While there was in most respects no social class difference in the kind of 'cognitive demands' that mothers made (see Chapter 8, page 164), there was one exception. This was with respect to a group of very difficult demands which involved the child in reflecting on the basis of her statement – e.g., 'I don't know what you mean', 'How do you know?' and 'What do you mean?' Sometimes these questions were asked rhetorically. However, in our study it was only the middle-class mothers who asked them with a pause, that is, an expectation that they would be answered. Examples of such questions can be found when Mina and her mother discuss tigers (page 89) and when Ann's mother tries to understand why Ann has said that children are not people (page 31).

In fact, demands of this type were beyond the capacity of most of the children. No child answered 'How do you know?' other than by saying ''Cause I know', while only two children could answer 'What do you mean?' Usually, when asked 'What do you mean?' they repeated their statement – Q: 'What do you mean, liquidy milk?' A: 'Liquidy milk.' One might therefore conclude that the mothers were foolish, or insensitive, to ask the questions. However, it is possible that being asked the questions, even though they could not answer them, conveyed to the children the idea that ambiguity can lead to failure in communication. The findings of a study carried out in Bristol by Peter and Elizabeth Robinson suggest that making this kind of demand on young children may have a long-term effect on their understanding of communication. The Robinsons found that children whose mothers had explicitly said to them, when they were two or three years of age, 'I don't know what you mean', were more advanced in their understanding of communication at the age of six than those whose mothers had not made this comment.[9]

However, although the mothers seemed to vary in the extent to which they encouraged explicitness in their children, *all* the mothers became explicit themselves when they wanted to be sure that there was no misunderstanding. In the following brief exchange one working-class mother spelled out the logical implications of her daughter's actions very clearly. Cindy had eaten most of her sweets and was wondering what to do with those that were left:

CHILD: I'll save these and eat them, right? [Possibly she meant that she would eat them later, but her mother wanted no misunderstanding]

MOTHER: You can't save them *and* eat them. You either save them and don't eat them, or you eat them. So what do you want to do? Save them? Or do you want to eat them?

CHILD: Save them and get another packet.

MOTHER: Where are you gonna get the money for the next packet?

It may be that social class difference in *what* is made explicit is as important as the extent of explicitness. Our study suggested, for example, that issues relating to money (who earned it, how it was spent, the scarcity of it) were more often spelled out explicitly in working-class homes.

Although there was evidence that all the mothers could become explicit when they wished, this was not the case with their children. In the following conversation Kelly is unable to explain that she wants a cup and straw of the same colour:

1. CHILD: I got the wrong straw. [She has a white cup and a yellow straw, while her sister May has a yellow cup and a white straw]
2. MOTHER: Huh?
3. CHILD: I got the wrong straw.
4. MOTHER: Why's that?
5. CHILD: That side that colour that [points to the cups].
6. MOTHER: What colour's that then [pointing to Kelly's cup]?
7. CHILD: That one?
8. MOTHER: What colour is it then?
9. CHILD: Red. [Incorrect – her cup is white]
10. MOTHER: White.
11. CHILD: White.
12. MOTHER: What colour's May's then?
13. CHILD: Blue. [May's cup is yellow]
14. MOTHER: Your dress is blue.

At this point, Kelly, having got nowhere by talking, resorts to direct action, and takes May's white straw to match her own white cup. May, not surprisingly, complains:

15. MOTHER: Give her back her straw before she hits you. [Gives white straw back to May]
16. CHILD: That must be mine [points to white straw].
17. MOTHER: Well go without then.
18. CHILD: I want that one. [The argument continues]

The mother makes an initial attempt to understand Kelly's meaning (turn 4), but Kelly can only produce an inadequate explanation of what is bothering her (turn 5). Her mother senses that the communication problem is in some way related to the child's ignorance of colour names (turn 6). At this point she abandons her attempt to understand Kelly, and initiates a question-and-answer teaching session. Kelly does not in fact know her colours well, but the lesson on colour-naming was not appropriately timed, since it did not coincide with her own motives in the conversation. Frustrated by the digression, she takes direct action (after turn 14), while continuing to attempt to justify herself (turn 16).

It should be noted that Kelly's difficulty was not that she lacked the concept of matching colours – note the emphatic use of 'That must be mine' in turn 16. Rather she was unable to express the concept in terms which her mother would understand, such as 'I should have the white straw to go with my white cup', or 'I want the same colour straw as my cup'. This difficulty was compounded by her mother's insensitivity or lack of patience. Mutual understanding was never achieved, and the conflict continued to escalate.

We should make it clear that this conversation was in no sense a 'typical' working-class conversation. Other working-class girls were more articulate, and other working-class mothers, for example, Joyce's mother, were much more sensitive. However, while children varied in their ability to express their meaning explicitly, it was our impression that some of the working-class girls had special problems in this respect.

Is there a social class difference in what is talked about?

In Chapter 3 we pointed out that most mothers, whatever their social class, discussed a wide range of topics with their children, often in the context of ongoing household activities. When we interviewed them, however, three-quarters of the middle-class mothers, but only a quarter of the working-class mothers, singled out this width of their curriculum as a central feature: 'She learns everything. How life is organized', was a typical middle-class answer.

These views were reflected in several aspects of the talk that we recorded. The middle-class mothers discussed a larger range of topics with their children than the working-class mothers. A significantly larger proportion of their conversations were concerned with topics that went beyond the 'here and now'. That is, they more often talked to their children about people who were not present, and about past and future events. Further, a larger proportion of their talk was concerned with conveying information to the children, and they gave their children more of the kind of information we classified as 'general knowledge' (science, history, geography etc.).

Perhaps related to this, the vocabulary they used in talking to their children was larger. Even in a very small sample of 200 words each, beginning with the first and the tenth page of each transcript, middle-class mothers and their daughters used a significantly larger number of different words than did working-class mothers and daughters. Another factor affecting vocabulary use may have been the value that the mothers placed on words. We had the impression that middle-class mothers were more concerned with deliberately extending their child's vocabulary, and encouraging them to use words correctly, as when Susan's mother corrected her use of the phrase 'a bit more' (page 75).

Some working-class mothers, in contrast, seemed content to work with a restricted vocabulary, provided that they could make themselves understood. The following conversation, for example, would be incomprehensible except to an observer, although the mother and child understood each other clearly. The mother is trying to persuade Tonia (aged three years and eleven months) to put on a cardigan:

CHILD: Don't want that one on, Mum.
MOTHER: Don't want that? Keep you nice and warm.
CHILD: Mummy? This. There. Put this on there. Put it on here. [She wants the belt tied round her dress, instead of round the cardigan]
MOTHER: No, I'll tie it round there. Put it on.
CHILD: I don't want it like this. Like that.
MOTHER: D'you want to go out in that [i.e., without the cardigan]?
CHILD: I wouldn't that. I want this, like this.
MOTHER: You have that round this [i.e., the belt should go round the cardigan].

And so on.

In this conversation meaning was perfectly communicated by means of pronouns and gestures, but a frequent resort to this type of communication seems likely to have the effect of restricting the size of the child's vocabulary. However, it should be stressed that the differences we found in vocabulary size and information content, although statistically significant, were very small. For example, on average, 36 per cent of the turns of talk of the middle-class mothers included information of some kind, compared with 32 per cent in the case of working-class mothers. Similarly, eighty-eight conversations about the past and future occurred in middle class homes, compared with sixty-eight in working-class homes. One kind of information occurred more frequently in the talk of working-class mothers than middle-class mothers – information relating to family, domestic and household matters – although this difference was not statistically significant.

Is there a social class difference in children's questions?

Some psychologists and teachers believe that young working-class children rarely ask questions out of curiosity. We found in our study that this was true if one observed the children at school (see Chapter 8). However, the social class difference was much smaller at home. The middle-class girls' talk to their mothers contained a slightly higher proportion of questions of all kinds: 7 per cent of all their turns of talk included a question, compared with 6 per cent for the working-class girls. This difference is tiny, although statistically significant. There was, however, a much larger difference in the *kinds* of questions asked. The middle-class girls asked their mothers more 'curiosity' questions (see Chapter 5, page 83), twenty-one per hour compared with twelve per hour in the case of working-class girls. On the other hand, working-class girls asked more 'business' and 'challenging' questions – the latter made up 13 per cent of their questions compared with 8 per cent for the middle-class girls.

Many of these challenging questions were 'Whys' and although not asked out of curiosity, usually gave rise to explanations. It might therefore be suggested that 'curiosity Whys' and 'challenging Whys' are equivalent, differing only in the context in which they appear. Nevertheless, when all 'Whys', whether classified as curiosity or challenging, are combined, it was still the case that the middle-class girls asked more 'Why' questions (nine per hour) than the working-class girls (five per hour).

'Passages of intellectual search' were also more common in the conversation of middle-class children. There were forty-one of these passages in the home transcripts of thirteen of the middle-class girls, compared with sixteen in the home transcripts of four of the working-class girls. Further, on average the middle-class girls' passages of intellectual search lasted for a longer period of time.

How are these differences to be explained? It could be argued that they are related to the finding that the middle-class girls scored higher on IQ tests. This point will be discussed on page 128. Alternatively, they could be the consequence of differences in the behaviour of the two groups of mothers. Middle-class mothers might 'reinforce' questioning by giving frequent and satisfying answers, while working-class mothers might fail to reinforce questions by not answering them at all. Or a completely different learning process might be responsible, with the middle-class mother 'modelling' question-asking by asking a great many questions herself.

Is there a social class difference in mothers' answer?

In order to look at the possibility that mothers of different social class gave different types of answers, we categorized mothers' answers to 'Why' questions as 'full', 'adequate', 'inadequate', and 'no answer'. A crude measure of a full answer was that it contained more than one clause. More precisely, by full answers we meant answers in which an event was explained in relation to a general principle, or a detailed explanation of a process was given, or a specific issue was set in a wider context. An example of a full answer to the question, 'Why is that there?' (indicating the pointer on a sundial) might be, 'It tells the time by the sun. The shadow of the pointer marks the hours. As the sun crosses the sky, the shadow moves.' Or, to the question, 'Why haven't we got a fireplace?' the mother might have answered, 'It was hard work carrying the coal from the cellar to the sitting room, and the coal fire made the room very dirty, so we blocked up the fireplace.'

A surprisingly small proportion of 'Why' questions (6 per cent altogether) received full answers. Life being short, and mothers having much on their minds, they were much more likely to give what we called 'adequate' answers (37 per cent altogether). These were answers which were focused on the question, but contained little by way of explanation – e.g., 'It tells you the time'; 'We blocked it up'. The third category of answers, definitely inadequate answers, were almost as frequent (32 per cent). These were implicit or oblique or irrelevant answers, or answers which gave associated information but didn't answer the question – e.g., in these cases, 'I haven't seen one of those for a long time'; 'Your father had enough'. A quarter of all 'Why' questions were not answered at all. Other possible ways of answering questions, for example, by saying 'I don't know', were, in practice, extremely uncommon.

There were significant social class differences in the frequency with which some types of answers were given. Middle-class mothers gave 'adequate' answers to 44 per cent of their children's questions, compared with only 27 per cent from the working-class mothers. Both groups of mothers gave an almost identical, very low, proportion of full answers (6 per cent), and both gave a similar proportion of inadequate answers.

Working-class mothers were, however, more likely than the middle-class mothers to ignore their children's questions (34 per cent compared with 28 per cent).

It is easy to suggest reasons for these differences. Sometimes children's questions are very difficult to answer. The adult must be in possession of, and confident enough to offer, the relevant information, and also be able to convey it in terms which the child can understand. Among the questions of this kind which we recorded were 'Why is this a round chair?' 'Why doesn't the battery work?' 'Why they hot cross buns?' 'How do they make him [puppet on TV] talk?' 'Why are there little ones [stars] as well as big ones?' It seems possible that highly educated mothers could tackle these questions with more confidence than those less well educated. However, only a small minority of 'Why' questions fell into this category.

A more important factor may be a social class difference in attitudes towards children's questions. When we interviewed the mothers some weeks after the recording, one question which we put to them was, 'Children do keep asking questions at this age. How do you feel about this?' The middle-class mothers were much more likely than the work-ing-class mothers to reply that they enjoyed answering questions, and to indicate that they thought answering questions helped their child's development. Typical comments were that the questions were interest-ing, that it was interesting working out how to answer them, or that they showed that the child was thinking. Four working-class mothers, but none of the middle-class mothers, said that they definitely *disliked* answering questions. They felt that the children never seemed to get to the end of questions, that it was a strain, that they tried their patience, and that children *would* ask them at the wrong time. Of course, as in all social class differences, there was a good deal of overlap in attitude.

On average, then, the middle-class mothers answered 'Why' questions more often, and more adequately. This finding would seem to be a sufficient explanation of their children *asking* these questions more frequently. However, if that were the case, one would expect the two measures to be correlated – those children who asked the most questions should have mothers who most frequently answered them or who gave the fullest answers. In fact, no such association occurred. It seems likely, therefore, that in individual cases the children's behaviour was influ-enced by other factors than how their mothers answered them.

One such factor appeared to be the mothers' propensity to ask questions themselves. Those mothers who asked a lot of quesions tended to have children who did the same. It looked, then, as though the children modelled themselves on their mothers in this respect. At school, as we will see, this was not the case.

Is there a social class difference in mothers' play with children?

It is often stated that working-class mothers rarely play with their children. In our study we found that all except two working-class and three middle-class mothers played with their children at some time during the afternoon, sometimes very briefly (see Chapter 3). All the mothers talked to their children about their play. There was no social class difference in the total time that mothers spent playing with their children, but differences between individual mothers were vast. Some mothers of both social class spent a large part of the afternoon in play, while others barely joined in play at all.

There was some evidence of a social class difference in the *kind* of play mothers joined in. When asked their views on play, most of the middle-class mothers mentioned the value of imaginative play. In fact, we observed six middle-class mothers, but only one working-class mother, taking a role in an imaginative game, and all these mothers introduced a great deal of educational input into the games. This did not necessarily mean that the working-class children played fewer imaginative games than the middle-class children, but only that their mothers less often took a role in their play. We found that they talked to their mothers about their imaginative play as often as middle-class children did. Davie, too, in her study in Stoke found no social class difference in the amount of children's imaginative play at home.[10] On the other hand, we observed exciting physical games between mothers and children more frequently in working-class than in middle-class homes. Eight working-class mothers, but only two middle-class mothers, played chasing and tickling games.

Most of the working-class mothers believed that children could learn from play. But they tended to see only certain kinds of play, particularly jigsaw puzzles, drawing, and any games involving numbers and letters as educational, while the middle-class mothers, intent on extending their children's general knowledge and thinking skills, saw imaginative play as another useful medium for learning.

All the children spent rather more than half their time at home playing, but the working-class children spent a greater proportion of the afternoon in play. This seemed to be largely because, unlike the middle-class children, they rarely sat down to eat a midday meal with their mothers. Instead, they tended to be given a snack to eat while they were playing. In these families, the main meal of the day was in the evening, when the father and other family members were present. As we saw in Chapter 5 *tête à tête* meals between mother and child were often the occasion for a topic to be discussed at length and in depth. This was because there were few distractions, and the mothers could give their full attention to the child. Those children who ran off with a sandwich to play gained in playing-time. They may also have gained in some feeling of family cohesion, and learned from family conversation, if they shared a general family meal in the evening. On the other hand, they missed the kind of educational opportunity that was possible in a *tête à tête* with their mothers.

Are there social class differences in the use of control?

It is widely believed that working-class mothers are constantly disciplining their children, and that their approach is very authoritarian: 'Do what I say or – ' While our study was not focused on discipline, we did analyse some aspects of mother–child interaction over this issue.

Life with a young child inevitably involves an element of control, because of the child's inexperience. However, we found an enormous range in the amount of control remarks used by mothers. By this we meant instructions to the child to do or not to do something, which the mother hoped would be obeyed, rather than suggestions. At one extreme we found two mothers who made only fifteen control remarks to their children in the course of the afternoon, while, at the other extreme, two mothers made respectively 137 and 153 control remarks. The range was particularly great among the working-class mothers, but on average there was no social class difference in the frequency or proportion of control remarks. However, there was some evidence that control was a more salient feature of life in the working-class homes, in that the working-class mothers were more likely to initiate conversations with control remarks than were the middle-class mothers.

There was very little social class difference in what the control was about. In both social classes, most control talk was concerned with the children's manners, with avoiding damage or waste to property, and with avoiding damage to people, usually the child herself.

We did not differentiate between positive control, that is, telling the child to do something, and negative control, telling the child to stop doing something. We did, however, look at disputes. These were occasions when either the child resisted the mother's control, or the mother resisted the child's demands. As described in Chapter 4, there was a great range in the number of disputes *within* social classes, with a small group of working-class families being extremely disputatious. This was reflected in the greater proportion of 'challenging Why' questions asked by working-class children (see page 122).

In just over a half of disputes (57 per cent) the working-class mothers justified their stance by an explanation. This happened rather more often (in 68 per cent of disputes) in the middle-class homes. Threats and bribes were uttered in 10 per cent of the disputes in working-class homes, and 7 per cent of the disputes in middle-class homes. Justifications by authority ('Because I say so') occurred in only 3 per cent of working-class disputes, and 1 per cent of middle-class disputes.

We found no evidence, then, of overall social class differences in the amount of control, or in the issues over which control was exercised. We also found little to justify the stereotype of the authoritarian working-class mother – in all the homes, what happened was very much a process of negotiation between mother and child. Middle-class mothers more often explained the reasons for their control, but the class difference in this respect was relatively small. The most striking social class difference was in the frequency with which the mother's control was disputed. Although disputes were rare in some working-class homes, they were a very prominent feature of life in others.

IQ and the child's talk at home

After the study was completed all the children were tested with the Stanford-Binet test by a clinical psychologist who knew nothing about the study. The average IQ score of the middle-class children was 122; that of the working-class children, 106. This large difference is typical of other studies of IQ and social class. The Stanford-Binet test for this age contains mainly language items, for example, naming objects in pictures, and asking such questions as 'Why do we have houses?' 'What is a chair made of?' Although usually considered a test of general intelligence, high scores depend on the extent of the child's vocabulary and general knowledge, as well as her grasp of more basic verbal skills, such as understanding the concept 'different'. Children's IQ scores may also be affected by other factors, such as the extent to which they understand the tester's intentions, and their ease and motivation in a test situation.

In our study there were no statistically significant associations between the children's IQ scores and the extent of their vocabulary or the frequency or proportion of complex usages of language in their talk, or of any particular type of complex usage. There were, however, some associations, but only within the working-class group, between question-asking and IQ scores. The working-class children with higher IQ scores asked a greater proportion of all types of question, including 'Why' questions, and 'curiosity' questions, than the working-class children with lower IQ scores. Within the middle-class group there was no such relationship. There was also no association within the middle-class group between IQ score and the frequency of 'passages of intellectual search'. These passages occurred in the conversations of only four working-class children. Their IQs varied from average to above average – they were 103, 104, 126, 135.

Our evidence about the relation between children's IQ scores and the nature of their spontaneous talk at home is thus conflicting and difficult to interpret. It is possible that there *is* an association, but that our measures of spontaneous language were not the right ones to reveal it. Because our study was not primarily concerned with assessing children's language skills, we did not make a comprehensive assessment of their spontaneous talk. Moreover, we do not know how reliable our measures of spontaneous talk were, in statistical terms. It was certainly our impression that the talk of the girls with the highest IQs, such as Beth, Susan and Ann, was more advanced than that of the other children, although none of our measures of spontaneous talk supported this impression. It is also possible, as we suggest above, that the large social class difference in IQ does not reflect, or only in part reflects, a difference in verbal skills. This was the conclusion reached by Wells, who found a similar discrepancy between test scores and spontaneous language.[11]

Overview

We started this chapter by pointing out that social class differences can be found in almost every aspect of childrearing. It was not surprising, therefore, to find them in several aspects of mother–child conversation, as well as in mothers' views about education at home, and play.

By no means all our measures showed social class differences. There was no social class difference in the amount of mother–child talk, the length of conversations, the frequency and nature of the mothers' questions and controlling remarks, or the amount that mothers played with their children. However, middle-class mothers tended to make more frequent use of language for complex purposes, and used a wider vocabulary in talking to their children. They more often gave their children information, of a wider range, and they more often took a role in their imaginative play. They also took their children's 'Why' questions more seriously than working-class mothers, that is, they less often ignored them and more often gave them adequate answers. The working-class mothers, on the other hand, tended to give their daughters more information on family, household and domestic topics than middle-class mothers did (although this difference was not statistically significant), and they more often played exciting physical and 'fun' games with them. Disputes between mother and daughter were very frequent in a minority of working-class homes, and explanations for control were offered rather less frequently.

There were similar, but smaller, social class differences in the children's talk. The working-class girls asked fewer 'Why' questions overall, but more 'challenging' questions. They less often used language for complex purposes, they used a smaller vocabulary, and fewer of them had 'passages of intellectual search'. They spent rather more time during the afternoon playing than the middle-class children did.

It is important not to exaggerate these differences. There was a wide range of behaviour within each social class group, with some working-class mothers and children using language in the same ways as middle-class mothers, and vice versa. Further, the differences were quite small. *All* the mothers made some use of language for complex purposes, and at times became very explicit and gave full explanations. *All* the children asked some 'Why' questions and on at least one occasion gave an explanation, made a comparison, and so on.

Both Bernstein and Labov contend that working-class children are as competent at conceptual and logical thinking as middle-class children. Our findings support this view. What we observed was a difference in the *frequency* of certain categories of talk. The differences were far too small to suggest that the working-class children suffered from 'language deprivation'. Our findings are more consistent with the notion of a difference in language *style*, related to a difference in underlying values and attitudes. The working-class mothers seemed to place less stress on introducing their young daughters to a wide range of general knowledge and information and extending their vocabulary, and on giving them adequate answers whenever they asked questions. On the other hand, they seemed to place more stress on helping their daughters to acquire domestic and mothering skills. These differences obviously make sense in terms of the different educational and occupational careers of the two groups of women.

So strong is the belief in a working-class language deficit that some teachers have been incredulous of our findings, arguing that in *their* schools children arrive 'hardly able to talk'. Quite reasonably, they have objected that our small sample, composed entirely of girls who attend nursery schools or classes, may not be representative of working-class children in general. Others have objected that our sample was not drawn from the lower social class, since two-thirds of our working-class sample had fathers who were skilled manual workers. In this respect, however, our study does not differ markedly from most British school-based studies of working-class children. Families with fathers in semi-skilled or unskilled occupations never constitute a majority in any school, even in deprived areas.[12] In fact, our two social class groups were exceptionally polarized, since the children were selected because their mothers had either unusually high or unusually low educational achievements.

Wells's study of spontaneous talk in the homes of 128 boys and girls from all social groups in Bristol also found no evidence of language deficit. Brief samples of their conversation were recorded at home with radio-microphones at intervals between the ages of fifteen months and five years. Like us, Wells found that social class differences in children's test scores were much larger than those in their spontaneous language. The aspects of language that he examined were not the same as in our study, but there was a good deal of overlap. The class differences he found were even smaller and fewer than ours. Although there were big individual differences between children, Wells was more impressed by 'the very great similarity between children in the amount [of language] they have learnt by the time they reach school age'. He concludes that 'with the possible exception of at most two children out of 128, all have developed mastery of the major meaning relations encoded in the sentences, and of the syntactic structures through which they are realized, and all are using language for a wide variety of functions'. Wells found no difference in any of these respects between boys and girls.[13]

Most linguists, in fact, are convinced that language acquisition is one of the most robust processes at work in childhood, although they disagree about whether the reason for this robustness is biological or social. This does not, of course, mean that all children acquire language at the same rate, or ultimately achieve equal mastery of it. It does mean that biologically intact children all master the basic verbal thinking skills. We suspect, therefore, that the children who are said to enter school hardly able to talk are almost always children who can talk perfectly well at home, but are initially too ill at ease to display the full range of their verbal skills when they enter school.

The question remains of whether, and to what extent, social class differences in language style of the kind we describe are likely to affect the children's subsequent achievements in school. This is an issue which our study cannot answer.

7

An afternoon with Donna and her mother

Up to this point we have presented our findings in a piecemeal fashion, one topic at a time. We thought, however, that it might be helpful to give an idea of how the various aspects of education at home that we have discussed coalesced in the case of one particular mother and daughter.

The selection of the family was necessarily arbitrary. Since all the children and their mothers were very distinct personalities, none of them could be considered in any sense 'typical'. We picked Donna because she is in many ways an extreme example, confirming many people's stereotyped impressions of working-class upbringing. As we shall see, Donna was very demanding, and much of the time was spent in wrangles and disputes. In addition, her mother did not engage in the kind of educational play valued by nursery teachers: indeed, there was little play of any kind during the afternoon. Yet the overall picture did not confirm any stereotypical view of the inadequacies of working-class language. Instead, our analysis of the afternoon makes clear that, despite the disputes and wrangling that go on, Donna's home provided a rich learning environment.

Donna was three years and ten months at the time of our recording, and of about average IQ (104). Her father was a carpenter. During the mornings, while Donna was at nursery class, Donna's mother worked as a cleaner in a pub, taking the baby, Kerry, with her. They lived in a small terraced council house, with a back yard. When we interviewed her some weeks after the recording, Donna's mother told us that she was anaemic. She said that she found it a strain looking after two young children, doing her cleaning job and keeping her own house clean and tidy, especially as she was very house-proud. The house was, in fact, spotless. She made it clear that Donna got on her nerves. Donna was very attention-seeking and moody, and her mother had not the patience for her endless questions. She also found Donna hard to manage. Donna did what she was told at school, but took no notice of what her mother told her at home. Still, her mother described her as a very lovable child, and she liked her independent character. Donna's mother said that during the recording she had made more effort than usual not to lose her temper, though she had done so on several occasions. She thought that Donna, too, had not got 'into a huff' quite as often as usual, and was perhaps a bit subdued. This self-account of their relationship sounds unpromising, but as we shall see, there was clear evidence in the recordings of Donna's mother's real concern for her, which led to many interactions of educational value.

Donna was certainly a demanding girl, and much of the first hour at home was dominated by this aspect of her personality. She had had lunch at school. At the start of the recording session her mother had just put the baby down for an after-lunch sleep; having spent the morning at her cleaning job, she now wanted to get on with her own housework. It would have suited her very well if Donna had played quietly by herself, but this was not to be. Donna spent much of the hour plying her mother with a series of demands, most of which were greeted with refusal and annoyance.

Donna started by getting her mother to sort out her dolls. However, she then only played with them for three minutes before embarking on a series of demands. She wanted to take off the special recording dress, but this request was, not surprisingly, refused. Her mother offered her an iced lolly which she accepted, but she wanted a biscuit as well. Donna's mother refused at first, but after many more demands eventually gave in. Donna next wanted to play with the baby's bottle, and when this was refused she asked for another biscuit. Her mother was by now getting annoyed, and threatened that if Donna 'kept it up' she would be sent to bed. It was clear that this threat had become part of their habitual way of interacting, for Donna's mother frequently shortened it to 'Keep it up, Don', a remark which was fairly meaningless without a prior history. But Donna did, however, keep up her series of demands: she asked for another lolly, she wanted some new plimsolls, she wanted to take off her T-shirt, and she asked her mother several times if she would play with her. Almost all these requests were turned down, and Donna usually responded with a moan or a whine. Other things happened which added to her mother's annoyance with her: she made snorting noises with her nose, and refused to blow it; she was told to stop shouting because of the baby; she discovered her slippers were broken, and her mother discovered she had managed to get grease on her clothes.

During this period Donna hardly played at all. She repeatedly and unsuccessfully tried to persuade her mother to play with her. Her mother, who was busy with housework, suggested a fantasy game for Donna to play with her teddy bear ('Go and give teddy some [iced lolly]'). When this was not taken up, and Donna's demands escalated, her mother frequently and angrily told her to 'Go and play'. Eventually, Donna decided to amuse herself by jumping about on the stairs, which brought another rebuke: 'Will you please go upstairs? You're getting on my nerves. Go on.'

Put like this, the first hour sounds fairly grim. Yet there were several things happening which indicated that the overall picture was not as bleak as this account suggests.

First, it was clear that throughout the wrangling and disputing that took up so much of this hour, Donna and her mother still shared a close and warm relationship with each other. From time to time this warmth broke through into their conversations. The following conversation took piece while Donna was sitting on the toilet; her mother was also in the bathroom, waiting for her to finish. Donna was talking in a loud voice, and her mother told her to stop shouting or else she would wake Kerry:

CHILD: Naughty boys scream, don't they, and wake their own babies up.

MOTHER: Mmm, they do, don't they?

CHILD: Even the naughty boys wake our baby up, won't they?

MOTHER: Mm . . . naughty boys that play outside.

CHILD: Yeah, and they mustn't, they must go to bed like me and Kerry.

MOTHER: Yeah.

CHILD: Me and Kerry don't scream when you take us to bed, do we?

MOTHER: No.

CHILD: Like all naughty children they scream in bed, don't they?

MOTHER: They do, don't they? . . . You re a good girl, ain't ya?

CHILD: So is Kerry . . . Well, she screams in the night. She usually screams.

MOTHER: Why?

CHILD: And I can't get to sleep when she screams, can I?
MOTHER: No, you can't.
CHILD: Or even cry.
MOTHER: Who cries?
CHILD: Kerry.
MOTHER: Ah, that's only if she's not feeling very well.
CHILD: Yeah. And she screams if she's not very well, don't she?
MOTHER: Still, she was a good girl last night, wasn't she?
CHILD: So was I.
MOTHER: You're always a good girl when you go to sleep. Sometimes when you get bellyache you do.
CHILD: Yeah, it don't matter when I cry or I got bellyache, does it?
MOTHER: Not if you really got a bellyache, no.

There was clearly a warmth between Donna, her mother and Kerry, which comes across in the concern they showed each other in this conversation. It showed itself, not only in the little remarks like 'You're a good girl', but also in the way Donna's mother was prepared patiently to follow along with Donna's thinking, as she progressed from naughty children waking up babies, through Kerry waking *her* up, to whether it mattered if she, Donna, cried when she woke up.

There were several other occasions during that first hour when Donna's mother showed the same concern. For example, she expressed an interest in Donna's life at school, asking her what she had had for lunch. Donna replied that she had had fish and chips and peas, and then added a very surprising remark, which her mother tried at length to elucidate:

CHILD: I have winkles on my tea.
MOTHER: Winkles? You can't have had winkles.
CHILD: Not for dinner.
MOTHER: What did you have them for, then?
CHILD: For afters.
MOTHER: Winkles for afters? Are you *sure* they were winkles?
CHILD: Going to ask my teacher tomorrow?
MOTHER: Well, if you say you had winkles, love. What did they look like? What colour were they?

The questioning continued for some time, Donna's mother finally deciding that she must have meant strawberries; winkles, she said, are 'rubbery fishy things that you don't like'.

This concern to understand what her little daughter was trying to say showed in a number of conversations. Donna, like many children of her age, was somewhat confused about time concepts. In the following conversation she expressed a puzzlement, which seemed to derive from a belief that the 'afternoon' was a specific point in time, rather than a longish period:

CHILD: Is it stafternoon yet, Mum? Is it stafternoon yet?
MOTHER: Yes, it's this afternoon.
CHILD: Has Aunty gone to pick Mary [her cousin] up now?
MOTHER: No, not yet, it's too early.
CHILD: Is it stafternoon?
MOTHER: It's this afternoon now, but it's too early to pick Mary up. Why?
CHILD: 'Cause she's still at school at afternoons?
MOTHER: Yes, till three o'clock. It's only about half past one now.

Donna's mother gave her many explanations in the course of the afternoon, often in the context of control. She did not usually turn her demands down flat, but for the most part gave some kind of reason or explanation for why she was doing so. True, these explanations were often fairly minimal or implicit, as when she said Donna could not play with the bottle ''cause it's glass' (and presumably might break, although this was not made explicit). But other explanations were detailed and explicit, and gave both Donna and us a clear picture of the constraints and realities of her life. Consider, for example, how she responded to yet another request by Donna to come and play with her:

MOTHER: I'm just going to do this work first, love. I've got washing to do.
CHILD: Yeah?
MOTHER: Got ironing to do.
CHILD: Yeah?
MOTHER: I got hoovering to do.
CHILD: Yeah?
MOTHER: Yeah, well it all takes time, love.
CHILD: And then you're finished?
MOTHER: Yeah, and then I'm finished.
CHILD: I don't want you to do hoovering, or washing, or . . . [Moans]

MOTHER: I'm sorry, but I've got to.

CHILD: Or ironing.

MOTHER: You know Mummy doesn't get much time Fridays. [Friday was the following day, so mother has to do more today]

CHILD: Oh . . . why did you have to do your washing up? [Donna presumably meant washing]

MOTHER: Well I didn't do none yesterday . . . We went out, didn't we, up Nanny's yesterday.

What is interesting here is not just Donna's mother's concern to give Donna an understanding of what she had to do, but her assumptions about what she might know or understand. 'You know Mummy doesn't get much time Fridays' was fairly opaque, particularly given that today was Thursday. She assumed that Donna would not only know that it was Thursday, but would also make the deduction that because she had not much time tomorrow, she would have to do more today. That in turn rested on a recognition that there was a fixed amount of housework waiting to be done. It was not clear, of course, how many of these inferences Donna actually made, or even whether she was capable of doing so.

While it may not be clear from the preceding conversation whether Donna understood the realities of her mother's working life, the following conversation suggests that she had some insight at least into the realities of her father's working life. Donna had finally managed to persuade her mother to go and sit on the step outside with her; even so, her mother was still feeling the constraints on what she could do:

1. MOTHER: I can't sit here for long. [Starts to fit Donna's slippers on her]
2. CHILD: Why?
3. MOTHER: Because your father'll be in soon.
4. CHILD: It's not dinner time yet.
5. MOTHER: It's gone dinner time, doesn't come here for lunch, does he? Not now. Works too far away.
6. CHILD: Why don't he come up here for lunch?
7. MOTHER: 'Cause it takes too long for him to get home and back to work again.
8. CHILD: And he's not allowed to?
9. MOTHER: No.
10. CHILD: Or he get, or he won't get lots of money?

11. MOTHER: No, he won't get lots of money, and then you won't get no new slippers.
12. CHILD: No, or new shoes?
13. MOTHER: Won't get them both this week, love.

This episode of persistent questioning did not amount to a 'passage of intellectual search'. It seemed more that Donna was confirming what she already knew, than seeking to understand something that puzzled her Turn 8, for example, suggests that she was aware that whether or not her father could take a long lunch break was something that he himself did not determine; rather it was determined for him. Moreover, if he did do something he was not allowed to, then he would not get paid (turn 10). Donna's mother lost no time in making the connection between her husband not getting paid and Donna's requests for new slippers and shoes. Thus the conversation rotated almost full circle: from Donna's demands that her mother sat with her on the step, to her demands for new slippers and shoes. En route, the economics of the family unit, and the constraints that it made on mother, father, Donna herself, had all been made clear.

Ths conversation, in fact, marked the beginning of a new phase in the afternoon's activities. Despite the large amount of housework pressing on her, Donna's mother stayed on the step with her for some time, and much of this was spent entertaining each other with stories and songs. (In the subsequent interview, Donna's mother told us that what she most enjoyed doing with Donna was singing.) She started by telling Donna about the dog at the pub where she worked; she promised to take Donna to see him some day:

CHILD: Does he bite you?
MOTHER: No, he likes to play. Threw his bowl at me this morning.
CHILD: Why?
MOTHER: Picked it up with his teeth and threw it at me.
CHILD: Why?
MOTHER: 'Cause he wanted some tea, and that was his way of telling me he wanted some tea.
CHILD: Does he say 'two teas'?
MOTHER: No, dogs can't talk, love.
CHILD: What do they say?
MOTHER: They bark.
CHILD: How?

MOTHER: Went 'woof woof' [pretends to bark].
CHILD: 'Woof woof'.
MOTHER: 'Woof woof'.
CHILD: 'Woof woof'.
MOTHER: Then he picked his bowl up with his teeth and he went 'Oogh!' Then he dropped it on the floor, right in front of me there. And I said to him, 'Do you want some tea?' and he went, 'Woof.' So I got the bowl and gave him some tea.
CHILD: You didn't! [Laughs]
MOTHER: I did! He doesn't have sugar in his tea, though . . . just the milk and tea.
CHILD: How does doggies drink tea, then?
MOTHER: He has it in a bowl and he licks it with his tongue. Like Auntie Doris's cat when it licks *his* milk up.
CHILD: Oh, like a cat.
MOTHER: Like a cat.

The story was a good one. At first sight it seemed far-fetched, yet Donna's mother made it sound very plausible: indeed, she introduced a strong note of reality when she said that dogs can't talk. It probably didn't matter whether it was true or not; what mattered was that the story entertained and captivated Donna, prompting her to ask further questions about the ways in which cats and dogs drink from their bowls.

The light-hearted mood was developed further over the next few conversations. Donna got off the steps and started jumping down from the steps on to the pavement. Her mother told her not to, as she would hurt herself, but Donna kept on jumping. Her mother kept on telling her off, but in a much more light-hearted manner than she was using earlier when they were inside:

MOTHER: You've only gotta fall and you'll hurt yourself . . . and you'll tell Daddy I've gone and beaten you up, won't you?
CHILD: I'm gonna tell him later on, when he comes in tonight.
MOTHER: If you're gonna tell him I'm *gonna* beat you up!! [Tickles child, who laughs]
CHILD: I'm gonna tell him!
MOTHER: What you gonna tell him?
CHILD: 'Cause Mummy's being beating me up.
MOTHER: Oh, ho ho ho fibber!
CHILD: Beat me up and then I *will* tell him.

MOTHER: Beat you up and then you will tell him, no [laughs].

CHILD: Beat me up and then I won't tell him, then.

MOTHER: Beat you up and you won't tell him? You want me to beat you up, do you?

CHILD: Yeah.

MOTHER: What, like this?

Donna's mother pretended to beat her up, and the two of them enjoyed some tickling and rough-and-tumble on the front step. They ended up with Donna sitting on her mother's knee:

MOTHER: Tell me a story.

CHILD: [Starts singing] 'Humpty Dumpty . . .'

MOTHER: No, that's a song, tell me a story. Tell me that one about the three bears, I like that.

CHILD: Three bears went out one day.

MOTHER: Yeah?

CHILD: In the forest.

MOTHER: Mm?

CHILD: And little girl came along.

MOTHER: What was her name?

CHILD: Poleck.

MOTHER: Goldilocks! [Laughs] Poleck!

CHILD: Goldilocks, and she eat baby's breakfast but was too sweet.

MOTHER: Mm.

CHILD: And she eat Mummy's breakfast, was too hot. Eat Daddy's breakfast, was just right.

MOTHER: Yeah? Go on . . .

CHILD: She eat it all up, she broke the chair, and she was in . . .

MOTHER: [Interrupts] Broke whose chair?

CHILD: Daddy's chair.

MOTHER: Baby's chair, you're getting mixed up.

CHILD: Baby's chair.

MOTHER: Yeah, go on then.

CHILD: And she got in baby's cot, and she said, 'Who's sleeping in my one? And who's sleeping with my one? And who's sleeping with my one?'

MOTHER: Yeah, well what about the three bears, have they come back yet?

CHILD: And they eat all the porridge up.

MOTHER: Who ate all the porridge up?
CHILD: Sarah and me! [Sarah was one of Donna's friends]
MOTHER: Goldilocks.
CHILD: Sarah did!
MOTHER: You're not, you're pretending, come on, tell me properly.
CHILD: I can't remember it.

Her mother then asked her to tell the story of 'Little Red Riding Hood', but Donna refused, and her mother told it to her instead. The version she told was somewhat idiosyncratic, in that the wolf was replaced by a fox. The fox ate both the Granny and Little Red Riding Hood, but all worked out in the end as the woodcutter chopped open the fox and out came the two gobbled-up characters. Donna's mother asked her to tell some of the stories she learned at school, but Donna claimed to have forgotten them all. Instead she sang some of the songs she heard at nursery. Her mother was familiar with many of these, and they sang them together. After they had exhausted their song repertoire, her mother said:

MOTHER: I used to learn numbers when I was at school.
CHILD: So did I!
MOTHER: Do you?
CHILD: Yeah!
MOTHER: Do you know any numbers then?
CHILD: One [and starts to count on her fingers].
MOTHER: Mm.
CHILD: Two, three, four . . . one, two, three, four . . . one, two, three, four . . .
MOTHER: Yeah, what's after four?
CHILD: Five, six, seven, eight, nine, ten.
MOTHER: Oh, clever, aren't you? What's after ten?
CHILD: One, two, three, four, five, six, seven, eight, nine, ten, eleven, five!
MOTHER: Ten, eleven, *twelve*.
CHILD: Ten, eleven, twelve. Fourteen, sixteen, nine, eighteen, sixteen, four, nineteen, seventeen, fifteen, twenty-one, twenty-two, twenty-three, twenty-six, twenty-eight.
MOTHER: Oh, that's not bad.

Her mother then asks her if she knows any letters:

MOTHER: You know, like A, B, C, or 'ah', 'buh', 'cuh'. Which way
   do you learn at school? Do you learn A, B, C, or do you learn 'ah',
   'boh', 'cuh'?
CHILD: A, B, C, C, Me.
MOTHER: A, B, C, D. Not A, B, C, Me.
CHILD: A, B, C, Me.
MOTHER: What does your name begin with? Hm? What letter?
CHILD: D.
MOTHER: D.
CHILD: I, I.
MOTHER: No, D, O.
CHILD: D, O.
MOTHER: N.
CHILD: N.
MOTHER: N.
CHILD: N.
MOTHER: A.
CHILD: A.
MOTHER: Donna Wetsock! [Donna's surname was Watson. This
   name – like Kerry's below – was obviously a family nickname]
CHILD: Ah, I'm not Donna Wetsock!
MOTHER: Yes you is! And Kerry's 'Kerrygold Butter'!

This teasing signalled the end of the lesson. It was clear that Donna's
mother was trying to help her with what she regarded as essential
learning: namely knowing her letters and numbers. In the subsequent
interview she told us that she was critical of Donna's nursery school for
providing only play, and that at home she was teaching Donna the
alphabet, and to spell and copy her name. Her approach was firmly
rooted in the traditional oral methods of teaching, which were probably
what she experienced herself when she was a child. Nowadays such
methods are frowned on by most teachers. Children who arrive at school
able to recite the alphabet are not particularly welcomed; their parents
are likely to be criticized for having taught their children the wrong
things. This is not the place to argue who is right; the important point is
that there is a large gulf between the methods which the school thinks
are appropriate and the methods which a mother such as Donna's is
likely to adopt when trying to help her child. There were signs here that
Donna's mother was aware of this possibility when she asked whether
Donna learned A, B, C, or 'ah', 'buh', 'cuh' (the more modern phonetic

approach). In fact, Donna learned neither at her nursery school – as we shall see in Chapter 9, her educational experiences at nursery were of a very different kind.

This long period on the steps ended with Donna's mother giving her a piggy-back down the stairs to the kitchen. She joked about Donna's weight, saying she would have to put her on a diet ('One meal a day . . . one cup of orange juice a day . . . no biscuits or lollies'). On arriving in the kitchen she pretended to put Donna in the washing machine, followed by the dustbin, and finally threatened to put her in the hutch with the rabbit. This playful period, however, soon came to an end, with Donna's mother having to do her washing, and we were back, equally inevitably, with Donna's demands. Her mother suggested she made a 'potato man', but Donna wasn't very interested at first. She asked instead to do some painting; when this was refused, she wanted to do some washing up; when this was refused, she wanted to do some hoovering; when this was refused, she finally agreed to make the potato man. However, she demanded a bigger potato than the one her mother was offering. When this was refused, she got very upset, and her mother very angry. Finally, she agreed to the little potato. The potato man idea was relatively successful, in that Donna's mother was able to combine her housework with a substantial involvement in the potato man construction: suggesting different parts of the body which Donna might use, helping with difficult bits, and so on.

As the recording session drew to a close, Donna and her mother sat down together to have a cup of tea and a biscuit (Donna: Can I have a biscuit? Mother: Seeing as I'm having one, I suppose you'd better!). They discussed what to do next. Donna's mother was going to make a pie, and there would be some pastry left over for Donna to do something with. Her mother suggested she made the pastry into cakes:

MOTHER: Do you remember the ones you made when Nanny came down?
CHILD: Mm.
MOTHER: With little currants in?
CHILD: Mm.
MOTHER: Could make some of them for Daddy tonight. You make 'em and I'll put them in the oven and cook them.
CHILD: I can't make them.
MOTHER: Remember, you gotta roll the pastry out.
CHILD: Mm.

MOTHER: Spread some currants on the top.
CHILD: Mm.
MOTHER: Then fold over your pastry, and roll it up in a ball.
CHILD: Mm.
MOTHER: And Mummy'll grease the tray.
CHILD: Mm.
MOTHER: And you put them in the tray, like you did before. They were nice.
CHILD: Oh, I know the little rock cakes!
MOTHER: Like you were making when Granddad come down that night.

Next they discussed how many they were going to make, and once more Donna's mother emphasized the crucial role of the father as breadwinner:

CHILD: I'm gonna eat them all.
MOTHER: Oh, you re being selfish, are you?
CHILD: And Daddy can have one?
MOTHER: That all? Poor old Dad's being working all day, getting some money, buy your slippers, and you only gonna give him one?
CHILD: Two.
MOTHER: Two? S' that all he's gonna get?
CHILD: Three.

They decided that Kerry would have two, that Donna and her mother would both have two as well, and that Daddy (presumably as the most important member of the family) would have three. They then tried to work out how many there would be altogether. This was a long and involved process, as Donna's mother wanted Donna to help work it out, and in the course of the calculations they got muddled up about the quantities involved:

MOTHER: Well, if you're gonna have two, and Daddy's gonna have two, how many's that? [Holds up two fingers, followed by another two fingers]
CHILD: Three.
MOTHER: No.
CHILD: Four.

MOTHER: That's right. And if Mummy's gonna have another two, what's that? Four, and two . . . [Holds up another two fingers]

CHILD: Four and [unclear].

MOTHER: If that's four [holds up four fingers] and that one makes [holds up another finger]?

CHILD: Five.

MOTHER: And that one makes [holds up another finger]?

CHILD: Four.

MOTHER: No, these are five [points to the five already up].

CHILD: Five.

MOTHER: Five and one more is . . .?

CHILD: Six.

MOTHER: S'right. Now if you're gonna have two, and Mummy's gonna have two, and Daddy's gonna have two, that's six, and if Kerry's gonna have two that's, that's six [holds up six fingers again] and one more makes . . .?

CHILD: Five.

MOTHER: No.

CHILD: Six.

MOTHER: Yeah, and what's after six?

CHILD: Eight.

MOTHER: No.

CHILD: Nine.

MOTHER: No.

CHILD: Ten.

MOTHER: No.

CHILD: Eight.

MOTHER: No, after six, what comes after six?

CHILD: Nine.

MOTHER: No, seven.

CHILD: No, not seven!

MOTHER: Nine doesn't come after six, definitely seven.

CHILD: My teacher says, 'One, two, then six.'

MOTHER: Well you gotta count 'cause you wanna know how many little cakes you gotta make . . .

Working on the assumption that they were each going to have two cakes, they eventually arrived at the total eight. Donna's mother, however, added a further complication, when she said that if they made ten Donna could have two to take to school the next day. Donna decided that she wanted to take five to school (holding up five fingers) and make five for today (held up the other five). Her mother explained that this meant they would all get less today – one each, in fact, with one over:

MOTHER: Who's gonna have the odd one?
CHILD: You.
MOTHER: Oh, I'm gonna have two, and you're gonna have one, and Daddy's gonna have one, and Kerry's gonna have one?
CHILD: Mm.
MOTHER: Oh, all right . . . glad we sorted that out.

It was clear that Donna had not followed her mother through the whole calculation; indeed, it would be surprising if a child her age had mastered all the additions involved. Yet she had some grasp of what her mother was doing, and seemed to understand the way her mother was representing the problem to her. Whether by intuition or design, Donna's mother had in fact used a number of good strategies for breaking the problem down, making it simpler and more concrete. She used her fingers to represent the cakes; fingers already up were those already counted, and new cakes were added on to these. Moreover, she broke down the addition of two cakes into two separate additions of one cake. At the same time, she linked the problem to Donna's knowledge of the number sequence (demonstrated earlier), by asking what comes after six, and so on.

Right at the end of the session, Donna and her mother were discussing going to Nanny's at the weekend and working in the garden. Donna's mother told her she could take her own little scissors and help cut the grass:

CHILD: They won't cut.
MOTHER: How do you know? You won't try them.
CHILD: I did yesterday.
MOTHER: No you didn't.
CHILD: I went, and they didn't cut.
MOTHER: Well, they're not really supposed to cut grass, are they? They're to cut paper with, and things like that.
CHILD: And cigarette box?
MOTHER: Pardon?
CHILD: Cigarette box?

MOTHER: Cigarette box, yeah. They cut cigarette box 'cause that's . . .

CHILD: [Interrupts] Mine don't.

MOTHER: What?

CHILD: Cut cigarette box.

Donna exposed the inadequacy of her mother's initial, rather far-fetched, suggestion that she could help cut the lawn with her scissors, finally showing that they would not even cut a cigarette box. At this point, her mother had no option but to change the subject, which she did by telling her to get down off the table.

Like most of the girls in our study, Donna talked to her mother a great deal – they had sixty-nine conversations during the afternoon – and asked a great many questions – seventy-seven, including twenty-eight 'Why' questions. She and her mother contributed nearly equally to initiating and sustaining the conversations. As is abundantly clear from our account, they belonged to the minority of very disputatious working-class families, where much of the mother–child talk was concerned with discipline. Two-thirds of the conversations which were initiated by Donna's mother started with a controlling remark. Nearly half the conversations initiated by Donna started with a demand. A third of their conversations included a dispute, and over half of Donna's 'Why' questions were 'challenges'.

Yet, as we have seen, this did not mean that language was only used for simple purposes, or that Donna was not given a good deal of information and explanation. In 60 per cent of their disputes Donna's mother justified her position. Both she and Donna made comparisons and generalizations, recalled events, discussed the future, gave explanations and used 'If . . . then' constructions.

However, perhaps because the context of so much of their talk was discipline, the range of information given to Donna was relatively limited. It centred round the behaviour of members of the family, and the constraints on her mother. Many of Donna's mother's explanations were brief and somewhat implicit, but when she considered it important she became very clear and explicit. She seemed to see her own educational responsibilities much more in the direction of encouraging formal school skills than extending general knowledge or vocabulary.

Donna's mother was one of a minority of working-class mothers who did not hold the view that play was important. She saw it more as a way of occupying Donna. Perhaps for this reason, she spent very little time either playing with her, or organizing or suggesting specific play activities for her to do on her own. When she did briefly play with Donna, it was to initiate tickling and pretend fighting games, which both of them hugely enjoyed.

We hope that this account of Donna's afternoon at home will sound a warning bell to those who believe that there is little educational content in homes like Donna's. True, Donna's mother rarely played with her, and constantly wrangled with her, but their style of interaction provided very real educational contexts.

8

How the children fared at nursery school

In this chapter we discuss how the children whom we have seen at home fared at nursery school. We describe the differences between the educational methods, curriculum and discipline of the nursery school and the home, and the ways in which the children's talk with their teachers differed from their talk with their mothers.

Two different worlds

The child moving from home to school enters a very different world. This is obvious if school is a formal classroom, but it is still true for the child attending an informal nursery school. Perhaps the most crucial difference for the child is that she moves from a very small social setting, in which she is a central character, and where she spends much of her time in contact with her mother, to a much larger group, where she is one of twenty to twenty-five children. Although kindly and welldisposed, the teacher has no special partiality for the child; moreover, she knows very little of her past, her life outside school, or her likely future.

Thus, while the child's life at home is centred on a very close relationship with an adult, at school adults become relatively unimportant in her life. This is particularly true in British nursery schools. The day is largely given over to free play, apart from a group story and possibly a music session, and the child can move freely between the classroom and the playground. Most of the child's experiences, therefore, are away from the teacher, with other children, and they are not shaped by adults, as they are at home. Indeed, her interactions with the staff may be almost incidental, and they are usually emotionally very low-keyed. What becomes important at school is her relationship with other children, and her play experiences. The schools in our study had a much larger range of play materials than any home, and the children obviously enjoyed the opportunities to paint, play with sand and water, and run and climb in the playground. All the children seemed happy at school.

Nursery teachers' aims and curriculum

Nursery teachers, however, aim to do more than provide children with a happy time. Superficially the teachers may appear to be simply supervising the children's play. In fact they give considerable thought to relating the organization of the play environment, and their interactions with the children, to their educational aims. Interviews with British nursery teachers have shown that they usually state as their most important aim furthering the children's social development, that is, helping the children to be members of a group and independent of their mothers.[1] Intellectual aims are put second, and the teachers typically state them in very general terms – 'developing the child's full potential', 'developing basic skills and understanding'. Nursery teachers usually give as their third aim assisting children's language development, mainly through conversation. Many teachers also mention as an aim preparing children for primary school by such means as encouraging them to listen to the staff and follow instructions.

Although clear about their educational aims, nursery school teachers are often puzzled if they are asked about their curriculum. This is because they do not have a curriculum, in the sense of a specific body of knowledge or skills to be taught within a given period of time. Indeed, they see themselves less as teaching, and more as providing the children with a rich learning environment. On further thought, therefore, they will usually say that the selection of play materials constitutes the curriculum. By this they mean that, for example, the provision of vessels of different size and shape for water play helps the child to develop concepts of volume; provision of bricks of different size and weight helps the child who is building towers to recognize causal relationships and develop concepts of balance. In addition, they will usually add that by talking to the child about her play they will help her to learn 'attribute' concepts, for example, size, shape and colour names. Very few nursery teachers, and certainly none in our study, teach reading or writing. They would, however, argue that they are laying the foundation for these skills by providing activities that develop pattern recognition and hand-eye coordination, by developing the child's spoken language, and by helping her to understand the relationship between stories and a printed text.

The teachers' stated educational aims are thus very different from the mothers'. The teachers saw themselves as 'encouraging development'; by this they meant providing a planned environment in which the children would learn by self-initiated play. The mothers, on the other hand, saw their own educational role much more in terms of 'teaching' the children; by this they meant imparting skills, such as reading, writing or road-safety, and providing children with information about a wide range of topics. The situation was thus somewhat ironic, in that it was the mothers, rather than the teachers, who were more likely to see themselves as 'teaching'.

Just as we found some correspondence between the mothers' stated curriculum and the kind of information they gave their children, we found that at school much the most frequent type of information given by the staff to children was about the child's play. The nursery world mainly consists of play. The staff typically asked the children what they were doing, made suggestions and discussed and demonstrated the use of play materials. They also taught the children 'attribute concepts' (size, number, colour, shape etc.) in the context of their play. Occasionally the staff played *with* a small group of children, organizing and taking the leading part in a fantasy game about hospitals, for example, or a board game, such as Picture Lotto. However, for any individual child, these occasions were rare: mothers played with children much more often than did staff, although a greater proportion of adult–child talk at school was *about* play.

On the other hand, the mothers gave the children much more information about family relationships, babies, and domestic and house-hold matters. The mothers also gave the children more 'general knowl-edge' (including science, history and geography) than did the staff, and, overall, discussed a wider range of topics with the children.

A further notable difference between school and home was that at school, because most talk concerned play, it was almost always con-cerned with the 'here and now'. At home, events outside the present context, including the child's own past and future, were more often discussed, and this was especially true in middle-class homes. The school curriculum was, in fact, considerably narrower than the home's – a smaller range of topics was discussed. Thus, in moving from home to school, the children encountered a different curriculum, one more concerned with their play activities and less concerned with family relationships, domestic matters and the social world.

Discipline at nursery school

Discipline at nursery school is so gentle, and usually so readily accepted by the children, that it is almost invisible in comparison with the often conspicuous wrangles at home. We were surprised, then, to find a very similar proportion of 'control' remarks in the talk of mothers and teachers. (The total *amount* of control was much greater at home, since the mothers talked much more to the children.) However, the control centred around rather different issues in the two settings.

The mothers' disciplinary efforts were mainly directed at preventing damage or waste to the contents of their home, teaching good manners, and protecting the child from danger. At school, other priorities obtained. The environment was set up for the use and safety of children, and mess and waste were tolerated, and, in a controlled way, encouraged. Teaching the children to say 'please' and 'thank you' was not a priority with the teachers, and most of their control was concerned with getting children to follow the school routine – to collect their milk, go to the playground, sit down for a story, wash their hands, and take their aprons on and off when instructed. They also expected children to put away the play materials they had finished with, a feat much less often attempted by the mothers.

The reason why control appeared to be relatively invisible at school was that it was so rarely challenged by the children. We showed in Chapter 6 that some of the girls spent a good proportion of their time at home wrangling with their mothers. At school, thirteen of the thirty children never disputed with the staff. On average, 15 per cent of adult–child conversations at home included a dispute; at school, the proportion was only 3 per cent.

Curiously, in view of the fact that most nursery school teachers give 'furthering the children's social development' as their first aim, relatively few staff–child interactions were concerned with this issue. As a form of control – telling children to take turns, share, be kind, not to quarrel etc. – it came up rather infrequently (on average 1.3 times an hour), much less frequently than instructions to follow the day's routine and to tidy up (6.5 times an hour). As a topic for information – for example, explaining how other children might be feeling, or making suggestions for positive interactions ('You can do it when John has finished'; 'If you put the book that way up, the others can see it') – it occurred very much less frequently than discussion about play, and about 'attribute concepts'. In fact, talk of this kind formed about the same proportion of teachers' talk as mothers' talk: in absolute terms, it happened much more frequently at home than at school. The explanation is probably that, while the teachers saw nursery school as providing a *setting* for the children's social development, they thought it best to allow this development to occur without adult intervention, where possible.

The children thus had to learn a new code of behaviour at school. Some issues that were insisted on at school were much less important at home – for example, tidying up, or sitting down when and where instructed. Behaviour that was unacceptable at home – for example, getting water or paint on the floor – was tolerated at school. Since there were very few instances at school of non-compliance on the part of the children, they must have found this transition relatively easy. It is sometimes suggested that softened forms of control are favoured by nursery staff – 'Would you like to come here?' – and that they present particular difficulties for working-class children used to a more direct approach. In fact, we found that nursery staff generally used a direct approach, especially when dealing with more than one child – for example, 'Come inside, please.' In any case, they rarely appeared to be misunderstood by the children, although difficulties may have occurred when they first started school – at the time of the recordings the children in our sample had all been at nursery school for some time.

The amount of staff–child interaction

A second difference between home and school which we have already touched on was the much smaller amount of adult–child talk at school. On average, the children took part in ten conversations an hour with the school staff, compared with twenty-seven an hour with their mothers. This count includes all conversations with groups of children of which our child was a part, except for the rare occasions when the teacher was addressing the whole class. A much smaller proportion of school than home conversations were one-to-one.

Many school conversations were very brief. Overall, two-thirds of all conversations were six turns or less, and only one-twelfth were over twenty-one turns. The average length of the conversations at home was sixteen turns, exactly twice the length of the average staff–child conversations. In all, therefore, there was four times as much adult–child talk, in terms of turns of talk, at home as at school.

This finding is not unexpected. The adult–child ratio is much smaller at school, and the children spend most of the time playing with other children, or on their own. It does, however, mean that the staff have little opportunity to get to know the children as individuals. It also raises problems for those who see sending children to school as a means of exposing them to more adult language. Of course, if the teachers' talk was in some sense much more 'educational' than the mothers', it might not matter that there was less of it. Later in the chapter we will try to assess whether this was the case. Meantime, it should be noted that the preponderance of very brief conversations at school immediately raises questions about their educational usefulness. It is not that there is any virtue in long conversations as such – a long conversation may be repetitive or desultory, while a brief conversation is often all that is required. Here are two examples of perfectly adequate brief conversations:

CHILD: Can you lift me down?
STAFF: Come on then, one, two, three.

STAFF: Will you put these away, that's a good girl.
CHILD: Why, are we gonna tidy up?
STAFF: Yes, we are, my love.

However, any exploration of meaning, or discussion of a topic from different standpoints, or attempt to tie together different areas of experience, takes time to develop, as we saw in Chapter 5.

Clearly, it is not easy for the teacher to hold long conversations. Because the children in her class are engaged in many different activities, she tends to spend her time moving from one child or small group to another. Even if the teacher did decide to spend longer in conversation with one child, her intentions might well be thwarted by the demands of other children for help and attention. Our findings are confirmed by a recent study in forty nursery schools which found that the average staff–child conversation lasted thirty-two seconds.[2]

Keeping the conversation going

Listening to the school conversations, it was evident that they were not only briefer, but much more adult-dominated than the conversations at home. It was the staff who tended to keep the conversation going, and who did most of the talking.

We looked at the question of who dominates the conversation in a number of different ways. First, we looked at each turn in the conversation and categorized it according to whether or not it 'sustained' the conversation. Examples of ways to sustain a conversation include commenting on the other person's contribution; making a spontaneous, but relevant, comment; and asking a question. On the other hand, simply answering a question or acknowledging a remark doesn't sustain a conversation. At home, the children, on average, contributed almost half of the sustaining comments (47 per cent). At school, however, they contributed only 19 per cent. The characteristic 'shape' of a school conversation was a question-and-answer session, with the children's role mainly confined to answering questions.

The staff also dominated conversations by the sheer quantity of their talk. They averaged fourteen words per turn, compared with five words per turn from the children. At home, the amount that mothers and children talked was much more equally weighted – the mothers contributed eight words per turn on average, while the children contributed six.

Another possible way to dominate conversations is for one participant to tend to initiate them. The staff did not dominate conversations in this way. Both at home and at school slightly more than half the conversations were started by the children. In both settings, their most frequent reason for starting a conversation was not, as it may seem to parents, to ask a question or to make a demand, but to convey information – often of the 'Look at what I'm doing' variety. Nearly half of the children's communications to adults started with an 'I've got something to tell you' purpose.

It may seem at first sight contradictory that the children were just as likely to initiate 'I've got something to tell you' conversations with their teachers as their mothers, yet the conversations at school were briefer and staff dominated. The explanation partly lies in the tendency for the staff to respond to the child's initial communication with a series of questions. Here are two examples:

CHILD: [Pulling a kite] It's flying.
TEACHER: Did it work?
CHILD: Yeah.
TEACHER: Did it blow behind you?
CHILD: Mm. [Sits down]

CHILD: [Playing with clay] I made a seat for the lady.
TEACHER: Ooh! That's a good idea. Do you want me to get the others back [referring to other clay models]? Are you going to make another? Do you want to put this lady on it?
CHILD: Yes.
TEACHER: Or d'you want to put another one?
CHILD: I want to put that lady on it.
TEACHER: Do you want to take the milk jug as well? Do you want to take this as well [the milk jug]?
CHILD: No.

In these two conversations the teachers responded to the child's communication in a positive way, but their questions and suggestions (particularly in the second example) took the conversational initiative from the child, and effectively cut short the conversation.

On some occasions the brevity of the school conversations seemed to be due to the staff's rather mechanical replies to the child's confidences. In an earlier study, one of us (BT) showed that a response such as 'Did you?' or 'How nice' tends to cut short communication with young children.[3] Conversations were also often terminated when the child's remarks were misunderstood, and the teacher did not detect the misunderstanding.

The teachers' educational methods: asking questions

A striking difference between the home and school conversations was the teachers' use of questions as an educational tool. It was this which resulted in the characteristic shape of the school conversations, which we have already noted. Typically, the teacher would move from child to child, questioning them about their play. This question-asking approach was probably particularly prominent in the nursery schools we studied because of the dominating influence at that time of the British educational psychologist, Joan Tough. Tough argued that an important role for nursery and infant teachers is to foster children's ability to use language by means of a special kind of dialogue. The kind of dialogue recommended is to ask questions which require for their answer the use of definite thinking skills. Questions of this kind have been called 'cognitive demands' by Marion Blank.[4]

Not all questions involve a cognitive demand. Suppose, for example, that the adult produces a tube of Smarties and asks, 'What colour Smartie would you like?' Here the cognitive demand on the child is minimal. True, she has to name a colour, but there is no reason why she cannot name any colour she chooses, and her answer (e.g., 'Green') tells us nothing about her understanding of the word 'green'. In contrast, suppose the child has chosen a green Smartie and is then asked, 'What colour is that Smartie?' The child is now being questioned about a specific cognitive skill: her ability to identify and name the colour 'green'. Of course a 'right' answer does not by itself prove that she fully understands the word 'green', any more than a 'wrong' answer proves that she does not. Further investigation would be required to establish the extent of her knowledge. Our point, however, is that the second question makes a specific cognitive demand on the child which the first question does not.

Cognitive demands vary greatly in their difficulty. We followed Marion Blank's classification of them according to the level of abstraction involved.[5] The lowest level of the scale involves questions which can be put to a child just starting to talk, while the highest level involves questions which will tax a five-year-old. At the lowest level – 'What is/ was that called?' – the child has only to use language to mirror her perception. At the next level she has to attach the correct verbal label to one attribute of the object – e.g., 'What colour is that?' A more difficult demand, which involves selecting and describing several aspects of experience, is to give a simple description: 'What is happening in the picture?' 'What did you do at school today?' At the highest level of abstraction the child is asked to use language to go beyond the perceptual information so as to predict, explain, compare, generalize and interpret: 'What do you think will happen next?' 'Why did he leave the room?' 'How will he get home?' In order to answer questions of this kind the child cannot simply describe her memories or perceptions. She must reflect on the implications of her experiences and on the relationships between objects and events, as well as express her understanding intelligibly in words. Such demands, in other words, usually require what we have called a 'complex use of language' if they are to be satisfactorily answered (see page 113).

Perfectly ordinary questions may, of course, include a cognitive demand, as when one asks a child, 'What were you doing in the garden?' or 'Why did you go upstairs?' The special characteristic of the teacher's use of cognitive demands was that about half of them were 'testing' demands, asked, not out of curiosity, but with the dual purpose of fostering and assessing the child's verbal thinking skills. Typically, they were concentrated in sequences and organized round an educational objective.

Using questions to stimulate thinking is a method hallowed since Socrates, and an important part of any teacher's repertoire. It certainly requires skill. Questions pitched at the right level can keep children alert and interested, while at the same time allowing the teacher to assess their knowledge. Later in this chapter we give an example of a successful conversation of this kind, centred round a book. However, there were many more occasions when the technique did not seem fruitful.

We will discuss two conversations which illustrate the kind of difficulties that are liable to occur when this approach is used with young children. In the first of these Joyce was rolling out clay when her teacher sat down next to her:

1. TEACHER: What's that going to be, Joyce?
   CHILD: [No reply]
   TEACHER: How are you making it?
2. CHILD: Rolling it.
3. TEACHER: You're rolling it, are you? Isn't that lovely? Oh, what's happening to it when you roll it?
4. CHILD: Getting bigger.
5. TEACHER: Getting bigger. Is it getting fatter?
6. CHILD: Yeah.
7. TEACHER: Is it, or is it getting longer?
8. CHILD: Longer.
9. TEACHER: Longer. Are my hands bigger than your hands?
10. CHILD: My hands are little.
11. TEACHER: Your hands are little, yes.
12. CHILD: It's getting bigger. Getting long. And long. Look.
13. TEACHER: Mmmm. What's happened to it, Joyce?
14. CHILD: Got bigger.
15. TEACHER: It has. My word.

This conversation is by no means untypical, and contains several features which crop up over and over again in teacher–child conversations at nursery school. For this reason it is worth analysing in some depth.

Consider first the context in which the conversation takes place. Why are the teacher and child talking at all? Clearly it is not because Joyce has anything she wants to say to the teacher at this particular moment. Rather, the conversation is taking place because the teacher sees an opportunity to introduce certain educational ideas (in this case, to do with size and shape) into the child's play.

The method which Joyce's teacher uses to carry out this educational aim is to ask her a series of 'testing' cognitive demands. Apart from the first question, 'What's that going to be?', they are all questions to which the teacher already knows the answer. Joyce does not respond with enthusiasm to this approach. She fails to answer the first question, and when she does respond her replies are fairly minimal. Apart from a brief moment in turn 12, when Joyce wants her teacher to see what is happening to the clay, the conversation is very much a one-sided affair.

As we have seen, the kind of questioning used here is justified on two grounds. First, it is suggested that the teacher benefits through learning what the child is capable of, what she knows and what she does not know. On this view, the questioning is primarily a type of *assessment*. The other justification is that the child is stimulated by such questions to think about aspects of the situation which had not previously occurred to her. Through answering the teacher's questions she will begin to develop her own cognitive linguistic skills. On this view, then, such questioning can constitute a means of *learning*.

On the strength of this particular conversation, it is hard to justify either of these claims. Take for a start the idea that the teacher is getting an accurate assessment of Joyce's capabilities. The problem here is that most of Joyce's replies are so ambiguous that it is impossible to say whether her understanding is deficient or not. In turn 4, for example, she says the clay is 'getting bigger' as she rolls it out. This might mean that Joyce really thinks there is more clay as a result of her rolling – as Piaget claims that children who fail his conservation tasks actually believe. On the other hand, she may simply be using the word 'bigger' in a loose manner to describe the increased length of the clay. Joyce's teacher picks up this ambiguity (turn 5) and asks if the clay is getting fatter, but again it is hard to interpret Joyce's reply. Does she really think the clay is increasing in width as she rolls it out, or does she simply assume that the teacher is using the term 'fatter' to refer to length? In turn 9 the teacher introduces a somewhat bizarre note into the conversation by asking Joyce, 'Are my hands bigger than your hands?' Presumably she is trying to check on Joyce's understanding of 'bigger', but the child's reply is not very informative. True, she says her hands are 'little', but it is not clear if she really understood that her teacher's hands are 'bigger'.

The problem of interpreting children's replies as a means of assessing their cognitive or linguistic development is one with which developmental psychologists have been struggling for years. Much ingenuity has been put into devising tasks which will establish what children understand by words like 'bigger' or 'more', yet the results are still inconclusive. This is not of course to discourage any teacher who wants to establish what her own pupils are capable of, but simply to point out the enormity of the task. In this particular case it is hard to see how anyone can be much the wiser after studying Joyce's replies to her teacher.

The other argument for questioning young children in this manner is that it will help to promote their cognitive or linguistic development. Is there any evidence that Joyce's development has been promoted here? Again it is hard to be sure, partly because we lack criteria of how to judge what Joyce might have learnt, and partly because we do not know what Joyce's teacher was trying to teach her. The teacher might have been trying to point out that clay gets longer and thinner as it is rolled out. If so, then it is not clear why she did not say so directly. Moreover, she had no reason to think that Joyce did not know this in the first place. But maybe the teacher was trying to establish that the word 'bigger' is inappropriate here, and to encourage the child to use the term 'longer'. If so, then she seems to have partly succeeded, for in turn 12 the child does spontaneously say the clay has got 'long'. This mastery is short-lived, however, for in turn 14 the child is back where she started: the clay has got 'bigger'.

On the face of it, it would seem that neither teacher nor child has learnt much from this conversation. Yet there is more than one kind of learning. What Joyce may well have learnt is experience in the kind of conversation she is expected to have with a teacher. As a preparation for what she will encounter later on in school, this may well be a useful lesson. For the teacher, this conversation may simply have confirmed what she and her colleagues told us before the recordings were made: namely, that Joyce was a girl whose language was 'poor'. Joyce's apparent confusion with size words, together with her general uncommunicativeness and minimal replies are all likely to perpetuate the picture which the teacher had already formed.

In fact, Joyce's conversations with her mother at home (see, for example, page 61) show that she had a much greater familiarity with language than one would expect from listening to her conversations at school.

As an educational technique, then, a series of cognitive demands may be unsuccessful in that neither teacher nor child appear either to enjoy or to gain from the conversation.

One variant of the cognitive demand session which we often observed at school was when the teacher tried to extract the 'correct' answer from a child. The following conversation illustrates this technique. June, the child whom we saw playing Knockout Whist with her mother in Chapter 3, has approached her teacher with a piece of paper:

1. CHILD: Can you cut that in half? Cut it in half?
2. TEACHER: What would you like me to do it with?
3. CHILD: Scissors.
4. TEACHER: With the scissors? [Child nods] Well, you go and get them, will you?
5. CHILD: Where are they?
6. TEACHER: Have a look round. [Child goes over to the cupboard, gets some scissors] Where do you want me to cut it?
7. CHILD: There.
8. TEACHER: Show me again, 'cause I don't quite know where the cut's got to go. [Child shows teacher where she wants paper cut] Down there? [Child nods; teacher cuts child's piece of paper in half] How many have you got now?
   CHILD: [No reply]
   TEACHER: How many have you got?
   CHILD: [No reply]
   TEACHER: How many pieces of paper have you got?
9. CHILD: Two.
10. TEACHER: Two. What have I done if I've cut it down the middle?
11. TEACHER: Two pieces.
12. TEACHER: I've cut it in . . .? [Wants child to say 'half']
    CHILD: [No reply]
    TEACHER: What have I done?
    CHILD: [No reply]
    TEACHER: Do you know? [Child shakes head]
    OTHER CHILD: Two.
    TEACHER: Yes, I've cut it in two. But . . . I wonder, can you think?

13. CHILD: In the middle.
14. TEACHER: I've cut it in the middle. I've cut it in *half*! There you are, now you've got two.

The teacher's intentions are clear enough. She does not simply want to comply with June's request, but tries to turn the situation into one of educational value by introducing a simple mathematical idea: namely, that if you cut a piece of paper into two equal pieces then you have cut it in 'half'. Nursery teachers are frequently encouraged to introduce mathematical vocabulary in this way: indeed many educational advisers would congratulate June's teacher on noticing the educational potential of this situation. The problem, however, lies in the way that she attempts to introduce this idea.

In turn 8 she first asks June how many pieces of paper there are, and then tries to elicit the word 'half' from her. June appears confused by this. In turn 11 she gives what she may feel to be an adequate, if somewhat condensed, reply to the teacher's request: if she has cut it down the middle she has produced 'two pieces'. This however does not seem to be the answer the teacher wants, for she keeps on questioning. Subsequently the teacher rejects two more answers, one suggested by the other child ('Two') and one by June herself ('In the middle'). Finally she reveals the correct answer, in turn 14, 'I've cut it in *half*!'

This use of cognitive demands to elicit a particular 'correct' response from a child is, of course, a common educational practice. Indeed, it might be argued that June is here getting useful preparation for school, and that the ability to work out what answer the teacher has in mind will serve her very well later on. There are, however, two important criticisms of the practice. The first is that the teacher may be so focused on the answer she wants to hear that she rejects other perfectly adequate replies. As a result, the child – as happens here – may lose confidence and start to doubt the limited amount of knowledge that she does have. The second criticism is that the child may in fact know the answer, but be so confused or inhibited by the questioning that she is unable to produce it when required. This is precisely what is happening here. If we go back to the very first turn of the conversation, we see that June's initial request to the teacher was that she should 'cut it in half'. In other words, June started the conversation by spontaneously using the very concept that she was unable to produce when being questioned.

The children's response to the teachers

As we have seen, the children frequently failed to respond to their teachers' cognitive demands. Over a third of the cognitive demands at school were simply not answered. This did not appear to be because of the difficulty of the question – the non-response rate was the same for all levels of difficulty and for both working-class and middle-class children. It seemed to be rather that the child was often either not interested or uncertain about how she was meant to respond. The children had a number of strategies for dealing with difficult questions. They very rarely said, 'I don't know' (on only 5 per cent of occasions). They were much more likely simply to repeat their statement, or evade the question in other ways. For example, in answer to the question, 'Why is that sticky?' one child simply asserted, 'Because it is.' On other occasions associated, but irrelevant, information was offered:

TEACHER: What do tigers look like?
ANN: They bite you.

TEACHER: Were you born in England or America?
ANN: I was born in my Mummy's tummy.

A quarter of all cognitive demands put to the children were evaded in this way. In all, then, the children gave focused answers to less than half of the teachers' demands.

Of course, the child's failure to meet the cognitive demand need not mean that the teacher was wrong to make it. The failure could constitute an educational challenge, by exposing the area in which the child needs help. In some cases such help could be quite straightforward – for example, the teacher quoted above could have found a picture of a tiger to discuss with the child. In other cases the gap between the demand and the child's ability to answer it was vast. Jane, quoted above, probably had no concept of the world being made up of different countries, or that she now lived in England but that her mother was American (see page 208). In such cases time and patience would have been required to ensure that the cognitive demand did in fact lead to an advance in the child's understanding. But it was very rare for a teacher to remain long enough with one child for this to happen.

Other difficulties with the technique have already been illustrated.

The child may become confused and lose confidence if the adult rejects a succession of answers, while probing for the 'correct' answer. Further, the child may simply not reply, perhaps annoyed at the intrusion into her activities of what seem to her irrelevant questions, or she may give ambiguous or conflicting answers. The adult is then faced with the choice of abandoning the child to her confusion, or spending what may turn out to be a great deal of time trying to clarify it.

For these reasons we are sceptical of the educational value of question-and-answer sessions with young children, and unhappy at the idea, put forward in some parent education courses, that parents should be encouraged to adopt them. Of course, questioning children, and even testing their knowledge, is a natural and ordinary thing to do, and we are not suggesting that it is totally undesirable. In the form of games for babies (e.g., 'Where's your nose?') testing demands have universal appeal. But if questions are to be asked for educational reasons, they seem likely to be most successful if two conditions are fulfilled. First, the child must be interested in answering the questions. This may be because they occur in a game of some kind, or, as in the conversation quoted on page 172, because they are centred on a story or other activity which the child herself wants to discuss. Secondly, the adult using them must have the skill and time to pursue any inadequacies which are exposed in the child's understanding.

We are not the only researchers who have come to doubt the value of questioning young children in this way. Similar findings have been reported by David Wood and his colleagues from the Oxford Pre-School Research Project. Wood's study was based on recordings of twenty-four preschool practitioners (mostly playgroup workers) talking with young children. Like us, Wood found that when the adult maintained the conversation mostly through questions, the children's answers tended to be terse and even monosyllabic. Wood also found that those practitioners who asked most questions had fewest questions asked of them, while those who held back on the questions, and offered the children more of their own ideas and observations, were likely to receive many more ideas and questions from the children.[6]

Cognitive demands at home

We do not wish to give the impression that only teachers made cognitive demands. Cognitive demands formed a much larger *proportion* of the talk of teachers than of mothers. But, because there was much more adult–child talk at home than at school, the overall number of cognitive demands was in fact larger in homes of both social classes than at school.

We looked not only at the number of cognitive demands made by the adults, but also at their level of difficulty. It might have been that the mothers made only very simple demands while the teachers' questions 'stretched' the children intellectually. This was not the case. All types of demands were made more often at home, except for those asking for colour, size and shape names. There was, however, a difference between home and school in what the cognitive demands were *about*. Mothers were especially likely to ask the child to recall past events, and also to ask about motivation and purposes: 'Why are you going upstairs?' 'Why do you want that?' That is, mothers' cognitive demands tended to be made in relation to people, their past and future and their motives, while teachers' cognitive demands tended to orient the children towards the properties of play materials.

Moreover, the mothers were more likely than the teachers to ask questions with no explicit educational intent. Instead, they were prompted more by curiosity – 'What did you do at the nursery this morning?' – or by the need for specific information – 'Where did you put your socks?' At other times they were aimed at getting the child to justify her actions – 'Why did you go outside?' – or explain her motivation – 'Why did you hit Susan?' In other instances – there are many illustrations in Chapter 5 – the mother was trying to elucidate the child's meaning. Nevertheless, even though these questions were not asked with educational intent, they placed cognitive demands on the child. In addition, the children did have some experience of 'testing' demands at home: all but one mother asked them in the course of the afternoon. Often testing demands at home arose because some error of the child's led the mother to test and correct her knowledge: 'What number is our house?' 'What colour is that?' 'What day is it today?' Others arose in the context of games.

An occurrence at home which was very unusual, however, was a concentrated sequence of testing questions of the kind we have described occurring at school. When they did happen – and we gave an example on page 119 – they tended to be as unsuccessful as most of such sessions at school.

The teachers' use of language for complex purposes

Psychologists often advocate attendance at nursery school as a means of assisting the language development of working-class children. What they have in mind is the benefit of exposing the children to the stimulating questions (cognitive demands) typically asked by the teachers, and also to the model provided by the teachers' own use of language for complex purposes – making comparisons, reasoning and so on – when talking to children.

We have already shown that the *proportion* of cognitive demands in teachers' talk was greater than in the talk of mothers, but because mothers talked to their child much more, the overall *number* of cognitive demands was greater at home. This was also true of the teachers' use of language for complex purposes. The teachers' talk was more densely packed with these usages than the mothers', but, overall, children of both social classes heard them more often at home. This was true both for all types of complex usage combined, and for each separate category – for example, the use of conditionals and generalizations. Further, just as mothers' talk covered a wider range of topics than teachers', it also contained a wider variety of language usages.

There was one category of language usage which occurred more often at home, not only in total, but also proportionately. This was the use of language to recall past events, and plan future events. This home – school difference was related to an aspect of nursery school life which we have already noted, its tendency to be almost exclusively concerned with the 'here and now'.

How the children talked to the staff

We have already noted that the children were much less likely to sustain conversation with school staff than with their mothers, and that they were much more likely to answer their mothers' questions than the nursery staff's questions. We will now consider some other character-istics of the children's talk to the school staff.

The children's failure to ask questions at school

Perhaps the most striking difference between the way in which the children talked to their mothers and their teachers was their failure to ask questions at school. Nursery schools are often seen as settings where children's curiosity can be both stimulated and satisfied, in a way not possible to the hard-pressed mother. We would agree with those who argue that this function is important for all children, and particularly for working-class children, whose mothers we found tended to answer their questions less readily and fully.

However, the teachers were in no position to satisfy the children's curiosity because the children hardly ever asked them questions. The girls asked their mothers on average twenty-six questions an hour, but they only asked two questions an hour of their teachers. Nearly half the children (fourteen) asked five questions or less during two mornings at school, and a further three children asked no questions at all at school.

Of those questions that *were* asked at school, a much smaller proportion were 'curiosity' questions and 'Why' questions, and a much larger proportion were 'business' questions, of the 'Where is the glue?' type, than was the case at home. 'Challenges' were very rare at school, and 'passages of intellectual search' were entirely absent.

Why did the children ask so few questions at school? It seems likely that part of the explanation lies in the teachers' reliance on brief bursts of question-asking as an educational technique. As we have seen, this resulted in an imbalance of conversation, with the teachers dominating the conversation by a series of questions, and then moving on to the next child after a very short time. Unintentionally, they must have transmitted the message that it was the children's role to answer, rather than to ask questions.

A further reason for the lack of questions may have been the fact that conversations at school tended to be centred around play activities, and were rarely concerned with events outside the school context. But at home, we found that both 'Why' questions and passages of intellectual search were hardly ever concerned with play. In addition to the conversations discussed in Chapter 4, we found that the kind of topics which provoked the girls' curiosity included such issues as why and how animals are killed at the vet's, why the Queen does not always wear a crown, when and why boats sink, and why the seats of chairs are of different shape. Conversations on such topics were very rare at school.

Flatness of children's communication to staff

So far we have pointed out that the children rarely asked questions at school, tended to give brief answers to the staff, and made little contribution to sustaining conversations with them. These were quantitative findings, but we will now go on to discuss some characteristics of staff–child conversations which are based only on impressions. The staff–child conversations tended to be characterized by a certain flatness, which the reader may already have noted. Perhaps this flatness arose from the relatively distant relationship between children and staff. We pointed out at the beginning of this chapter that the children's nursery school experience was primarily with other children. Their contacts with the staff were relatively few, and staff and children did not know each other very well. In consequence, the children did not seem to feel the same urge to communicate significant experiences and feelings to the staff as they did with their mothers. Equally, the staff seemed to be less involved in what the children had to say.

The impression of flatness can be illustrated by comparing the conversations which Carol, one of the working-class children, had with her teacher and with her mother about an incident at school. During the morning, a strong wind came up and blew the buckets in the sandpit about. Carol was clearly excited by this event. When she went inside the school she did not describe it to her teacher, but she did confide her intention to tell her mother about it:

CHILD: I'm telling Mummy that the buckets rolled away.
TEACHER: Pardon?
CHILD: I'm telling Mummy that the buckets rolled away when we were not looking.
TEACHER: Are you?
CHILD: Yeah.
TEACHER: That's nice.
CHILD: A-and the sand went a-all in my eyes.
TEACHER: In your eyes? Were they sore? Are they still sore now? Oh, you poor old thing. Do you think if you had a piece of apple, it would make them feel better?
CHILD: It was in there.
TEACHER: Okay, well let's wash it out. [Teacher and child go to bathroom]

In fact Carol did not tell her mother about the incident, until her mother brought up the topic herself:

1. MOTHER: It's very windy today, isn't it? Was the wind blowing the sand at your nursery?
2. CHILD: Yeah.
3. MOTHER: Hm. The sand is all dry now and when it's windy . . .
4. CHILD: And it went right in my eyes, and Mummy I want to tell you something. And it's funny, um, the buckets rolled away and . . . and, we wasn't looking there . . . and we said . . . and we weren't able to catch the buckets.
5. MOTHER: Weren't you?
6. CHILD: No.
7. MOTHER: And what was making the buckets run away? Because they haven't got legs, have they?
8. CHILD: No.
9. MOTHER: Then what was making them run away?
10. CHILD: Rolling.
11. MOTHER: Were they rolling?
12. CHILD: Yeah. Yeah. They were rolling . . . see, they were standing up, and we was not looking, 'cause, we was making sandcastles.
13. MOTHER: Mm.
14. CHILD: And then it tumbled over, the buckets, and then it went roll, roll, roll, roll. 'Cause the wind blow huff.
15. MOTHER: Oh gosh. Very strong the wind, isn't it?
16. CHILD: Yeah.

The note of urgency and excitement in Carol's communication to her mother is certainly missing at school. At school, in fact, the child quickly enters a dependent, help-seeking relationship with the teacher which, as we show in the next chapter, was particularly characteristic of the working-class girls at school. The reader will note that in turns 7 and 9 Carol's mother makes, and repeats, a 'testing' cognitive demand of a 'teacherly' type. However, when Carol fails to meet the demand she does not persist or correct her, but allows Carol to talk about what was clearly important to her.

The children's difficulties in communicating to staff

All the children in our study had some communication difficulties, even at home, for reasons we discussed in Chapter 5. At school, these difficulties increased because they had to make themselves understood to strangers. This task is both inevitable and important, and if children can be helped to master it, their communication skills will improve. The task, however, is made much more difficult if children have to communicate with a large number of strange adults who know very little about their activities. This was the situation in 'open-plan' schools where the children could play in any of two or three classrooms and came into contact with up to ten staff. Inevitably, most of the staff would not know in any detail what the children had been doing, and sometimes misunderstood or failed to understand what the children said.

An example of this kind of difficulty occurred with Joyce, who attended an open-plan school. One teacher showed a group of children how to thread coloured beads on elastic to make necklaces. Partly because the elastic was frayed, Joyce found the task very difficult. Despite numerous injunctions to manage on her own, she required a lot of help to thread each bead. The teacher, having other children to help, eventually cut short the exercise and tied up the elastic to make a bracelet. Joyce must have been disappointed, since she immediately asked the teacher to make her a necklace. The teacher, moving on to other duties, asked the nursery assistant to help. The nursery assistant, not knowing the long struggles Joyce had already been through, tried to get her to thread the beads herself, and then left the area. Joyce, having by now tried unsuccessfully many times, gave up and put the beads away. At this point another teacher came up and asked:

TEACHER: Is that what you made? [No reply from child] What is it?
CHILD: A bracelet.
TEACHER: A bracelet? Where do you wear it?
CHILD: On your arm.
TEACHER: On your arm. Isn't that pretty? Aren't you clever?

Joyce then went into the playground and up to another nursery assistant:

CHILD: Look what I got, a bracelet.
STAFF: Did you make it?

CHILD: Mm. But I didn't do it up.
STAFF: You didn't do it up. You are a clever girl.
CHILD: I didn't do it up.

Joyce then set off to get her milk, and met another teacher:

TEACHER: What have you been doing?
CHILD: I been make, making a bracelet. But I didn't make mine necklace.
TEACHER: Oh dear. Perhaps when you've finished your milk you can go and make a necklace.
CHILD: Mm.
TEACHER: Think you could? Is this your bracelet? Look at all those colours. What colours have you got in there?
CHILD: Yellow . . . and green.
TEACHER: Yes, and what else?
CHILD: Match that matches that. [Her fingernails were painted pink]
TEACHER: That bead matches your nails, doesn't it?
CHILD: Mm.

Joyce drank her milk, played in the playground and went inside. She approached two further members of staff, each time showing her bracelet and commenting that 'I didn't do it', or 'I didn't make a necklace'. Each time the staff responded by asking her for colour names, or suggesting that she now made a necklace. Joyce was unable to explain adequately what for her was clearly the dominant aspect of the experience, her disappointment and frustration that she had been unable to thread the beads without help, and had only achieved a bracelet, not a necklace. Since none of the staff had been present throughout the activity, they were unaware of her feelings, and unable to help her to verbalize them. It must also be said that they failed to pursue the leads she did offer.

The children's communication difficulties were much greater when it came to talking to the staff about their home life. This point will be discussed further in Chapter 10.

Stories at school: an illustration of an educational approach

We will end this chapter by discussing some of the story-reading episodes at school. These episodes illustrate a number of the points we have made, especially the tendency of the teachers to use every opportunity to ask the children 'stimulating questions'; the children's frequent failure to respond to these questions, and their tendency to be confused by them; and the children's failure to ask questions of the staff.

In almost all the schools the teacher read a story to the whole class during the morning. We did not record these sessions, but we did analyse the occasions when the staff read to 'our' child, either individually, or as a member of a small group.

In Chapter 3 we discussed the somewhat chaotic story-reading we observed at home. Story-reading at school had a very different flavour. At school, even if the children's attention wandered, physically they remained with the staff throughout. The episodes never ended, as they sometimes did at home, with adult and child arguing or refusing to continue because one or other was bored, nor was the reading constantly interrupted by the child's demands for a change of book. However, although the story sessions were much better ordered at school than at home, the children made a much less active contribution to them. In the nine story sessions at home, the mothers asked sixty-one questions, the children seventy-eight. In the eight story sessions we recorded at school, the staff directed sixty-three questions to the child we were observing, while these children asked the staff only three questions. Because the teacher dominated the proceedings in this way, the story became, in fact, a lesson. Sometimes the lesson seemed successful, as in the following example. The teacher came up to Kelly, who was looking through an illustrated version of Aesop's fable about the fox and the raven.

TEACHER: Who's he? [Points to fox in picture]
CHILD: A fox.
TEACHER: What's he doing?
CHILD: He in the hole, its big hole.
TEACHER: What's he doing?
CHILD: Look, tries to get the ducks.
TEACHER: What's he trying to do with the ducks?
CHILD: Trying to bite his tail.

TEACHER: Yes, isn't he? Has he managed it?

CHILD: No. He tried to, tried to take his nose off.

TEACHER: Trying to get the rook's nose, his beak, is he?

CHILD: Yeah, he's trying to get his, he try, the fox try get his tail. He try to get the mouse.

TEACHER: Will he manage to get down there?

CHILD: He can't get down there.

TEACHER: Why not?

CHILD: 'Cause it's too big.

TEACHER: Who's too big?

CHILD: For that.

TEACHER: Who's too big?

CHILD: [No reply]

TEACHER: The fox is too big?

CHILD: Yeah.

TEACHER: Mm ... I think he is. He's too fat to get down that narrow path, isn't he?

CHILD: He try get that.

TEACHER: What is that?

CHILD: I don't, he got cheese.

TEACHER: Oh yes, the raven has cheese.

CHILD: Yeah, he got a cheese.

TEACHER: What does the raven do with the cheese?

CHILD: Eat it, and drop it.

TEACHER: He *drops* it, doesn't he?

CHILD: Yeah, and the fox pick it up. Eat it, his dinner, look!

TEACHER: Mmm.

CHILD: That's the end of the story. [Teacher goes off. Child carries on looking at book]

This was one of the longest conversations recorded at school, and was an example of sustained adult questioning in which the child's interest was maintained. This interest was shown both by the spontaneous contributions made to it by the child, and by her willingness to answer the teacher's questions. Often, however, the staff's questions appeared to come between the children and the story to an undue extent. This was particularly the case when the teacher was determined to extract a particular answer from the children.

In the following example, the teacher has read a story called 'Ruth and Martin Go to the Park' to several children, including Erica.

Throughout, the reading was punctuated by a large number of questions from the teacher. The story ends with the main characters falling into a pond. The last page has no words on it, and is simply a picture of Ruth and Martin's boots drying in front of the fire. The teacher wants to make sure that the implicit meaning of this picture is understood.

1. TEACHER: Where are the words on that page? Are there any words?
2. OUR CHILD: No.
3. OTHER CHILDREN: No.
4. TEACHER: There aren't any words, it's just a picture. What's the picture for? What does the picture tell you? [No reply] Well, where are the boots?
5. OTHER CHILD: [Points] There's Martin's boots, there's Ruth's boots.
6. TEACHER: That's right. Why are those boots there, do you think? Where are they, where are the boots? [No reply]

At this point the children appeared to be puzzled, since the reply given by the child in turn 5 ('There') and accepted by the teacher in turn 6 ('That's right') is apparently, after all, not satisfactory. They have no way of knowing that the required answer is 'By the fire'.

7. TEACHER: Where are the boots?
8. OTHER CHILD: [Points] There.
9. TEACHER: Yes, but where are they?
10. OUR CHILD: [Points] There.
11. TEACHER: Where are they? Are they in the garden? [No reply] Are they in the garden? [Child continues to point]
12. OTHER CHILDREN: Yes. There they are.
13. TEACHER: Is that the garden? [Points to the fire]
14. CHILDREN: No.
15. TEACHER: Where are they then? Tell me where they are.
16. OTHER CHILDREN: There. Inside.
17. TEACHER: But whereabouts inside?
18. CHILDREN: Inside.
19. TEACHER: Are they beside the sofa?
20. OTHER CHILD: No.
21. TEACHER: Where are they then?
22. OTHER CHILD: In the kitchen.

23. TEACHER: Where are the boots, then?
24. OTHER CHILD: By the fire.

It has taken 18 turns to extract this phrase, apparently because the children were slow to guess what the teacher wanted them to say. Almost certainly they did not really think the boots were in the garden (turn 12), but were so confused by this time that they believed that this was what the teacher wanted them to say. The teacher has not yet attained her goal, however:

25. TEACHER: That's right. Why are they by the fire?
26. OTHER CHILD: Cause they're wet.
27. TEACHER: But if they're wet, why would you put them in front of the fire?
28. OUR CHILD: 'Cause they were all wet.
29. TEACHER: What would the fire do?
30. OTHER CHILD: Make them dry.
31. OUR CHILD: Make them dry.
32. TEACHER: It would dry them out, wouldn't it?
33. OUR CHILD: Yes.
34. TEACHER: I'd better go and sort those children out [referring to quarrelling children in another part of the room].

The teacher's aim was to extract an explicit explanation of why the boots were by the fire. This is a perfectly legitimate educational aim, but the children were apparently mystified throughout by the teacher's questions. It seems probable that they understood the picture, and that they could have given the explicit explanation, but were confused about what was required of them. Eventually the right answer was produced, but it is doubtful what had been achieved in the process.

Whereas at home children commented freely on the book that their mother read to them, they have to learn to inhibit this tendency at school. This is partly because there are other children's needs to be considered, but the main consideration was often that spontaneous comments are likely to cut across the teacher's educational goal. In the following example, the teacher is reading a book called *Big Sweets and Little Sweets* to a small group of children, and pauses to ask Lynne a question:

TEACHER: What sorts of sweets do you like?

Either Lynne does not understand what the teacher means by 'sorts of sweets', or she cannot recall their names. Her answers in turns 3 and 5, particularly, suggest that she is evading questions she cannot answer by making irrelevant responses.

1. CHILD: Lots of sweets.
2. TEACHER: Lots of them? Do you like any of them specially?
3. CHILD: I've got some indoors.
4. TEACHER: Have you? What kind?
5. CHILD: Got a packet.
6. TEACHER: A packet of them? What, Smarties? Are they Smarties?
7. CHILD: They're in a bag.
8. TEACHER: In a bag? Smarties are in a box, aren't they?

The teacher continues reading the book, and a little while later again tries to extract the 'right' answer, in this case the word 'sweets':

TEACHER: [Reading] 'I like . . .' What's the word for all kinds of jelly babies and Smarties? What do we go to buy? We say I'm going to buy some . . .

Whether or not Lynne was able to produce the 'total class' concept, sweets, in response to this question is impossible to tell. Again, she answers irrelevantly, this time with some resentment, perhaps because her earlier remarks had been dismissed by the teacher in turn 8:

CHILD: I *have* had some Smarties [indignantly]
TEACHER: Can you think of the word?
CHILD: But I *have* had some Smarties.
TEACHER: What sort of a shop do you go and buy Smarties from?
ONE CHILD: A children's shop.
ANOTHER CHILD: No, a sweetie shop.
TEACHER: A sweet shop. [Continues to read] I like sweets . . .'

It is worth noting that Lynne, who appears to be very immature in these conversations, is the same child who, on page 43, was questioning her mother about the processes of growth and development. We do not necessarily want to imply that she was capable of giving better answers than she did to the teacher's questions – it is impossible to know. We do, however, suggest that there is a good deal more to Lynne than the teacher might have guessed; in particular, a lively intellectual curiosity. It is this aspect of the children which is so little in evidence at school, and which is unlikely to be revealed in a teacher-dominated situation.

The different 'flavour' of story-reading at home and at school was partly due to the fact that the teacher was labouring under the twin disadvantages of coping with several children, and having a less intimate knowledge of the children than their mothers have. It was also because at school the staff tended to use the stories to pursue their educational aims. This was to some extent also true of the mothers, especially the middle-class mothers, but in their case much of the educational input was under the control of the children, since it was given in response to their questions. In the case of the staff, their educational aims tended to be pursued quite independently of the children, and often without any relation to their interests. In the process delight and excitement in the story must surely have been lost.

Overview

We began this chapter by pointing out that in moving from home to nursery school, the child moves from a setting where her life is centred on her mother to one where adults play a much more minor role. Nevertheless, even if they have less contact with the children than their mothers do, the staffs' interactions with the children are influenced by definite educational aims.

The teachers' aims, and their interactions with the children, were much more focused on play than was the case at home. In consequence, the 'curriculum' of the nursery school was rather different from that of the home, and narrower in scope. The discipline of the nursery school was also focused on issues rather different from those focused on at home. The teachers were particularly concerned to shape the children into being 'pupils', while the mothers placed more emphasis on trying to rear well-mannered children who could be trusted not to damage their homes. The children were much less likely to dispute the teachers' control than their mothers'.

Adult–child conversations were much fewer and briefer at school. The structure of teacher–child conversations was also typically very different from conversations at home. At school, the teachers contributed much more to the conversation than did the children, while at home the contributions of mother and child were more nearly matched. Staff conversations with children characteristically took the form of a series of questions organized round the educational objectives of assessing and fostering the children's language and thinking.

We were sceptical whether these objectives were reached, because the children so often failed to respond to the staff, answered ambiguously, or appeared confused. Moreover, this educational approach seemed to choke off the children's own questions, and their spontaneous talk to adults. The children asked very few questions, especially 'Why' questions, at school. 'Passages of intellectual search', in which the children raised questions, and thought through and discussed the adults' answers, did not occur at school. Particularly in schools with large numbers of staff, the children sometimes had difficulty in communicating about their play activities, and the conversation tended to have a 'flat' emotional tone. An analysis of some of the story episodes at school illustrated the strengths and weaknesses of the teachers' approach.

In the next chapter we will show how the working-class girls were at a particular disadvantage in the school setting.

9

The working-class girls, including Donna, at school

Why, in every country of the world, do the children of manual workers tend to have lower educational achievements than the children of white-collar workers? In Chapter 6 we pointed out that the most widely accepted current explanation among psychologists and teachers is that lower achievement is due to verbal deprivation at home. A minority view, argued forcefully by the American linguist Labov in relation to black ghetto children, is that, on the contrary, they grow up in a rich verbal culture. They only appear to be verbally incompetent in the alien social setting of the school or clinic. Their low educational achievements must be due to factors within the school or the wider society, not to their personal inadequacies.

In Chapter 6 we showed that, for the working-class children in our sample, the notion of 'verbal deprivation' was indeed a myth. Their mothers talked to them as much as middle-class mothers did to their children. They asked them to predict, explain and compare. All the working-class mothers themselves made comparisons, offered explanations, and used 'If . . . then' constructions when talking to their children. They discussed a wide range of topics with them, especially those that impinged on domestic and family matters.

At the same time, there were some social class differences in the style of mother–child interactions. A proportion of working-class families were very disputatious. The working-class mothers tended to be less concerned about answering their children's questions and extending their general knowledge than the middle-class mothers. They also seemed generally less concerned that their children should use language clearly and explicitly, and they used a rather smaller vocabulary in talking to them. The children, for their part, asked fewer 'Why' questions than middle-class children, used a smaller vocabulary, and made rather less frequent use of language for complex purposes.

We have no way of knowing whether differences of this kind – if they are representative of those in larger groups – could account for working-class children's underachievement at school. This would require an analysis of the exact nature of the demands of the primary classroom, and of the problems children have in meeting them. We do have evidence, however, which we will discuss in this chapter, in support of Labov's contention that working-class children are adversely affected by the school setting. This evidence came from comparing the way in which children from the two social class groups behaved at home and at school. As we saw in the last chapter, all the children, irrespective of social class, behaved differently towards adults in these settings. There was, however, evidence that the working-class children were much more strongly affected – in statistical terms, there were interactions between social class and setting.

Keeping the conversation going: working-class children

At school, it was the staff who tended to keep the conversation going, and who did most of the talking, whereas at home conversations were more evenly balanced between mother and child. This effect was particularly pronounced for the working-class children. They contributed only 15 per cent of sustaining remarks in conversation with the staff, compared with 23 per cent in the case of middle-class children. At home, children in both social class groups contributed half of the sustaining remarks.

Further, while at home the length of the mothers' and children's remarks were nearly equally matched, at school the children spoke more briefly, the teachers at much greater length. This discrepancy between the proportion of adult talk to child talk at home and at school was significantly greater in the case of working-class children.

Use of language for complex purposes

Perhaps because of this tendency for the working-class girls to make a minimal contribution in their conversations with the staff, they used language for complex purposes less frequently when talking to their teachers than to their mothers. For the middle-class girls, there was no such difference. They used the same proportion of comparisons, explanations and so on in their talk with their mothers and their teachers. But in two mornings at school, four of the fifteen working-class girls made either no use of language for complex purposes in talking to teachers, or only one use, yet in half that time at home they made respectively thirty-one, twenty-eight, fifty and seven such uses. A typical conversation that Cindy held with her teacher was as follows:

TEACHER: That's beautiful [looking at drawing]. What's this [points at figure]?
CHILD: A dog.
TEACHER: A dog?
CHILD: But he hasn't got no legs.
TEACHER: Just didn't want any legs, did he? What's that bit there?
CHILD: I dunno.
TEACHER: Will you write your name on it? [Child doesn't reply; teacher writes child's name on drawing]

At home, Cindy showed command of most of our coded complex uses of language. She used several in the following conversation, which took place while she was making a pool of water in the earth in her garden:

CHILD: Is it leaking?
MOTHER: Looks like it.
CHILD: Why is it? [No reply] Is it, does it leak now?
MOTHER: Yes, it's all soaking in the ground.
CHILD: Oh well, we better put some stones in then. Better get a little chunk of dirt so it won't go down. That one won't do, this is better. There. That'll save it. Now it won't go away, will it?

Why the children approached the staff

It was not the case that the working-class girls kept their distance from the staff. They were just as likely to approach the staff as the middle-class girls, and there was no difference in the number of conversations they held with them. There was also no difference in the length of these conversations, no doubt because almost all the conversations were kept going by the staff. But there was a social class difference in their reasons for approaching the staff.

The working-class girls were much less likely to approach the staff with a question than were the middle-class girls. As we saw in the last chapter, all the children showed a noticeable reluctance to ask questions of the nursery staff. While they bombarded their mothers with questions, the proportion of questions in their talk to staff was much smaller. This was especially true of 'Why' questions and 'curiosity' questions. The working-class children were particularly affected in this respect. While half of their questions at home were 'curiosity' questions, this was the case with only a quarter of their questions at school; 70 per cent of their questions at school were routine 'business' questions. Ten of the fifteen working-class girls did not ask a single 'Why' question in two mornings at school, although all asked several during one afternoon at home.

The working-class girls, then, did not regard the nursery staff as people to whom their curiosity should be addressed. Instead, they tended to turn to them for help and assistance, especially in relation to other children. The working-class children initiated more than twice as many conversations with the staff as did the middle-class children by appeals for help. Appeals to help in disputes with other children – 'Miss, he's hit me', 'She's taken my spade' – were especially frequent. At home, there was no social class difference in the frequency of appeals for help. The middle-class children, on the other hand, were more than twice as likely as the working-class children to initiate conversations with the staff by a question, although, again, there was no social class difference in this respect at home.

There was also a tendency for the working-class girls to have fewer disputes with the school staff than the middle-class girls. All the children were much less inclined to dispute with the nursery staff than with their mothers. On average, 18 per cent of the working-class girls' conversations with their mothers included a dispute, but only 2 per cent of their conversations with their teachers. In the case of the middle-class children, on average 12 per cent of their conversations with their mothers included a dispute, and 4 per cent of their conversations with the staff. Although this difference is small, and not statistically significant, it is consistent with the other social class differences we found at school. School disputes were usually concerned with the staff's attempts to make children follow the class routine, for example, to come in from the playground for a story, or to wash.

References to home life at school

There was also a social class difference in the topic of conversation. The middle-class children were much more likely to initiate talk about their home life to the staff than were the working-class children. Such conversations occurred nearly twice as often in the transcripts of the middle-class girls. At home, there was no difference in the frequency with which middle-class and working-class girls discussed what happened at school.

As we shall see in the next chapter, the discussions that did occur about home at school were not particularly fruitful, and this was especially true in the case of the working class children. Our impression was that the staff were more knowledgeable about the home circumstances of the middle-class children, and thus better able to talk to them about their home life. This may have been because the middle-class mothers talked more freely to the teachers, or because the middle-class children were more successful communicators.

Why were the working-class girls so affected by school?

Compared to the middle-class girls, the working-class girls showed a greater difference between their behaviour to their mothers and their teachers in a whole range of respects. These included the length of their remarks to adults, and the extent to which they sustained conversations, asked 'curiosity' questions, used language for complex purposes, talked about their 'other' life, and asked the adult for help.

The net effect of these characteristics was to make the working-class girls appear particularly unassertive, subdued and immature at school.

The middle-class girls, whose behaviour was much less affected, thus appeared noticeably more assertive, at ease and confident.

This appearance of self-confidence showed itself in many small but revealing ways, other than those we have already described. For example, the middle-class girls were quite prepared to correct the teachers in no uncertain manner. Thus, when Valerie's teacher looked at the model she was making and commented, 'That's a good garage', Valerie replied, 'It's a boat, actually.' On page 78 we quoted a conversation with Beth, in which the staff asked her where she would be when she left nursery school: 'Be? In a different school, of course,' was the tart reply. Lesley, when she hit another child, defended herself calmly: 'Well, he did something wrong.' Jane commented to the teacher about a boy who had just splashed her with his tricycle, 'I wish he wasn't in this school.' 'Don't you like him?' 'No, not very much.' Very few working-class children had the confidence to advance their opinions in this way, or to contradict the teacher.

The effect of nursery school on the working-class children's behaviour is particularly striking when one considers that the schools were in no way formal or intimidating. All the nursery schools in our study were happy and relaxed places where the children were free to choose their play activities and their friends. The children had been in the nursery for nearly a year, and none of the effects could be ascribed to the difficulties of settling in. We can only suggest a number of factors that may have been involved.

First, the school must have seemed much more foreign to the working-class than to the middle-class children. The decorative schemes, pictures and furniture were in accord with middle-class taste. The books and play equipment used at school were often to be found in the middle-class homes. While some kinds of play equipment were found in almost all the homes – dolls, dolls' prams, tricycles, jigsaw puzzles, pencils, play-dough – many of the middle-class mothers bought other, more 'developmental' toys from the same specialized catalogues as the teachers. Like the teachers, too, they tended to buy their children's books from specialized bookshops, and the middle-class children often remarked at school that they had the same book or toy at home. The working-class mothers, on the other hand, tended to buy a rather different selection of books and toys from the local toyshop and supermarkets.

Another factor which may have affected the confidence of the working-class girls was the contrast between the speech style of the nursery staff and their mothers. Many of the working-class mothers had strong regional accents, and they used some non-standard grammatical constructions. In contrast, the teachers were mostly from middle-class backgrounds, and their speech style and approach to the children was much closer to that of the middle-class mothers.

Perhaps, too, the children were influenced by the attitudes of their own mothers to the teachers. When we interviewed the mothers some weeks after the recording, we found the working-class mothers much less confident about their educational role *vis-à-vis* the school than the middle-class mothers. To the questions, 'Who do you think draws the children out more, the nursery teacher or the mothers?' and 'Who do you think tells the children more things?', ten of the working-class mothers, but only two of the middle-class mothers, answered, 'The teacher.' Similarly, when we asked, 'Do you think the children learn more language at nursery school or at home?' twelve of the middle-class mothers, but only two working-class mothers, answered, 'The home.'

These answers make depressing reading. They suggest that the middle-class mothers had a realistic and accurate picture of the relative contributions made by teachers and mothers to the children's language development. The working-class mothers, on the other hand, shared the teachers' belief that they, the mothers, were offering their children inadequate language stimulation. In the same way, they had a highly inflated notion of what the teachers were offering the children at school.

There was also evidence that the working-class mothers were more likely to caution their children about how they should behave to the teachers. Ten of the working-class mothers, but only four of the middle-class mothers, said that they had warned their child not to misbehave at school. Donna's mother, for example, when asked, 'Did you say anything to her about how she should behave, and about the teachers?' answered, 'I told her to do as she was told, and never be rude to the teacher. I told her if she had a problem with other children, don't hit them, go to the teacher.' She added, however, that she had recently changed this latter injunction, as she had decided that the teachers did not have the time to sort out the children's quarrels. The middle-class mothers were more likely to give such replies as, 'I didn't tell her anything special, except that it would be fun', or 'except that she should say if she wanted to go to the lavatory'.

It is also possible that social class differences in the children's self-chosen play activities brought them into different relationships with the nursery staff. The working-class girls spent the majority of their free playtime playing with sand and water, or in physical activities outside, particularly running around, climbing and playing on the slide. The middle-class girls, on the other hand, were much more likely to spend their time painting, doing handcrafts, listening to stories, and playing board and other table games. (One of us, BT, found a very similar picture in a much larger study of play in nursery schools).[1]

Although in theory all nursery school activities lend themselves to 'educational' conversations with the staff, in fact, as Sylva has shown,[2] these are more likely to occur in the course of the kind of activities preferred by the middle-class children. Sand and water play and chasing around, on the other hand, are more likely to produce conflicts between children, and consequent appeals for the staff to intervene.

Whether any or all of these factors played a part in enhancing the confidence of the middle-class girls at school, and depressing that of the working-class girls, it is impossible to say. It seems likely that several factors interacted. Whatever the reason, it is surprising that a different attitude to the teachers was apparent in these very young children at the outset of their school career.

The teachers' behaviour towards the working-class girls

The children's lack of confidence and apparent immaturity was matched by a difference in the teachers' approach to them. It was as though they adjusted their own speech style to a lower level when talking to the working-class girls. Thus they made less frequent use of language for complex purposes when addressing the working-class girls than the middle-class girls. They were more likely to initiate conversations with working-class children by questioning them, and their 'cognitive demands' were pitched at a lower level. They gave a more restricted range of information to the working-class children. They were less likely to ask the working-class children for descriptions and more likely to ask them intellectually easy questions concerned with labelling objects and naming their attributes (e.g., 'What's that called? What colour is it?').

Asking children for colour names was, in fact, a particularly frequent staff conversational gambit with the working-class girls. It was certainly the case that a number of the working-class children did not know many colour names. Given that the staff saw 'naming colours' as an important educational aim, this approach could be justified. In a wider context, however, doubts arise. By focusing on this intellectually simple task they failed to provide the children with opportunities for more advanced conversation. At the same time, the low-level conversations that ensued must have reinforced their own belief that the children were only capable of simple dialogue.

Some of these differences may have been due to the greater tendency of the middle-class girls to choose activities which evoked relatively complex language from the staff. They were more likely, for example, to play matching and sorting games with the staff, and to ask them for stories. But even in casual conversation the staff tended to use more complex language in talking to them. Louise, for example, was doing handwork near her teacher when she noticed another child speak to her.

CHILD: What? What did he want?
STAFF: He wanted to take some milk home with him today.
CHILD: Well, he mustn't.
STAFF: Not when you've been at school a long time.
CHILD: Mm.
STAFF: You don't take milk home then, do you? When you first start school, and you don't drink the whole bottle, you can.
CHILD: Dan's drunk it all up, the whole milk.
STAFF: Well, then, there's none left to take home, is there?
CHILD: No.
STAFF: But if Jimmy had only drunk a little drop of his bottle, he could take the rest home.
CHILD: I was a baby once. [She began to discuss this topic]

Joyce, a working-class girl, triggered conversation at a lower intellectual level from the same teacher, probably because of her awareness that Joyce was unsure of colour names.

CHILD: Where's Joan [her friend]?
STAFF: Joan is over . . . Oh no, she isn't. I thought she was painting.
CHILD: I did one painting, a long one.
STAFF: You and Joan?
CHILD: Mm. [In fact, the two girls had not been painting together]
STAFF: What colour did you paint with?
CHILD: I had red and blue, dark blue.
STAFF: Blue, isn't it? [Looks at turquoise paint on Joyce's arm]
CHILD: Mm, blue.

STAFF: [Jokes] I don't think you painted a picture, I think you painted yourself.

CHILD: I did paint a picture. That looks like green. [She looks at her arm which has red and turquoise paint on it]

STAFF: Green? No, that's red – look, there it is.

CHILD: Yeah. That looks like blood running out of my arm, doesn't it? [Points to red paint on arm]

STAFF: Yes, you're bleeding, aren't you? Does that one look like blood? [Points to turquoise paint on arm]

CHILD: Mm.

STAFF: Mm? Is that the right colour for blood? What's that colour? [Joyce doesn't answer]

The reader will note that it was Joyce, not her teacher, who raised the level of the conversation by introducing a simile.

A tendency to adjust one's conversational level to the perceived level of the partner's speech is an almost universal tendency of both adults and children when talking to young children, and probably assists the child's language development. In the situation we are describing, however, the effect can only be to reinforce the children's use of more immature language. Thus, far from the nursery school providing a compensatory language environment for the working-class children, both the quantity and quality of the language addressed to them at home was superior.

Our evidence thus supports Labov's contention that working-class children give a misleading impression of their abilities to school staff. This may well be one factor in the children's underachievement at school. If, as we found, teachers respond to their apparent rather than their real abilities, they will tend to underestimate what the children can achieve and present them with inappropriately low-level tasks. An initial setback of this kind can soon become cumulative. Other factors, for example the children's disinclination for sedentary occupations, the different language styles used at home and at school, may, of course, be involved.

Donna at school

In Chapter 7 we described how one working-class child, Donna, spent an afternoon at home. Donna was not chosen as a 'typical' working-class girl – there was far too wide a range among the working-class families for any one family to be considered typical. Nevertheless, Donna's upbringing showed some stereotypical working-class characteristics. Indeed, in a number of respects, she and her mother represented one extreme of the social class continuum. As we shall show, Donna's experiences at school were also in some ways typical of what happened to the working-class children, although she was more assertive than most of them in her relationships with the staff.

Our account of Donna's time at school largely leaves out what must have been the most important aspect for her – her play on her own, and her interactions with other children. Conversations with the staff, on which we focus, played a relatively minor part in her morning. At nursery school she spent most of her free playtime outside, chasing other children, on the slide, on a tricycle, or in the sandpit. At home, the reader may remember, she spent most of her time indoors, hanging around her mother and talking to her, except when they both sat on the step together.

This difference was reflected in the sheer quantity of their talk. Donna and her mother between them exchanged 1471 turns of talk during one afternoon. In two mornings at school, Donna's conversations with the staff amounted to 201 turns. Two of Donna's conversations at home (those discussing nursery rhymes and counting rock cakes) together produced more talk than all her conversations with the staff combined.

The following account of one morning at school includes almost all her conversations with the staff. We chose the second morning because the conversations were longer and less routine than those of the other morning.

Donna arrived at school that morning clutching a doll; on the previous day she had brought her teddy bear. A number of children used this device to bridge the gap between home and school, and it usually led to some anxious minutes when the toy was mislaid. When Donna arrived at school she found that the staff had prepared an unusual activity for the children. Donna was persuaded to put her doll down and try it. Bowls of paint had been placed on the paint table, and the children were shown how to blow bubbles in the paint using a straw. When they had blown a large collection of bubbles to the top of the bowl, they were to place a piece of paper on top of the bubbles, and the pattern of the bubbles would be transferred to the paper. Donna had difficulty getting enough bubbles, and the nursery assistant who was supervising this activity instructed her how to do it:

STAFF: You've got to get that right to the very top, Donna, move it
nearer to you. Like a little bit more, just to get it up a bit more.
Well, you've got to keep blowing till it goes right to the top. It's
not coming up properly . . . do it again [Donna blew more bubbles].
Blow that right to the top and then we do a pattern with your
bubbles [staff pointed to another child's more successful bubbles].
Look, right to the very top . . . look, like this, Donna, look so they
come right to the top of the bowl. [Donna got some bubbles to the
top of the bowl and put a piece of paper on top. She showed the
staff her paper – it didn't have much of a pattern on it]

CHILD: E'y'are.

STAFF: [Laughed when she saw child's paper] You didn't blow it
hard enough. You didn't get it high enough, did you?

The assistant went away and returned with more dry paint to add to the
bowls and some brushes to mix it with. Donna mixed her paint until the
nursery assistant decided it was well enough mixed.

STAFF: That's all right, you don't need these brushes any more. It's
all been mixed. [Donna blew some more bubbles and started to
put her paper on top]

CHILD: Look! Look!

STAFF: I don't think it's high enough, Donna. Bit more. Bit more.
[Donna blew more bubbles and tried to show staff]

CHILD: Look! Look! Oh, s'gone down again! [Donna was annoyed
with herself. She blew more bubbles and tried to attract the staff's
attention] Look! Look! [Staff made no response as she was busy
with the other children. Eventually she came back to Donna]

STAFF: Do you want to do another one? [Donna nodded] You
haven't done one yet, have you? This one's not turned out yet, has
it? You haven't got the bubbles up here.

CHILD: I did have it up there. [She turned to her friend, Kevin, next
to her] Didn't I, Kevin? [She started blowing again, and did well
that time]

STAFF: [To other child] Oh look, Donna has! [To Donna] Come on
then, Donna, put your paper on quick before the bubbles disappear. [Donna put the paper on and took it off to show staff]

CHILD: Look!

STAFF: Better, isn't it? Try again, you could do it again then,
couldn't you? [Donna got her bubbles up again]

CHILD: Look! [Staff gave Donna her first piece of paper again]
STAFF: Put this one on again 'cause it's not . . . clear. Don't press it
in the middle, will you?
CHILD: [Took the paper off] Can I do another one?
STAFF: No, we'll let someone else do it now. [To Donna and Kevin]
So you two go and wash your hands, you've been here a long time.

Donna washed her hands, and went to the dry sand container on the
other side of the room.

The nursery assistant had helped Donna to acquire a specific skill,
that of making patterns from bubbles of paint. Donna enjoyed this
activity, and there is little doubt that she would not have produced an
attractive pattern without the staff's instruction. Nursery school activities of this kind seemed to be aimed at showing children how to use
material in new and creative ways. It is hard to know whether Donna's
creativity was enhanced by this experience: she would certainly have
been punished if she had tried to repeat the activity at home.

Donna then spent about twenty minutes playing with dry sand and
talking to the other children. During this time the only conversation she
had with any of the staff was when she was quarrelling with Kevin over
one of the spades. The nursery teacher came over and pointed out
another spade she might use:

STAFF: There's one, all right?
CHILD: [Moans] I don't want that one.
STAFF: You have to share. I think Kevin was using it first, Donna.
CHILD: [Moans] *I* was.
STAFF: You sure?
CHILD: [Moans] Yes.
STAFF: You have it back in a minute, all right? [To Kevin] When
you're finished. [To both] You can go and have your milk in a
minute, anyway.

Donna accepted this, and carried on playing in the sand. After a while
she went to the milk table, supervised by a student teacher, and picked
up a whole bottle of milk:

CHILD: I have half a bottle.
STAFF: That's not half, they're [i.e. the half bottles] in the crate, all
right, Donna? [But Donna started drinking from the whole bottle]

Wait a minute, Donna, wait a minute. Will you wait a minute, Donna . . . put it back in the crate. Go and put it back in the crate. [Donna eventually put the whole bottle back in the crate and picked out a half bottle. She drank it all up and showed the student]

CHILD: Look!

STAFF: That's better, Donna. Go and put your bottle away.

Donna put her milk bottle away, then remembered the doll she brought to school that morning. She asked the student teacher:

CHILD: Where's my dolly? My dolly?

STAFF: I don't know where it is.

Luckily, her teacher was passing by and heard Donna's question:

STAFF: I put it on my table for you, see, 'cause it was getting all painty, really.

CHILD: Mm.

The teacher took Donna's hand, and they went together to collect the doll. Donna picked up her doll and went outside to play in the sandpit. She spent over thirty minutes there, and most of the time was spent playing and talking to other children. However, the sandpit was being supervised by a student nursery nurse, and several brief conversations took place. At one time Donna said softly to herself, 'Sandals, sandals, sandals.' Then, more loudly to the student:

CHILD: You can't make sandals out of sand.

STAFF: No, it's too soft, isn't it?

Later, Donna commented to her friend, who was playing next to her:

CHILD: We've got the same spade.

STAFF: Yes, same colour aren't they? And everything!

A little later, some of the other children pretended to feed the student nurse with 'cakes' made of sand. Donna, however, didn't get involved in this game. Later, another child, Jimmy, tried to take Donna's bucket. Donna called out, 'No', 'No', 'No', repeatedly, apparently trying to get help from the student nurse. The nurse rebuked the aggressor, but Jimmy then tried to take Donna's spade. Donna again called out, 'No! I got that spade first', but this time the student nurse ignored her, and eventually Donna used another spade. Subsequently, the nurse helped Jimmy turn out a bucket of sand. Donna's aggression welled up, and she smashed it with her spade. The student took it very gently:

STAFF: You've broken our cakes? Oh dear. How are we going to eat them now?

Donna shrugged her shoulders and didn't reply. She returned to quarrelling with Jimmy, and ignored an invitation from the student to have 'a piece of cake'. Later, however, she did get involved in a fantasy game with the student. One of the other children pretended she was making 'apple pie' out of sand, and Donna said she was too:

CHILD: So I.
STAFF: You're making apple pie as well. Ooh, I shall have to have some then, 'cause I love apple pie. [Donna pushed her full bucket towards the student]
CHILD: Here's some.
STAFF: What's this? [No reply] Is that apple pie and custard? [Donna nodded] Ooh, I love apple pie and custard. Ooh, that's beautiful. [She pretended to eat] You had a piece? [She offered Donna the bucket: Donna pretended to eat some]
CHILD: I'm making some more now.
STAFF: You're making some more? What you gonna make this time?
CHILD: Some more apple pie and custard.
STAFF: Some more apple pie and custard?
CHILD: Yes.

The student went inside, and Donna continued to play in the sandpit. When the student returned to sweep up the sand, Donna told her that she had filled her bucket. The nurse saw Donna's doll sitting on the side of the sandpit, and offered to put it inside.

When she returned, the other children in the sandpit offered her more 'cake'. Donna joined in the game:

CHILD: Some more for you!
STAFF: And what kind of cake's this one?

CHILD: Um . . . white.
STAFF: White cake. Oh that's lovely.

Donna dropped out of the fantasy game at that point, and returned to filling containers with sand. Eventually, after a long spell in the sandpit, Donna played on the slide, then went over to the student and held her hand. The student suggested several things she might do, but Donna just shook her head. Soon it was time to go in for a snack and story. The student teacher told Donna to wash her hands, but she refused.

CHILD: Don't wannoo.
STAFF: Why's that then?
CHILD: I washed my hands at home.

Donna went to the washroom, all the same, along with the student nurse and some other children. The student nurse also attempted to get her to wash her hands:

STAFF: Donna, come and wash your hands.
CHILD: I washed them at home.
STAFF: Come on!
CHILD: I washed them at home.
STAFF: Wash them here as well. Donna, use the toilet.
CHILD: Don't need to.
STAFF: You try.

Donna went to the toilet, washed her hands and went off to snack and story. Afterwards she wandered round for a bit, then went over to the sandpit again. She spent some time in the sandpit, then went back inside to wait with the other children until it was time for a music session, which ended the morning.

Donna seemed to enjoy her morning at school. She had probably benefited from running around, mixing with other children, and from her long relaxed sessions on her own and with others in the sandpit. She was also learning to follow school rules, and to take part as a member of a large group in story and music sessions. Both she and her mother probably benefited from a period of lessened emotional tension away from each other.

Intellectually, it is difficult to see that the school was offering Donna much. The specific teaching activity at school, showing the children how to make patterns from paint bubbles, was intended to enhance creativity by demonstrating the diversity of ways in which familiar materials can be used. Activities of this kind (for example, foot painting, finger painting) are not uncommon in nursery school, and they are enjoyed by the children. The fact, however, that they run so counter to the values and priorities of the home must serve to widen the gap between school and home for both parents and children, and from this point of view they may be unproductive. The rather narrow intellectual horizons of Donna's world were not extended at school. Nothing occurred on either of the mornings we recorded to enlarge her general knowledge, her vocabulary, or her understanding of her own world. It is true that the staff encouraged Donna to engage in fantasy play, but her participation was so minimal and imitative that her imagination was hardly stretched.

Donna's behaviour with the staff was subdued. It was not that she avoided the staff – 40 per cent of her conversations with the staff was initiated by herself, and half of these conversations were initiated by telling the staff about what she was doing. However, her further contributions to the conversations were very limited: 84 per cent of the conversaions lasted only six turns or less. The reader will have noted that her remarks were very brief. She contributed only 23 per cent of remarks that sustained conversation when talking to the staff, compared with 49 per cent with her mother. She asked no 'Why' questions, and made only nine uses of language for complex purposes in two mornings at school. But in one afternoon at home she asked twenty-seven 'Why' questions and used language for complex purposes ninety-two times.

Nonetheless, Donna clearly sought some contact with the staff, especially the student nurse. Several times she joined the other children, however briefly, in offering the student fantasy food, and when she was tired she stood silently next to her, holding her hand. However, something of the disputatious Donna her mother knew appeared at school. She was much more inclined than most of the working-class girls to resist school discipline and to contradict staff remarks, and in this respect she was atypical.

If the reader looks again at the account of Donna's afternoon with her mother (Chapter 7), they will find a striking contrast. There is a depth and intensity running through the home conversations which is almost entirely absent at school. Donna's struggles to understand her world, and her mother's concern that she should understand, have no parallel at school. Her mother's educational intentions, whether with respect to Donna telling a fairy story correctly, learning letters and numbers, or understanding why her mother cannot play with her and her father cannot come to lunch, seem much more serious and committed than any of the staff's intentions.

Overview

In this chapter we have shown how the working-class children in general, and Donna in particular, fared at school. We confirmed Labov's contention that these children were adversely affected in their relationships with adults by the school setting. That is, in a wide range of respects they appeared more subdued and immature at school than at home.

Because the teachers adjusted their demands to the perceived immaturity of the children, they in no way 'compensated' for any inadequacies in their homes. On the contrary, both the quantity and the quality of the language addressed to them at home was superior, while the school staff did not generally provide the extension of the children's general knowledge and vocabulary that would have complemented the education of the home.

Our findings suggest possible factors involved in the origin of differences in the educational attainment of these two groups of children. We cannot tell from this study which, if any, of the factors are involved. What we do know is that the working-class children were already appearing at a disadvantage in nursery school.

10

The gap between home and nursery school

'If only parents understood what we are trying to do at school, it could be "nursery" for the children all day at home.' This remark, made by a concerned nursery school teacher, expresses a point of view that is very widespread. It implies that professionals know better than parents how to educate children. It also implies that parents should model themselves on teachers. In this book we have tried to show that these views are mistaken. Home is by no means an inferior substitute for school. On the contrary, it provides a powerful learning environment for young children, but one that is very different from school. In this chapter we will discuss the gap that exists between these two worlds, and the very real difficulty of bridging it.

The nursery schools and classes in our study created a child-centred play environment in which children had relatively few encounters with adults. When they did encounter the school staff, they found that the staff's expectations of them were very different from their mothers'. Some activities were encouraged which would invite punishment at home – for example, playing with water, making footprints or blowing bubbles in paint. On the other hand, the children had to learn that other activities allowed at home were not permitted at school. For example, decisions which they made themselves at home, or negotiated with their mothers – when to wash their hands, come inside, have a story – were made by the staff as part of the school routine the children must learn to follow.

Further, the staff addressed them in a way that was very different from their mothers. Their encounters with the staff were usually very brief. The staff expected them to answer a great many questions about what they were doing. Their talk to the children was mainly concerned with play, rather than the wide range of topics that cropped up in the course of daily life at home. Unlike many of their mothers, the staff usually remained very calm and even-tempered, even if the children contradicted them or disputed their authority. And, as we shall show in this chapter, the children often had difficulty in making themselves understood to the staff.

The children responded to the difference in these two settings by behaving differently themselves. They tended to answer the staff's questions briefly, or not at all, They rarely asked the staff questions of their own, or made the kind of spontaneous remarks that keep a conversation going. These characteristics were particularly marked in the case of working-class children.

These findings emerged from an overall comparison of the children at home and at school. But the extent to which the children's behaviour was affected at school varied from one child to another. There were no significant correlations between the children's behaviour at home and school – for example, children who talked a lot to their mothers did not necessarily talk more than other children to their teachers. Some did, and some did not.

Attempting to bridge the gap: the children's attempts at school

All the parties involved – staff, parents and children – made attempts to bridge the gap between home and school. As we shall see, this feat was harder for the teachers than the mothers.

Most of the children made active attempts to link their home life to school. One way in which some of them did this was to bring a favourite toy, doll or teddy bear to school. Most of the schools in our study were very tolerant of this practice. Another way attempted by the children was to talk to the staff about their life at home. This often happened when the staff read to the children.

At the end of the morning most teachers read to the whole class. These sessions were in many ways intended to be a forerunner of the kind of experience the children would meet when they moved on to primary school. Some children listened intently to the stories, others fidgeted and looked bored. For many children this was a time to sit back and recharge their batteries. Thumbs were sucked, hair twiddled, teddy bears clutched. Others attempted to make themselves more comfortable by commenting on the links between the story and their home experience. For example, the story might concern a pet cat. One or two of the children would call out, 'We've got a cat at home', 'Our cat's stripey like that one', and so on. The teacher's problem was that if she responded encouragingly to these offerings, she was soon deluged with more and more contributions from the children on the same or related themes – 'We've got a dog, miss', 'Our budgie died last week', and so on. In order to proceed at all with her story session, the teacher would soon have to call a halt to the children's contributions. The opportunity to create explicit links between the child's own experience and the story was thus almost inevitably lost.

More intimate story sessions, when the staff read to only two or three children, might seem to offer a better possibility for linking home and school experiences. Usually, however, the children's comments were ruled out of order on these occasions too, because the staff were pursuing their own educational aims. They might, for example, be intent on getting the children to predict what would happen next in the story, or to explain what a word meant. Even if they themselves asked the children to make a link with their home life ('Does your cat sleep on the sofa?'), they soon realized that they must close the floodgates on the replies if they were to pursue their main aims.

Some of the children approached the staff at other times with confidences about their home life. During our observations, twelve middle-class and seven working-class children started at least one conversation in this way. Giving confidences of this kind called for rather advanced communication skills, since the staff usually knew almost nothing about the children's home circumstances and experiences. In the first place, it required that the children appreciate what the staff would need to be told in order to understand them. We showed in Chapter 5 that some of the children had already gone some way to acquiring this skill, but there was a considerable range in this respect amongst them. It also required that the children should know how to give the staff the appropriate information in a clear and comprehensible form. They could be helped if the staff asked the right questions, but this did not always happen.

The following conversation failed to establish communication, because Lynne did not explain that Polly was her grandmother's dog who had just spent a night with her, and the nursery assistant did not ask who Polly was, or where her home was:

CHILD: Polly's back. Polly comed up yesterday, but she's gone home. Polly.

STAFF: Polly?

CHILD: Yeah, my Polly.

STAFF: Oh!

CHILD: We had some biccies up there. When we taked her home. She bringed us some sweeties.

STAFF: Oh, that was nice.

CHILD: A packet.

STAFF: A packet? What kind? [Child did not reply, and staff talks to other children]

Even very articulate children, talking to staff who tried to help them clarify their meaning, could run into difficulties, as was the case with Cathie:

CHILD: My grandma's got a humper-dumper [large plastic sheet with handles, used for collecting garden rubbish].

STAFF: What's a humper-dumper?

CHILD: You put all the rubbish on it.

STAFF: Humper-dumper?

CHILD: Yes.

STAFF: For all the rubbish from the garden?

CHILD: Mm.

STAFF: Oh . . . what happens to it when it's full up?

CHILD: Well you see . . . they take . . . Tara took so much . . . that it all fell . . . that some of it fell out.

STAFF: Did it?

CHILD: Mm.

STAFF: Oh dear. You'll have to get another one.

CHILD: But it did . . . didn't matter 'cause it didn't run out. She's still got the humper-dumper.

STAFF: That's lucky.

Such conversations should be compared with those between the same child, Cathie, and her mother (for example, page 64) which flowed effortlessly along because they were based on a shared set of experiences.

There is a further difficulty for children of this age in communicating with someone who has not shared their experiences. This is the inadequacy of some of their basic conceptual frameworks, an issue which we discussed in Chapter 5. For example, they find it very difficult to describe where a place is, because of their patchy knowledge of the spatial relationships between places. Erica almost managed this task. She was not helped by being misheard by the staff. The nursery assistant was sewing in the book corner when Erica approached her:

CHILD: Daddy takes me to the zoo.
STAFF: Which zoo's that? London Zoo?
CHILD: No, the terrace zoo.
STAFF: Terrace? Where's that? Is it near you?
CHILD: Yes, it lives a long way out.
STAFF: Far from here?
CHILD: Yes. It's nearer here than it's nearer our house.
STAFF: It's nearer your house, is it?
CHILD: Nearer your house. Nearer the school than it is to my house.
STAFF: What did you see at the zoo? [The conversation continued]

Communication sometimes broke down because of the child's inadequate or faulty grasp of the concepts she was using. This happened to the most intellectually advanced and articulate child in our study, Beth, whose 'sloping roofs' conversation was quoted in Chapter 5. In the following conversation it emerged that Beth not only had a mistaken notion about what was to happen at school in the future (no event was planned), but that she was giving the wrong meaning to the word 'museum', and had a very restricted understanding of what a church is.

Beth was talking to a nursery assistant who was mending some equipment when, out of the blue, she asked:

CHILD: Well, when will the museum have gone?
STAFF: What museum, darling?
CHILD: The museum that's going to be in this school.
STAFF: The museum that's going to be in this school? I don't know. Whereabouts is the museum in the school, then?

Beth was impatient with the assistant for misunderstanding the tense that she used, and rephrased her statement:

CHILD: I mean the museum that's going to come, but it's coming later.

STAFF: We're having a museum here, later?
CHILD: Yeah.

At this point the assistant decided to check on Beth's understanding of the word 'museum':

STAFF: Well, what sort of things do you get in a museum, then?
CHILD: Just get married. That's all you get in museums, you just get married.
STAFF: Well, what do you do in churches, then?
CHILD: Sing hymns.
STAFF: Don't you get married in church?
CHILD: No.
STAFF: Have you been to a museum, Beth?
CHILD: Yeah.
STAFF: Well, in museums they have all sorts of very old things, like tables and chairs and clothes. But in a church . . . lots of things happen in church.
CHILD: What?
STAFF: You get christened in church.
CHILD: And you sing hymns.
STAFF: You sing hymns, yes, you go to church on Sundays.

The rest of the conversation was concerned with what happens in churches. The mystery of what Beth meant by a museum and why she thought one was coming to the school was never resolved.

The communication difficulties we have described are not unique to children – conversations between adults can fail for all the reasons we have discussed. The difficulties are, however, much more acute in young children, because of their inexperience, ignorance and greater intellectual limitations.

The communication difficulties are also not unique to the school – we shall describe similar difficulties at home – and they can certainly not be blamed on the staff. The difficulties are, however, accentuated at school by the lack of shared experience between staff and children, which makes the communication task more difficult. The inevitable problem that results provides the school staff with an important educational opportunity; it can be argued that one of their basic tasks should be to help the children improve their communication skills.

The attempt by the school staff to bridge the gap

Some of the school staff tried to bridge the home–school gap from
their end by asking the children questions about their home life. This
well-intentioned effort was liable to run into difficulties. We have
already discussed the difficulty that arises from not understanding the
child. A more serious problem was that the staff had no means of
evaluating the children's replies. Often they were uncertain whether or
not to believe them. This was the case in the following conversation,
which took place while the teacher was helping Louise with some craft
work:

STAFF: What sort of car have you got, Louise?
CHILD: A silver one. And a red one.
STAFF: Not *two* cars? [Incredulously]
CHILD: Yeah. Because my daddy drives the one to work in the . . .
[Fades out]
STAFF: Daddy needs one to drive to work?
CHILD: Yes!
STAFF: And who uses the other one?
CHILD: Me! To go to school!
STAFF: You drive it to school?
CHILD: No, no. Daddy drives the red car, we drive the silver car.

The teacher continued to probe, but was clearly left uncertain about the
truth of Louise's story.

In the following conversation the teacher was even less inclined
to believe Mina's answer, but was also uncertain how to handle
her. The teacher had been discussing babies with a small group of
children:

STAFF: What does your baby do, Mina?
CHILD: She can walk. [The baby is only six months old]
STAFF: Mina! [In a 'you're joking' voice]
CHILD: She can. She can now. Not yesterday she couldn't.
STAFF: She couldn't yesterday.
CHILD: No, but she can now.
STAFF: You're teasing me.
CHILD: Not.

Mina seemed to enjoy inventing tall stories about her home life, but other children seemed to be pushed into invention more out of a desire to please the staff. Carol, for example, had recently moved house. In answering the nursery assistant's questions about her new bedroom, she ended up claiming furniture which in fact she did not have:

> STAFF: What's in your bedroom?
> CHILD: Um . . . toys.
> STAFF: Toys, what else? What do you sleep on?
> CHILD: A bed.
> STAFF: A bed. Have you got a dressing table?
> CHILD: No.
> STAFF: No? What do you put all your clothes in, then?
> CHILD: Er . . . a dressing table [hesitantly].
> STAFF: How nice. Has it got a mirror?
> CHILD: No. [In fact she had no dressing table]

Communicating about school at home

Because the mothers were familiar with the school routine, conversations at home about school tended to present fewer difficulties than conversations about home at school. This was certainly the case with the more articulate children. Rosy and her mother were having lunch, when her mother asked her what she had done at school. Rosy began to list the morning's events:

> CHILD: . . . and then I danced, and then I had my story, and then we . . .
> MOTHER: Did you dance to music? Did Mrs Smither put her tape-recorder on?
> CHILD: Not her tape-recorder, her record-player.
> MOTHER: Oh.
> CHILD: And, um, then, um, then I got my shoes and then I, you came to collect me.
> MOTHER: What was the story today? Had you heard it before?
> CHILD: I've heard it at school. I don't think you know it – the tiger. A tiger.
> MOTHER: 'The Tiger Who Came to Tea'?

CHILD: No, a different tiger. But I can't remember how it goes.

MOTHER: What happened to the tiger?

CHILD: Um ... the tiger ... um ... I can't remember what the tiger did.

MOTHER: Forgotten it, have you?

CHILD: Yes, I always forget [laughs].

MOTHER: You don't listen properly [a little scornfully].

CHILD: I *do* listen, that why people make a noise at school.

MOTHER: Oh. Who makes a noise at school? Is it always the same people? [The conversation continued]

The children were also helped to link home and school experiences by their mothers' ability to tune in very sensitively to the meaning of their remarks. Mary was eating chocolate peanuts at home and talking about them, when her talk began to be more about the story that she had heard at school than about what she was doing. The story, 'The Tiger Who Came to Tea', describes the unexpected visit of a tiger to a little girl and her mother. The tiger ate up all the food in the house, and drank all the water from the taps. Mary did not explicitly state that she was referring to a story, but her mother was able almost at once to interpret her remarks:

1. CHILD: I really do like it, and I eat it all up.
2. MOTHER: You do, you eat most things up.
3. CHILD: [Shifting to the story] No. I eat all the food up. I eat all your food up.
4. MOTHER: You're a good girl.
5. CHILD: Mm. If you haven't got any food left ... like the tiger who came to tea ...
6. MOTHER: What tiger who came to tea?
7. CHILD: You know, at school we got it.
8. MOTHER: Oh, I haven't read that one. What happened to the tiger that came to tea?
9. CHILD: Well, he ate all the food up ... and ... when, when the olden days ... but, in the olden days, tiger, you know it, well if tigers ... who came to tea, not in the olden days, well, whoever came to ... our house who ate all the ...

Mary's incoherent reply shows that she found it difficult to answer her mother's 'What happened?' question in turn 8. But when her mother substituted a series of more specific prompts she was able to retell the story:

MOTHER: Who did he go to tea with?
CHILD: Sylvia and her mother [impatiently].
MOTHER: And he ate all the things? That . . .
CHILD: [Interrupting] And the more of the food up.
MOTHER: Sylvia's tea as well?
CHILD: Yes.
MOTHER: And the Mummy's tea?
CHILD: And Daddy's and all the things . . . and all the things in her cupboard, he drunk all the water from the bathroom tap . . . and the sink.
MOTHER: I don't think they'll ask him to tea again.
CHILD: No.
MOTHER: Or did he turn into a good tiger in the end? Did he learn how to behave?
CHILD: No, he didn't come to tea ever again.

Another way in which the mothers helped the children to talk about their life at school was by an imaginative projection on their own part. In Chapter 8 we quoted Carol's conversation with her mother, which was facilitated by her mother's interest in envisaging the effect of the wind on the school sandpit. Joyce's mother was also interested enough to project into situations in this way. As they came home from school, Joyce told her that there had been no milk at school that day. When they got home, Joyce reverted to this unusual event. Her mother seemed just as interested in this topic as Joyce, and set about imagining its implications:

CHILD: No milk at all.
MOTHER: That's funny, that is.
CHILD: Yeah.
MOTHER: I don't understand why it didn't come. So what did everyone do – sit down round the little table and drink water?
CHILD: No.
MOTHER: What, then?
CHILD: I wasn't thirsty.
MOTHER: Did they say to you, 'You going to have a drink of water, Joyce'?

CHILD: No. [She kicks her shoe off, is rebuked, and the subject changes]

Of course, mothers were not always successful in establishing communication about school. In Chapter 7 we described Donna's mother's long, but largely unsuccessful, attempt to understand whether Donna had been given 'winkles' at school. Briefer, somewhat inconclusive, conversations like the one with Tonia that follows were not uncommon:

CHILD: Jan's not allowed to play with me.
MOTHER: Jan's not allowed to play with you? [Surprised]
CHILD: No. Jan doesn't play with me.
MOTHER: Doesn't *want* to play with you?
CHILD: No. I've got nobody to play with.
MOTHER: Didn't you?
CHILD: No – Mummy, watch me [plays with coin].

Perhaps because they were at ease at home, and felt no special need to make a link with their school lives, the children made more references to home when they were at school than to school when they were at home. Further, we saw no sign at home of the children doing an activity or following an interest that had arisen from school, and only one occasion in which a child asked a question at home about a remark made to her at school. Jane's mother was American, and while the teacher was showing Jane a book about Red Indians she asked:

TEACHER: Were you born in America? [No reply] Or were you born in England? Do you know?
CHILD: I was . . . I was born in Mummy's tummy.
TEACHER: You were born out of Mummy's tummy, yes. I wasn't sure whether you were over in this country.

It seemed unlikely that Jane had any clear concept of different countries, or of her relationship to them, but she was evidently aware of, and troubled by, this area of ignorance. (In Chapter 5 we suggested that this awareness of confusion was a characteristic of four-year-olds.) In the afternoon, while she was paddling in a pool in her garden, she brought up the topic with her mother:

MOTHER: Where you were born? If someone says, 'Where were you born?' that means, 'Where were you when you came out of your Mummy's tummy?' Well, you were born in England. But, do you know what nationality you are?

CHILD: Pardon?

MOTHER: Do you know what nationality you are?

CHILD: No? [In a tone of interest]

MOTHER: You're British, and you're American. You're all British and you're all American.

At this point Jane's younger brother called her mother away, so it is impossible to know whether Jane's understanding has been enlarged, or her confusion increased.

Overview: the implications of the home–school gap

Our study suggests that school and home make very different demands on children, and that children behave differently in the two settings. It may be argued that children derive considerable benefit from moving between these two different worlds, and that, in any case, school and home must necessarily place different demands on children. We will discuss these points in Chapter 11.

In this chapter we have been mainly concerned to describe the attempts made by staff, parents and children to link home and school through conversation. We have shown that the parents' lack of knowledge of school, and the staff's even greater lack of knowledge of the children's homes, made this process difficult, especially since the children's communinication skills were limited. Some schools have attempted to tackle this problem by encouraging the staff to visit the children at home, and the mothers to spend time in school, and by giving the parents detailed information about the children's daily activities. These practices were not widespread in the nursery schools and classes in our study.

11

Young children learning

Our study of four-year-old girls at home and at school raises some fundamental questions about how young children think and learn, and the role which adults can play in helping them. These questions are important for any consideration of the kind of care and education that should be provided outside the home. They are also relevant to the question of what kind of parent education, if any, we should provide.

In this chapter we will summarize our main findings, and discuss their implications.

The home as a learning environment

It was clear from our observations that the home provides a very powerful learning environment. Indeed, its potentialities for learning must be considerably more extensive than we were able to show, because we did not by any means witness all the children's important experiences. We did not observe them with their fathers or grandparents, with older brothers and sisters, with their friends, or on their excursions into the neighbourhood. Nevertheless, even from the limited sample of their lives that we observed, it was clear that they were learning a great deal at home.

We found that this learning covered a very wide range of topics, but was especially concerned with the social world. Play, games, stories and even formal 'lessons' provided educational contexts, in the course of which a good deal of general knowledge, as well as early literacy and numeracy skills, were transmitted. But the most frequent learning context was that of everyday living. Simply by being around their mothers, talking, arguing and endlessly asking questions, the children were being provided with large amounts of information relevant to growing up in our culture.

Why does the home provide such varied and effective learning contexts? Five factors seem to us to be particularly significant.

The first is the extensive range of activities that take place within, or from the base of, the home. Within the home meals are planned, cooked and cleared away; clothes washed and ironed; babies are cared for; pets and gardens tended; shopping is planned; money and wages are discussed; relatives and neighbours call; letters are written; bills paid, and telephone calls made. In addition, the home is the centre of many links with the wider world. Parents go back and forth to work, and older children to school; expeditions are made to shops, banks, clinics, libraries, markets, garages, cafés, parks and swimming pools; friends and relations are visited; activities in the street are watched and discussed; trips are made by car, bus, caravan and rail.

All these events provide the child with an opportunity to learn about a wide range of topics, especially about the social world in which she lives. They also provide her with models of adults, especially women, engaged in a variety of activities.

Secondly, at home parent and child share a common life, stretching back into the past, and forward into the future. This vast body of shared experience helps the mother to understand what her child is saying, or intending to say. It also facilitates a task essential for intellectual growth – helping the child to make sense of her present experiences by relating them to past experiences, as well as to her existing framework of knowledge.

A third significant aspect of the home environment is the small number of children who have to share the adult's time and attention. Only 11 per cent of British families contain more than two children under the age of sixteen.[1] The child's mother is thus very salient to her, constantly available to answer questions, provide information and act as a conversational companion. Moreover, the smaller the family, the more the opportunities for prolonged one-to-one conversation. As we have seen, such conversations are a particularly powerful way in which children's understanding can be enhanced in a manner closely matched to their intellectual level and to their interests.

The fact that most mothers have only one or two children to attend to also makes it possible for them to teach their children relatively advanced skills. Given sufficient undivided attention, even young children can be taught skills which would be difficult for a teacher to teach to a group of children of the same age.

A further characteristic of the learning environment at home is that the learning is often embedded in contexts of great meaning to the child. Making a shopping list, helping with the baby, writing to Granny, deciding how many cakes are needed for tea, playing card games, are activities that, because of their interest to the child, make it easy for her to learn. This principle is well understood in primary education, but it is much easier to put into effect in the home than in the school. Because school activities tend to be divorced from the rest of living, teachers often have to devise rather artificial learning devices. For example, the teacher may introduce a threading activity to encourage hand–eye coordination. At home, the mother may have taught the child to wind up a vacuum cleaner flex in a figure of eight. Her intention was simply to teach the child the proper way to complete the cleaning job. Nevertheless, she has also incidentally helped to develop difficult motor skills in a context where the child is highly motivated to learn, because of her wish to behave like an adult.

A final significant characteristic of the learning environment of the home is the close, and often intense, relationship between mother and child. This may at times hinder learning – we saw how stories and games were often interfered with by the child's demands. It does, however, keep the child near her mother and in consequence able to learn from her, and it allows the child to express her questions, puzzles and anxieties freely. The mother's concern for her child means that she will almost certainly have definite educational expectations, which she is likely to pursue with whatever energy she has available. The 'curriculum' of the home differs from one mother to another, but each is likely to have very high expectations in one or other area – whether this is general knowledge, logical thinking, reading, baby care or social skills. It was a matter of great personal concern to most mothers in our study that their child should acquire the skills, knowledge and values that they believed to be important. It is this parental concern that converts the potential advantages of the home into actual advantages.

The learning potential of the home is therefore not a necessary attribute of all family settings. It may be reduced if the family is very large, or isolated from the community. It may be reduced if a close relationship does not obtain between mother and child, or if the mother is so preoccupied with her own problems that she has little interest in her child. Equally, it seems likely that the learning potential of the home will be reduced if a child is looked after by a childminder or nanny who does not have a strong educational concern.

The working-class home as a learning environment

The characteristics of the home environment which we have discussed are present in working-class as well as middle-class homes. The working-class mothers were just as concerned to teach their children as the middle-class mothers were. There was, however, some evidence of a difference in values, attitudes and educational priorities in homes of different social class. The working-class mothers seemed to place less stress on introducing their daughters to a wide range of general knowledge, information and vocabulary, encouraging them to be explicit, and answering their questions. On the other hand, some placed more stress on helping their daughters to acquire domestic and mothering skills, and understanding the role of money and work in the family's activities. They tended to favour more 'traditional' approaches to teaching literacy and numeracy. Although they spent just as long as the middle-class mothers playing with their children, the working-class mothers were less likely to use play as a vehicle for education.

These differences seemed to us to amount to a difference in language style and educational approach, rather than to a 'language deficit' in working-class homes. All the basic language usages were observed in all the homes; the social class difference was in the frequency of the usages. Further, the differences we have described refer to group averages. Within each social class group, there was a wide range of language usage.

The child as a thinker

Our analysis of the conversations at home led us to an enhanced respect for the intellectual activities of four-year-olds. Although the home provides a very powerful learning environment, children are by no means passive absorbers or recipients of this environment. On the contrary, their own intellectual efforts are an essential part of the learning process. Even with the most attentive mothers this process was not always easy. In all the homes many questions went unanswered, much was left implicit, misunderstandings were often undetected by the mothers, full explanations were rarely given, and many explanations were definitely misleading. Armed only with their curiosity, logic and persistence, the children tackled the task of making sense of a world they imperfectly understood. Because of their inexperience they could rule out few inferences or explanations as implausible: almost everything had to be treated as possible until shown to be otherwise.

We believe that persistent intellectual curiosity is a particularly prominent feature of four-year-olds. This is because of the flexible and incomplete structure of their conceptual framework, and also because of the children's growing awareness of the many confusions and misunderstandings that occur. At an earlier stage in their development children lack the ability to express their difficulties. At a later stage, their conceptual framework is better able to cope with their experiences. But between the ages of about three and five years, a state of intellectual disequilibrium exists.

These observations led us to question some of Piaget's theories. Thus, while we fully accept Piaget's notion of the child as an active learner, we believe that he underestimated the role of verbal exploration – that is, puzzling and thinking – in four-year-old children. We also believe that he underestimated the importance of the child's interest in the social world of adults, and the role which adults can play in helping the child towards understanding through dialogue. Our study suggests that the kind of dialogue that seems to help the child is not that currently favoured by many teachers in which the adult poses a series of questions. It is rather one in which the adult listens to the child's questions and comments, helps to clarify her ideas, and feeds her the information she asks for.

Further, while we agree with Piaget that the young child's thinking differs from that of an adult, we do not accept that they are incapable of 'decentred' or logical thinking. The model of the world with which they operate seems to us limited and distorted by their lack of experience and knowledge, and by their incomplete conceptual framework, rather than by an absence of logic.

The nursery school as a learning environment

Just as we missed much of significance that happened to the child at home, so we were also able to focus only on the learning experiences of the child with the nursery staff, not with other children or with the play equipment. Even with this limited focus it was, however, clear that the learning environment of the nursery school is very different from that of the home. In the first place, the nursery staff have to socialize children into the world of school. The child has to learn a new code of behaviour; she must also learn to follow the school routine. Further, she must learn how to make herself understood to strangers, and how to understand the intentions and communication requirements of the school staff.

However, the most striking difference between home and nursery school is the way in which the school focuses on play. The children learn social skills through playing with each other. By experimenting with sand, water, bricks, paints and so on, they acquire an understanding of the physical world which many regard as the necessary precursor of mathematical and scientific knowledge. For anyone holding a Piagetian model of learning, this environment is ideal.

A child-centred play environment has obvious advantages for children, in addition to the learning opportunities it provides. Society in general is designed for the needs of adults, and does not provide for children's needs to explore, run around, make a noise, play with 'messy' materials and so on. The inevitable disadvantage, however, of providing an environment entirely geared to play is that the possibility of children learning by watching and taking part in the adult world is thereby excluded. The staff's role becomes one of watching over and talking to the children, rather than themselves engaging in adult activities, which might serve as interesting and challenging models to the children.

At the same time, the other prominent theme in present nursery training, the importance of fostering language by questioning children, means that staff–child interaction tends to be dominated by this aim. The dialogue that ensues is very different from conversation at home, and often seems educationally ineffective. This is because the children frequently fail to answer, or become confused by the staff's questioning, and fail to contribute to the conversation themselves. The puzzling mind of the four-year-old has no outlet in a setting where the child's basic role is to answer and not ask questions.

Further, because staff–child conversation focuses on play, it tends to be concerned with the 'here and now' to a greater extent than conversations at home. This situation is somewhat paradoxical, since one function of schooling is to extend the child's intellectual horizons. It was, however, the mother who linked the child's present to her past and future, and to the world beyond her own experience. Because the staff know little of the child's life outside school, and almost nothing of her past and future, they cannot integrate her experiences in the way that is possible for a parent.

There are other constraints on school staff which make it difficult for them to be as educationally effective as parents. The relatively large numbers of children in relation to the number of adults reduces the opportunities for one-to-one discussion. The low-keyed emotional relationship between staff and children reduces the likelihood of the children seeking out the staff, and of the staff having a personal educational concern for them.

Since our study took place in nursery schools and classes we are not in a position to compare them with playgroups. However, it is clear that playgroups share a number of the characteristics of nursery schools that we have described. Wood's research suggests that adult–child conversations in playgroups are very similar to those we have described in nursery schools.[2]

Our analysis of the educational role of the nursery school admittedly runs counter to widespread current beliefs. Many politicians and professionals believe that nursery school stimulates intellectual growth and language development, and gives socially disadvantaged children a head start in school. There is very little British research evidence to substantiate these claims. Certainly this study suggests that children's intellectual and language needs are much more likely to be satisfied at home than at school. Indeed, with the staff–child ratio obtaining in nursery schools and classes, the staff could not be expected to rival the contribution of the home. With these numbers, the teacher's role must inevitably be largely managerial. For children with special needs – for example, those whose first language is not English, or children suffering from severe neglect – special individual attention is required instead of, or as well as, nursery education.

The working-class children at school

The working-class girls in our study were particularly affected by the nursery school setting. In their relations with the nursery staff they tended to be much more subdued, passive and dependent than at home. The staff responded to this perceived immaturity of the working-class children by pitching their talk to them at a lower level. Far from compensating for any inadequacies of their homes, the staff were in fact lowering their expectations and standards for the working-class children. The overall effect was that the working-class children already appeared to be at an educational disadvantage in school.

We have suggested a number of factors that, singly, or in a complex interaction, might be responsible for this situation. Without a better understanding of the cause, it is difficult to suggest how it can be remedied. However, if teachers knew more about the interests and skills that children display at home, they might be better able to see where the school could complement the strengths of the home.

Assessing children in different contexts

The difference in the behaviour of the working-class children at home and at school which we have just discussed is an instance of a wider issue, the effect of context on children's behaviour. Although this issue is well understood by academic psychologists, its practical implications are rarely followed through. Teachers continue to make judgements of children on the basis of their classroom behaviour alone, doctors and psychologists on the basis of a clinic interview and test, perhaps supplemented by observations in school.

Joan Tough, for example, an educational psychologist who has had a powerful effect on inservice training for British teachers, cites the following conversation between a teacher and a five-year-old child, Paul, who is playing with a toy farm, to show 'the difficulty that many children have in taking part in conversation':[3]

TEACHER: Tell me what is happening, will you?
CHILD: That's a farm.
TEACHER: Oh, that's a farm here, is it? Who lives in the farm, I wonder?
CHILD: Them lot [points].
TEACHER: Oh, who are they?
CHILD: The people.
TEACHER: What sort of people live in a farm? [Child shrugs] What do we call the man who lives in a farm, do you know?
CHILD: Farmer.

At no point does Tough consider the possibility that Paul's limited contribution to this conversation might reflect his social unease or defensiveness, rather than his limited grasp of language, or suggest that the teacher might learn from listening to his conversation in an out-of-school setting, or by transforming the social situation between teacher and child.

Similar instances abound in the writings of other clinical and educational psychologists. Our study suggests that judgements on children's language abilities should be very tentative until a context is found where they talk freely and spontaneously. We suspect that the same caution should be exercised when pronouncing on other aspects of children's behaviour, such as their play.

How valid are our findings?

At several points in this book we have discussed the issue of the validity and generalizability of our findings. Doubts must inevitably be felt about the 'naturalness' of people's behaviour in the presence of microphones and an observer. Slightly more than half of the mothers told us that they had felt rather ill-at-ease during the recording. It is reasonable to imagine that both mothers and school staff gave the observed child more attention than might ordinarily be the case. Yet it was clear from the transcripts that the activities we observed at school and at home were not out of the ordinary. The games played were obviously familiar to the children, the ordinary household routine of meal preparation, baby care and housework went on as usual. The mothers by no means behaved like saints – some of them lost their tempers, swore at, and slapped the children. Much of what happened at home was, in fact, controlled by the demands and behaviour of the children. Our own opinion was that both school staff and mothers probably tried to live up to their conception of a 'good' mother or teacher. This may have affected the proportion of 'good' behaviour that they displayed, but nothing in the transcripts suggested that they acted in unusual or uncharacteristic ways.

Another source of doubt arises from the very small size of our sample. Might it be in some way completely unrepresentative? The main reason why we have confidence in our findings is that they are consistent with those of other recent observational studies. Findings about staff–child conversations at nursery school are similar to those found in an earlier, much larger, study by one of us (BT), and to Wood's findings in playgroups.[4] Our findings about the children at home are consistent with the much larger studies of Wells and Davie.[5] These studies differed from ours in that in one case conversation was not recorded, and in the other case, only ninety-second samples of conversation were recorded. But both included boys and girls, and, like our study, both found little evidence of many of the common stereotypes about home life.

Implications for parents

Some parents will be worried by our findings. If the home environment is so favourable to learning, should their children attend nursery class or playgroup at all? Are children at day nurseries or with childminders missing an important dimension of experience? Other parents may be concerned that they are impeding their child's development by being too impatient with their questions, or not spending enough time talking to them.

We should make it clear that children have a variety of educational needs, some of which cannot be met within the home. They need to learn how to get on with other children, to be a member of a group, to separate from their families, and to relate to, and communicate with, strange adults. They need opportunities to run around, and they enjoy the variety of play equipment offered by nursery classes and playgroups. The strong emotional environment of the home fosters some kinds of learning, but may be detrimental to other kinds. The more detached atmosphere of the nursery or playgroup can be a calming influence on the child, as well as giving the mother a valuable respite; and learning to follow the nursery routine helps to prepare the child for the demands of primary school.

Moreover, we have no reason to suppose that the process of education through one-to-one dialogue that we have described needs to take place all day and every day. It may be that one episode of real concentration on a child each day, or one question seriously answered, is as valuable as hours of less focused attention. In any case, we do not believe that parents must always answer their children's questions, and constantly engage in long conversations with them. Children have to learn that adults have other concerns, and cannot be constantly available to them. Indeed, it is possible that even if parents discourage questions and rarely talk to their children at length, sooner or later, from a variety of sources, their children will acquire the knowledge and conceptual framework necessary for them to function adequately. We suspect, however, that children whose parents tend to answer their questions more fully, who are usually alert to detect and clear up misunderstandings, and who sometimes have time for leisurely, thoughtful conversations will make more rapid intellectual progress.

Implications for nursery schools

It could be argued that our findings have no particular implications for nursery schools or playgroups. For example, it might be concluded that the process of fostering intellectual development can safely be left to the home, while the nursery class meets the social and physical needs of the children. This is a very reasonable point of view, which many parents and playgroup leaders might put forward. Most nursery teachers, however, would not want to abdicate responsibility in this way for the children's intellectual growth. They might reasonably challenge us to suggest ways in which nursery schools could change in order to meet the children's intellectual needs more adequately.

The school's problem, as we see it, is how to foster, harness and satisfy the interest and curiosity which children show at home. An environment is required which will allow the 'puzzling mind' to flourish, and which will help the young child to overcome her considerable ignorance and misinformation, develop her intellectual structures, and improve her communication skills.

In our view, this would mean changing staff priorities. Instead of the present emphasis on fostering play, on devising ingenious ways of using play materials, and on questioning the children about their play, a higher priority would have to be given to widening the children's horizons, extending their general knowledge, and listening to them talk. We found that most of the intellectually challenging conversations at home took place at times of relative leisure for both mother and child, usually during a *tête à tête* meal, or when the mother was drinking coffee, or during a one-to-one story session. They rarely happened while the child was busy with an activity. Nursery schools and playgroups, however, tend to be very activity-oriented, with the staff uneasy if they are not moving from one child to another, seeing that the children are busily occupied. On the rare occasions when we observed long conversations at school, the staff were usually anchored in one spot for a long time, mending or making apparatus, while a child stood by, chatting to them.

A further difficulty schools and playgroups have to overcome is their tendency to underestimate children's abilities and interests. This tendency derives from a number of sources. It is fostered by the belief that children mainly learn through play, and from the Piagetian theory of the child's limited intellectual powers. It is also fostered by the belief that working-class children do nothing at home except watch TV. In fact, our transcripts show that young children's interests extend to any aspect of life that impinges on them – the neighbours, money, electric lights, the structure and arrangement of houses, parents' work, God, the death of pets, doctors. If school staff are to stimulate and pursue these interests, they must revise their ideas of what children can understand, and feed them with a great deal more general knowledge.

This may involve going beyond the school walls more than is usual at present. In the famous Malting House School, started in Cambridge in the 1930s by Susan Isaacs,[6] the staff did just this. One child's question, 'What is wood made of?' led to a visit to a sawmill; another question, 'What is material?' led first to the introduction of simple cardboard looms, and later to a shopping trip to see big rolls of material. In some respects, schools have a potential advantage over homes in following through children's interests, since the staff can give these priority, while mothers are usually preoccupied with domestic tasks. A visit to the shops, for example, is a routine occasion at home, sometimes enjoyable, at other times an occasion for disputes. At school, it could be a planned educational experience. The teacher, for example, might be able to persuade the shopkeeper to allow a small group of children to see the goods stacked at the back of the shop, or arriving by lorry. The process of receiving change, which many young children believe is a source of wealth to their parents, could be discussed at length.

However, we do not want to suggest that 'outings' are in themselves necessarily valuable. Without someone familiar and trusted at hand both to answer and to stimulate their questions, new experiences, however challenging, are likely either to wash over young children, leaving little impact, or else add to their confusions. This is because matching the level of explanation and information given to a child to her present level of understanding is a delicate process, which to be successful requires a close knowledge of the individual child. It also requires a willingness on the part of the child to ask questions about what she does not understand.

This quality of adult–child communication is difficult to achieve with the ratios of 1:10 or 1:15 which obtain in British nursery schools and classes. The size of many nursery classes militates against the possibility of staff and children getting to know each other well, and having leisurely conversations. This is especially true in open-plan nursery schools or units, with forty to sixty children moving freely through them. They were inspired by the 'Piagetian' model of education, and designed to give children access to the largest possible range of play materials. Such an environment makes the educational approach we have in mind almost impossible to achieve.

The constraints of too few staff and too large classes are compounded by the almost universal system of half-day school. Different children attend school in the morning and afternoon: it would be extremely difficult, with the best will in the world, for staff to get to know all these children well. It is hardly surprising that the staff we observed knew so little about their pupils, and that the children did not know the staff well enough to ask them questions, or talk to them freely.

The gap between home and school

We have placed considerable emphasis in this book on the gap between the worlds of home and school. The learning experiences, the discipline, the communication requirements, the physical and social environments of these worlds are very different, and the question arises of whether and how this gap should be bridged.

It may be argued that such a gap is not necessarily a bad thing. An important function of the school, according to this view, is to introduce children to new ways of thinking and knowing. Thus the fact that they must communicate with adults who have not shared their past and know little of their background may act as a spur to greater explicitness. Moreover, since children must operate in milieus outside their homes, it can only help them to learn that different codes of conduct and styles of communication obtain at home and at school.

More fundamentally, some psychologists would argue that school must necessarily be different from home because it is a setting in which the child's home learning has to be 'decontextualized'. At home, for example, the child may learn to count in relation to rock cakes or card games. This knowledge is not necessarily available to her in other contexts. The child who can play Monopoly at home may not necessarily be able to use the mathematical skills involved when tackling the school's mathematics scheme. It is the school's role to introduce children to a way of thinking and knowing the world which is independent of their own experiences. The goal of education, as Margaret Donaldson argues in *Children's Minds*, is to produce people who are capable of ignoring their own individual knowledge and experiences and can instead think in a logical and 'disembedded' manner, freed from the constraints of their own particular viewpoint.[7] In order to achieve this, it might be argued that children need to learn right from the start of school that they are indeed in a new environment, where they will have to acquire new skills and new ways of talking.

We would not want to argue with the view that 'disembedded' thinking and academic skills are important goals of education. Our objection is to the notion that these goals are best served in ignorance of the skills and interests that children manifestly possess at home. Our observations of children at home showed them displaying a range of interests and linguistic skills which enabled them to be powerful learners. Yet observations of the same children at school showed a fundamental lack of awareness by the nursery staff of these skills and interests. There is no doubt that, in the world of school, the child appears to be a much less active thinker than is the case at home. We do not believe that the schools can possibly be meeting their goals in the most efficient manner if they are unable to make use of so many of the children's skills.

Moreover, if children are unable to bring these skills and interests into school, then a split will inevitably arise between what they are learning in the two locations. We saw in our study how the detailed knowledge of the world which the children had built up since infancy through their interactions with their mothers was no longer relevant in their interactions with the nursery staff. Any tentative links that the child might make between her home experiences and those she was presented with at school tended to be suppressed in group discussion or misunderstood in individual discussion. Thus, if the child started to tell staff about some event at home, the communication was often unsuccessful because the staff did not have enough background knowledge to sort out its meaning. If the staff asked the children about their home, the conversation was often equally unfruitful because the staff did not know what to make of the children's answers. As a result, the children effectively moved in two different worlds, with little opportunity to transfer knowledge or skills gained in one domain across to the other. The split in children's learning between home and school was already visible at the age of four.

This split is not, of course, a special characteristic of nursery schools, but applies throughout the educational system. 'School learning' may become increasingly separated from any learning which takes place outside the classroom. Knowledge may be acquired in school for the purpose of passing examinations which is unlikely to be applied to real life problems away from school. Similarly, the child's experience and knowledge of the world gained outside the classroom may not be seen as relevant to the academic learning taking place inside the classroom.

At the nursery level, the gap could to some extent be bridged by a much greater involvement of parents in schools, and a much greater knowledge on the part of the school staff of the children's out-of-school lives. This would involve the same kind of changes that we have already advocated on other grounds, that is, organizing smaller groups in nursery schools, avoiding open-plan schools, and perhaps 'assigning' particular children to particular members of staff. It would also involve a recognition by the staff of the *importance* of knowing about the children's out-of-school interests and learning.

However, a big obstacle to the integration of the two worlds of home and school in the preschool years is the young child's relatively poorly developed communication skills. We saw in Chapter 10 how difficult it was, even for the more articulate children, to communicate about home when at school, and about school when at home. They frequently made incorrect assumptions about what the person they were talking to knew about their other life, and what they would need to know in order to understand them. An important educational task for the nursery school is to help children improve these communication skills. Some kinds of games may be useful here, but once again the sensitivity of the adult and her knowledge of the child would seem to be crucial factors.

Do parents need educating?

During the past ten years there has been a growth of home-visiting schemes. These schemes, some run by schools, others by voluntary organizations, and others by local authorities, provide for a home visitor, or education visitor, to make regular visits to families with under-fives. Most schemes are directed towards families believed to be in special need of support. While the schemes vary greatly in emphasis, almost all aim to improve the quality of interaction between parents and children. Most involve encouraging parents to play with their children, and emphasize the role of parents as educators, although some lay more stress on befriending and supporting the mothers.

There is no doubt that many mothers appreciate this interest and support. What concerns us, however, is the assumption that professionals know how parents should interact with, and educate, their children. This is also the assumption underlying most parent education courses, which can be found attached to schools, antenatal and child health clinics. In fact, the knowledge basis for parent education is very slight. There is no real evidence that parents need to interact with children in any *particular* way; often the advice offered seems to be based on ideas about what a 'good' middle-class parent does. Even more worrying is advice which seems intended to make parents behave like teachers, for example, by suggesting that they ask their children 'open-ended' and 'stimulating' questions, and teach them colour, size and shape names.

Our study suggests that the exchange of views and questions, equally balanced between adult and child, that makes up conversation at home is better attuned to young children's needs than the question-and-answer technique of school. It also suggests that no particular home context or activity is especially 'educational'. It is the concern of the parent for the child to understand, and the child's own curiosity and persistence, which promote learning. Even such umpromising contexts as parent–child disputes may be at least as conducive to learning as play. And while it is obviously useful for children to learn colour and shape names, focusing on this task may lead to a neglect and underestimation of their deeper and more complex interests.

We found no reason to believe that parents should be encouraged to play with their children if they don't want to. Other forms of interaction, especially leisurely conversation, may well be more intellectually stimulating. Nor is there any good educational reason why parents should provide children with sand and water play, bricks and so on – although the children may well derive great pleasure from these activities. The mathematical and scientific concepts which these materials are intended to help develop can be acquired from play with the ordinary materials of the home – food, bath water, cardboard boxes and so on.

However, parents themselves may well want information and help of various kinds in educating their child. Sharing experiences with other parents is a valuable form of support and learning, often not available to isolated families. Some parents want well-informed advice about toys and books, others want to know when and how best to teach reading and writing. Almost all parents respond with interest when someone knowledgeable shows an individual concern for their child and points out to them aspects of her development which they had been unaware of. We can therefore see a useful role for parents' groups, and for advice and information centres which respond to these needs, but none for attempts by professionals to alter the way in which parents carry out their educational role.

Indeed, in our opinion, it is time to shift the emphasis away from what parents should learn from professionals, and towards what professionals can learn from studying parents and children at home.

Statistical appendix

These tables are printed in the order in which the findings are first mentioned.

Hourly rate of conversations

	Working class	*Middle class*
Home	27.0	26.4
School	10.9	9.1

Location F = 119, p<0.001; social class NS; interaction NS.

Length of conversations

| | *Percentage of all conversations which are:* | | | |
	short *(2–6 turns)*	*medium* *(7–21 turns)*	*long* *(22+ turns)*	*Mean no.* *of turns*
Working class at school	65	28	8	7.7
N	(333)	(141)	(38)	
Middle class at school	62	29	8	8.3
N	(396)	(184)	(54)	
Working class at home	43	38	18	16.5
N	(398)	(351)	(167)	
Middle class at home	42	38	20	16.1
N	(400)	(354)	(187)	

Proportion of short, medium and long episodes: location χ^2 = 141, p<0.001; social class NS; interaction NS. *Mean episode length*: location F = 54.8, p<0.001; social class NS; interaction NS.

Length of adult and child turns

	Adult	Child
	Mean number of words per turn	
Working class at school	14.0	4.8
Middle class at school	14.5	5.4
Working class at home	6.5	5.8
Middle class at home	8.6	5.8

Based on 11 randomly chosen conversations per child per setting.
Mean adult words per hour: location $F = 37.5$, $p<0.001$; social class NS; interaction NS.
Mean child words per turn: location $F = 4.8$, $p<0.05$; social class NS; interaction NS.
Proportion of adult-to-child talk: location $F = 50.8$, $p<0.001$; social class NS; interaction $F = 3.97$, $p<0.06$.

Information content of talk to children

Mean hourly rate	Home		School	
	Working class	Middle class	Working class	Middle class
Control remarks[1]	30.6	23.3	5.9	6.0
Other information[2]	140.5	158.9	30.2	45.8
Mean number of information categories in adult talk[3]	24.9	27.4	18.7	22.1
General knowledge[4]	3.9	7.6	0.9	1.4

Percentage

Proportion of turns of talk containing information[5]	32	36	35	45
Proportion of turns of talk containing control[6]	7.8	5.3	8.2	6.7
Proportion of talk with information about play[7]	7.4	8.5	12.1	17.1
Proportion of talk with domestic family information[8]	5.1	3.1	0.8	1.1
Proportion of talk informing child about social behaviour[9]	1.3	1.8	1.6	2.1

1. F (location) 166, $p<0.001$; social class NS: interaction NS.
2. F (location) 105, $p<0.001$; social class NS; interaction NS.
3. F (location) 43.7, $p<0.001$; F social class 5.1, $p<0.05$; interaction NS.
4. χ^2 using categories; location 24.4, $p<0.001$; social class 5.2, $p<0.05$.
5. F (class) 6.4, $p<0.05$; location NS; interaction NS.
6. No significant differences.
7. F (location) 8.7, $p<0.01$; social class NS; interaction NS.
8. F (location) 24.8, $p<0.001$; social class NS; interaction NS.
9. No significant differences.

Adult–child disputes

| | Home | | School | |
	Working class	Middle class	Working class	Middle class
Proportion of conversations with dispute	17.9	11.9	2.3	3.5

Social class at home: T = 1.55, NS; F value for difference in variances 12.1, p<0.000.

Frequency of children's questions

| *Hourly rate* | Home | | School | |
	Mean	S.D.	Mean	S.D.
Working class	24.0	13.4	1.4	1.5
Middle class	29.0	16.1	3.7	3.4

Percentage of turns of talk

| Working class | 5.6 | 2.3 | 2.0 | 1.9 |
| Middle class | 6.6 | 2.1 | 4.0 | 3.2 |

(Hourly rate) *Home vs school*: F = 77.4, p<0.001; social class F = 1.8, NS;
interaction F = 0.2, NS. (Percentage of turns of talk) *Home vs school*: F = 26.5, p<0.001;
social class F = 5.6, p<0.05; interaction F = 0.7, NS.

Setting and motivation of questions

Hourly rate	'Challenges'	%	'Business'	%	'Curiosity'	%
Working class at school	0.1	7	0.9	70	0.3	24
Middle class at school	0.1	2	1.3	36	2.3	62
Working class at home	3.2	13	7.9	34	12.3	53
Middle class at home	2.1	8	5.8	20	20.6	72

Proportion of each type of question in different settings: home vs school, χ^2 = 47.5, d.f. =
2, p<0.001; social class χ^2 = 97.9, d.f. = 2, p<0.001; interaction χ^2 = 7.7, d.f. = 2, p<0.02.

Frequency of 'Why' questions

	Hourly rate	Percentage of all questions
Working class at school	0.2	15
Middle class at school	0.8	22
Working class at home	5.2	22
Middle class at home	8.8	31

'Why' questions as a proportion of all questions; home vs school, $\chi^2 = 6.0$, d.f. = 1, $p<0.01$; social class $\chi^2 = 20.4$, d.f. = 1, $p<0.001$; interaction NS.

Children's passages of persistent questioning

	Number of passages	Number of children
Working class at home	16	4
Middle class at home	41	13

$\chi^2 = 8.7$, d.f. = 1, $p<0.01$. There were no passages at school.

Adults' total complex uses of language

	School	Home	School	Home
	Mean hourly rates		Mean percentage of total turns	
Working class	11.4	38.4	14.3	8.8
Middle class	17.4	51.5	17.2	11.6

(Hourly rates) *School vs home*: F = 79.4, $p<0.001$; social class F = 5.0, $p<0.05$; interaction NS. (Percentage of total turns) *School vs home*: F = 21.4, $p<0.001$; social class F = 5.2, $p<0.05$; interaction NS.

Children's total complex use of language

	School	Home	School	Home
	Mean hourly rates		Mean percentage of total turns	
Working class	2.2	17.1	2.4	3.8
Middle class	5.0	20.1	4.6	4.4

(Hourly rates) *School vs home*: F = 110.1, p<0.001; social class F = 6.3, p<0.05; interaction F = 5.5, p<0.05. (Percentage of total turns) *School vs home*: F =6.2; p<0.05; social class F = 9.7, p<0.01; interaction F = 6.2, p<0.05.

Number of different words used by mothers and children in 200 words of talk

	Children		Mothers	
	Working class	Middle class	Working class	Middle class
Mean	89.5	92.9	94.7	101.2

Social class F = 12.0, p<0.01.

Adequacy of adults' answers to 'Why' questions

	Inadequate replies	Adequate + full	No reply
Working class at school	3	8	0
Middle class at school	14	25	7
Working class at home	60	56	61
Middle class at home	89	146	59

Analysis of deviance: location adequacy χ^2 = 5.7, d.f. = 2, NS; social class: adequacy χ^2 = 10.7, d.f. = 2, p<0.005; location: class: adequacy X^2 = 6.6, d.f. = 2, p<0.04.

Adult play with children

Mean hourly rate	Home		School	
	Working class	Middle class	Working class	Middle class
Conversation about play[1]	5.8	5.1	2.1	2.7
Adult play suggestions[2]	3.2	3.8	1.8	2.2
Percentage of play conversation concerned with fantasy play[3]	29%	32%	8%	8%
Total number of games adult plays with child[4]	3.3	2.4	1.3	1.4
Proportion of session child spends playing[5]	49%	41%	59%	52%

1. F (location) 25.2, p<0.001; social class NS: interaction NS.
2. F (location) 11.3, p<0.01; social class NS; interaction NS.
3. Too many zeros to carry out a statistical analysis.
4. Home vs school F = 24.3, p<0.001; social class 1.4, NS; interaction 1.6, NS.
5. F (location) 7.1, p<0.01; F (class) 4.3, p<0.05; interaction NS.

Sustaining the converstion

	Percentage of conversation sustained by child N=165	Child does not respond Mean percentage
Working class at school	15	15.6
N	(24)	
Middle class at school	23	11.4
N	(38)	
Working class at home	48	6.6
N	(79)	
Middle class at home	45	7.1
N	(74)	

Based on 11 randomly chosen conversations per child per setting.
Child sustains: location χ^2 = 58.5, d.f. = 1, p<0.001; social class NS; interaction χ^2 = 3.61, d.f. = 1, p<0.01. *Child doesn't answer*: location F = 21.1, p<0.001; social class NS; interaction NS.

Frequency of cognitive demands

	School		Home	
	Working class	Middle class	Working class	Middle class
Cognitive demands per 100 turns of talk[1]	9.3	8.5	3.3	4.5
Cognitive demands per hours[2]	7.6	7.9	14.8	19.6
'Testing' demands per 100 turns[3]	4.0	4.7	1.0	2.3
'Testing' demands per hour[4]	3.6	4.5	5.3	9.6

1. *Home vs school*: $F = 26.6$, $p<0.001$; social class $F = 0.1$, NS; interaction $F = 1.1$, NS.
2. *Home vs school*: $F = 23.2$, $p<0.001$; social class $F = 1.1$, NS; interaction $F = 1.3$, NS.
3. *Home vs school*: $F = 11.5$, $p<0.01$; social class $F = 1.6$, NS; interaction $F = 0.2$, NS.
4. *Home vs school*: $F = 5.7$, $p<0.05$; social class $F = 2.2$, NS; interaction $F = 1.5$, NS.

Proportional use of each type of cognitive demand as a percentage of all demands

	School		Home	
	Working class	Middle class	Working class	Middle class
Labels[1]	34	25	25	22
Attributes descriptions[2]	28	17	16	9
Recall, narration[3]	13	23	24	27
Explanations, generalizations[4]	20	27	24	19
'3 Rs'[5]	6	9	10	23

1. *Home vs school*: $F = 0.5$, NS; social class $F = 0.4$, $p<0.1$.
2. *Home vs school*: $F = 7.0$, $p<0.01$; social class $F = 14.4$, $p<0.001$.
3. *Home vs school*; $F = 6.7$, $p<0.02$; social class $F = 2.7$, NS.
4. *Home vs school*: $F = 0.7$, NS; social class $F = 0.6$, NS;
5. *Home vs school*: $F = 1.5$, NS; social class $F = 1.2$, NS.
There were no signficant interactions.

Additional tables can be found in the following published articles:

M. Hughes, H. Carmichael, G. Pinkerton and B. Tizard (1979) Recording children's conversations at home and at nursery school: a technique and some methodological considerations. *Journal of Child Psychology and Psychiatry*, **20**, 225–32.

B. Tizard, M. Hughes, H. Carmichael and G. Pinkerton (1980) Four-year-olds talking to mothers and teachers. *Journal of Child Psychology and Psychiatry*, monograph supplement no. 2.

B. Tizard, M. Hughes, H. Carmichael and G. Pinkerton (1982) Adults' cognitive demands at home and at nursery school. *Journal of Child Psychology and Psychiatry*, **23**, 2, 105–16.

B. Tizard, M. Hughes, H. Carmichael and G. Pinkerton (1983) Children's questions and adults' answers. *Journal of Child Psychology and Psychiatry*, **24**, 2, 269–81.

B. Tizard, M. Hughes, H. Carmichael and G. Pinkerton (1983) Language and social class: is verbal deprivation a myth? *Journal of Child Psychology and Psychiatry*, **24**, 4, 533–42.

Notes

Foreword

1. Bryant, P. E., Bradley, L., Maclean, M. and Crossland, J. (1989) Nursery rhymes, phonological skills and reading. *Journal of Child Language*, **16**, 407–28.
2. Callanan, M. A. and Oakes, L. M. (1992) Preschoolers' questions and parents' explanations: causal thinking in everyday activity. *Cognitive Development*, **7**, 213–33. And Callanan, M. A., Shrager, J. and Moore, J. L. (1995) Parent-child collaborative explanations: Methods of identification and analysis. *The Journal of the Learning Sciences*, **4**, 105–29.
3. Scarborough, H. S., Dobrich, W. and Hager, M. (1991) Preschool literacy experience and later reading achievement. *Journal of Learning Disabilities*, **24**, 508–11.
4. Astington, J. W. (1993) *The Child's Discovery of the Mind.* Cambridge, MA: Harvard University Press.
5. Dunn, J., and Brown, J. (in press) Emotion, pragmatics and developments in emotion understanding in the preschool years. In D. Bakhurst and S. Shanker (eds.), *Jerome Bruner: Language, culture, self.* Sage Publications. And Meins, A., Fernyhough, C., Russell, J. T., and Clarke-Carter, D. (1998) Security of attachment as a predictor of symbolic and mentalising abilities: A longitudinal study. *Social Development*, **7**, 1–24.
6. Lagattuta, K., and Wellman, H. (submitted) Differences in early parent–child conversations about negative versus positive emotions: Implications for the development of emotion understanding. Thompson, C., Barresi, J., and Moore, C. (1997) The development of future-oriented prudence and altruism in preschoolers. *Cognitive Development*, **12**, 199–212. And Haden, C. A., Haine, R. A. and Fivush, R. (1997) Developing narrative structure in parent–child reminiscing across the preschool years. *Developmental Psychology*, **33**, 295–307.

7. Hickling, A. and Wellman, H. M. (in press) The emergence of children's causal explanations and theories: Evidence from everyday conversation. *Developmental Psychology*. Dunn, J. and Brown, J. (1993) Early conversations about causality: Content, pragmatics, and developmental change. *British Journal of Developmental Psychology*, 11, 107–23. And Scholnick, E. K. and Wing, C. S. (1992) Speaking deductively: Using conversation to trace the origins of conditional thought in children. *Merrill-Palmer Quarterly*, 38, 1–20.

8. Dunn, J., Cutting, A. L., and Demetriou, H. (2000) Moral sensibility, understanding other, and children's friendship interactions in the preschool period. *British Journal of Developmental Psychology*, 18(2), 159–78.

9. Siegal, M. (1996) Conversation and cognition. In R. Gelman (ed.), *Perceptual and Cognitive Development. Handbook of Perception and Cognition* (2nd edn.) San Diego, CA: Academic Press.

10. Rogoff, B. (1990) *Apprenticeship in Thinking*. Oxford: Oxford University Press.

11. Vygotsky, L. S. (1962) *Thought and Language*. Cambridge, MA: MIT Press

12. Evans, G. W., Maxwell, L. E., and Hart, B. (1999) Parental language and verbal responsiveness to children in crowded homes. *Developmental Psychology*, 35, 1020–23.

13. Cutting, A. L., and Dunn, J. (1999) Theory of mind, emotion understanding, language and family background: Individual differences and interrelations. *Child Development*, 70(4), 853–65.

14. *Curriculum Guidance for the Foundation Stage* (2000) London: DfEE/QCA.

15. Gregory, E. (1996a) Making Sense of a New World: learning to Read in a Second Language. London: Paul Chapman. Gregory, E. (1996b) Learning from the community: A family literacy project with Bangladeshi origin children in London. In S. Wolfendale and K. Topping (eds.), *Family Involvement in Literacy*. London: Cassell. And Gregory, E. (1998) Siblings as mediators of literacy in linguistic minority communities. *Language and Education*, 12(1), 33–54.

16. Heath, S. B. (1983) *Ways with Words: Language, Life and Work in Communities and Classrooms*. Cambridge: Cambridge University Press.

17. Greenhough, P. and Hughes, M. (1998) Parents' and teachers' interventions in children's reading. *British Educational Research Journal*, 24(4), 383–98.

1 Why we studied children learning

1. Wells, C. G. (1984) *Language Development in the Pre-school Years*. Cambridge University Press.

2. Hess, R. D. and Shipman, V. C. (1965) Early experience and the socialisation of cognitive modes in children. *Child Development*, **36**, 869–86.

3. For example, Dunn, J. (1982) *Siblings*. London: Grant McIntyre. And Davie, C. E., Hutt, S. J., Vincent, E. and Mason, M. (1984) *The Young Child at Home*. Windsor: NFER/Nelson.

4. Tizard, B., Mortimore, J. and Burchell, B. (1981) *Involving Parents in Nursery and Infant Schools*. London: Grant McIntyre; Ypsilanti: High Scope Press.

5. Bullock Report (1975) *A Language for Life*. London: HMSO.

6. Bryant, P. E. (1974) *Perception and Understanding in Young Children*. London: Methuen.

7. Donaldson, M. (1978) *Children's Minds*. London: Fontana.

8. Dunn, J. (1983) Sibling relationships in early childhood. *Child Development*, **54**, 787–811.

9. Bates, E. (1975) Peer relations and the acquisition of language. In M. Lewis and L. A. Rosenblum (eds.), *Friendship and Peer Relations*. New York: John Wiley.

2   How we carried out this study

1. *General Household Survey, 1977*. London: HMSO.

2. Wells, C. G., *op. cit.*; Davie, C. E. *et al.*, *op. cit.*

3. Wells, C. G., *op. cit.* Also Wootton, A. (1974) Talk in the homes of young children. *Sociology*, **8**, 277–95. And Bernal, M. E., Gibson, D. M., William, D. E. and Pesses, D. I. (1971) A device for automatic tape recording. *Journal of Applied Behaviour Analysis*, **4**, 151–6.

4. Hughes, M., Carmichael, H., Pinkerton, G. and Tizard, B. (1979) Recording children's conversations at home and at nursery school. *Journal of Child Psychology and Psychiatry*, **20**, 225–32.

5. Johnson, S. M. and Bolstad, O. D. (1975) Reactivity to home observation. *Journal of Applied Behaviour Analysis*, **8**, 181–5. Connolly, K. and Smith, P. K. (1972), Reactions of preschool children to a strange observer. In N. G. Blurton Jones (ed.), *Ethological Studies of Child Behaviour*. London: Cambridge University Press.

6. Purcell, K. and Brady, K. (1966) Adaptation to the invasion of privacy. *Merrill Palmer Quarterly*, **12**, 242–54. Bernal *et al.*, *op. cit.*

7. Johnson and Bolstad, *op. cit.* Bernal *et al.*, *op. cit.*

3   Learning at home: play, games, stories and 'lessons'

1. Tizard *et al.*, *op. cit.*

4 Learning at home: living and talking together

1. Dunn, J., *op. cit.*
2. Davie, C. E. *et al.*, *op. cit.*

5 The puzzling mind of the four-year-old

1. Piaget, J. (1926) *The Language and Thought of the Child*. London: Routledge and Kegan Paul.
2. Isaacs, S. (1930) *Intellectual Growth in Young Children*. (Appendix by N. Isaacs.) London: Routledge and Kegan Paul.
3. For example, Davis, E. A. (1932) The form and function of children's questions. *Child Development*, 3, 57–74.
4. For a brief presentation, see Piaget, J. (1970) Piaget's theory. In P. H. Mussen (ed.), *Carmichael's Manual of Child Psychology*, vol. 1. New York: John Wiley.
5. Hughes, M. and Donaldson, M. (1979) The use of hiding games for studying the co-ordination of viewpoints. *Educational Review*, 31, 133–40.

6 Working-class verbal deprivation: myth or reality?

1. See a very useful sourcebook: Reid, I. (1977) *Social Class Differences in Britain*. London: Open Books.
2. Newson, J. and Newson, E. (1968) *Four Years Old in an Urban Comnuunity*. Hemel Hempstead: Allen and Unwin.
3. Davie, R., Butler, M. and Goldstein, H. (1972) *From Birth to Seven*. London: Longman.
4. See Rutter, M. and Madge, N. (1976) *Cycles of Disadvantage*. London: Heinemann Educational Books.
5. Bullock Report, *op. cit.*
6. Labov, W. (1969) The logic of non-standard English. In P. P. Giglioli (ed.) (1972) *Language and Social Context*. Harmondsworth: Penguin Books.
7. Tough, J. (1976) *Listening to Children Talking*. London: Ward Lock Educational.
8. Bernstein, B. (1971) *Class, Codes and Control*, vol. 1. London: Routledge and Kegan Paul.
9. Robinson, E. J. and Robinson, W. P. (1981) Ways of reacting to communicating failure. *European Journal of Social Pychology*, 11, 189–208.
10. Davie, C. E. *et al.*, *op. cit.*
11. Wells, *op.cit.*
12. Barnes, J. and Lucas, M. (1975) Positive discrimination in education. In J.

Barnes (ed.), *Educational Priority Vol. 3. Curriculum Innovation in London's EPAs*. London: HMSO.
13. Wells, *op. cit.*

8   How the children fared at nursery school

1. Clift, P., Cleave, S. and Griffin, M. (1980) *The Aims, Role, and Deployment of Staff in the Nursery*. Windsor: NFER Publishing Co.
2. Ibid.
3. Tizard, B., Cooperman, O., Joseph, A. and Tizard, J. (1972) Environmental effects on language development. *Child Development*, **43**, 337–58.
4. Blank, M. (1973) *Teaching Learning in the Pre-school*. Columbus: Charles E. Merrill Publishing Co.
5. Blank, M., Rose, S. A. and Berlin, L. J. (1978) *The Language of Learning: the Pre-school Years*. New York: Grove and Stratton.
6. Wood, D., McMahon, L. and Cranston, Y. (1980) *Working with Under Fives*. London: Grant McIntyre.

9   The working-class girls, including Donna, at school

1. Tizard, B., Philps, J. and Plewis, I. (1976) Play in pre-school centres, I and II. *Journal of Child Pychology and Pychiatry*, **17**, 251–74.
2. Sylva, K., Roy, C. and Painter, M. (1980) *Childwatching at Ploygroup and Nursery School*. London: Grant McIntyre.

11   Young children learning

1. *Social Trends*, 11 (1981). London: HMSO.
2. Wood *et al.*, *op. cit.*
3. Tough, J. (1977) *Talking and Learning*. London: Ward Lock Educational.
4. Tizard, B., Philps, J. and Plewis, I. (1976) Staff behaviour in pre-school centres. *Journal of Child Pychology and Pychiatry*, **17**, 21–33. Also Tizard *et al.* (1976), *op. cit.* And Wood *et al.*, *op. cit.*
5. Wells, *op. cit.*, and Davie, C. E. *et al.*, *op. cit.*
6. Isaacs, *op. cit.*
7. Donaldson, *op. cit.*

Index of children

middle class

Ann 30–2, 117, 163
Beth x, 38–9, 59, 67, 68, 77–8, 99–100, 184, 201–2
Cathie 63–5, 71–3, 116, 200
Erica 74–5, 88, 173–5, 201
Helen 24, 67
Jane 163, 184, 207–8
Lesley 184
Louise 187, 203
Mary 37–8, 68, 69, 205–6
Mina 59–61, 82–3, 89–91, 117, 203–4
Penny 38, 39, 91–3, 94–5
Rosy x, 44–6, 61, 95–9, 204–5
Ruth 24, 69, 88–9, 102, 105
Susan 27–30, 57–8, 73–4, 75, 93–4, 95
Valerie 184

working class

Carol 86–8, 168–9, 204, 206
Cindy 33, 118, 181
Donna 75, 83, 99, 132–48, 185, 188–96, 207
Elaine 76
Joyce 32–3, 40–1, 61–3, 114, 158–61, 170–1, 187–8, 206–7
June 34–7, 40, 161–2
Kelly 70, 76, 117, 119–20, 172–3
Lynne 42–4, 67, 87, 104–5, 175–7, 199–200
Pauline 50–3, 54–7, 58–9, 61, 103–4, 117
Samantha 47–9, 65–6, 104, 115
Sandra 115
Tina 49
Tonia 121, 207
Vida 104
Wendy 33

General Index

alphabet, learning 142–3
arithmetic *see* number skills

babies, living with 58–61
Bernstein, B. 116, 129–30
Blank, Marion 157
Bruner, J. 1
Bryant, Peter viii–ix, 7
Bullock Report 6, 109

Callahan, Maureen ix
card games 34, 35–8, 40
cheating at games 39–40
child as thinker ix–x, xv, 6–7,
    212–13
children's questions *see* questions
Christmas presents 91–5
class *see* social class
cognitive demands 117–18, 157–65,
    186
communication difficulties at school
    170–1, 199–202
competitive games 39–40
complex use of language 112–16,
    128, 166, 181
confidence, lack of 183–6
control 23–4
    see also disputes

school discipline 152–3
social class and 126–7
conversations
    dominance 155–6, 180
    home-school differences 153–6,
        180, 182–3
    information in 24–5
    initiation of 23, 156
    length and frequency 23, 153–4
    social class and 112, 180, 182–3
    with teachers 153–6, 180, 182–3,
        189–96, 216–17
    turns of 23, 24
counting 36, 37–8, 56, 73–4, 141,
    144–6
    see also number skills

Davie, C.E. 13, 66, 125, 218
disputes 69–70, 127, 129, 152–3
    see also control
    at school 152, 183
    explanations following 70, 127,
        129
    social class and 69–70, 129, 180,
        183
Donaldson, Margaret 7, 222
Dunn, Judy vii–xi, 61

egocentrism 34, 51, 58, 101–3
explanations following disputes 70,
     127, 129
explicitness 116–20, 212

Father Christmas 91–5
fathers
     see also parents
     involvement of 2
     occupations 111
Froebel, Friedrich 25
future and past events 61–6, 151–2,
     166, 201, 210, 214–15

games
     see also play
     at school 151
     bodily contact 40
     card games 34, 35–8, 40
     cheating 39–40
     competitive 39–40
     counting 36, 38
     educational 37, 125
     for fun 40–2
     Hunt the Thimble 34
     I Spy 34–5
     Knockout Whist 34, 35–7, 40
     with rules 33–40
     Stepping Stones 38–9
     word games 37, 41
gap between home and school
     197–208, 221–3
     see also home-school differences
     attempts to bridge 198–202
     teachers 203–4
     talking about home at school 183,
          199–200, 203–4
     talking about school at home
          204–8
general knowledge and information
     24–5, 44, 70, 77–8, 120, 121,
     151, 212
Gregory, E. xi

Heath, Brice xi
Hess, R.D. 4
home
     learning aty see learning at
          home
     as learning environment 3–5,
          76–8, 209–12
     school comparedy see gap
          between home and school;
          home-school differences
     talking about home at school 183,
          199–200, 203–4
     talking about school at home
          204–8
home-school differences 2, 8
     see also gap between home and
          school
     aim and curriculum 150–2
     amount of talk 153–4, 166
     children's questions 167
     cognitive demands 117–18,
          157–65, 186
     control 152–3
     conversations 153–6, 180,
          189–96, 197–8
     difficulties in communicating with
          staff 170–1
     discipline 152–3
     disputes 152, 183
     flatness of communications 168–9
     games 151
     information 151
     intellectual search 167
     language, use for complex purposes
          166, 181
     observer effect 17–18, 217
     past and future events 151–2,
          166, 214–15
     play 150, 151, 214
     questions by children 167
     range of topics 151, 167
     social development 150, 152–3
     story-reading 172, 177

home-school differences (*cont.*)
  use of language for complex
    purposes 166, 181
home-visiting schemes 223
housing 111–12
Hunt the Thimble 34

I Spy 34–5
imaginative play 26, 27–33
implications for home and school
  nursery schools 219–21
  parents 218–19
implicitness 116–17
information and general knowledge
    24–5, 44, 70, 77–8, 120, 121,
    151, 212
intellectual search 91–100, 122, 167
IQ scores 127–8
Isaacs, Nathan 84
Isaacs, Susan x, 80, 220

Knockout Whist 34, 35–7, 40

Labov, William 109–10, 111, 116,
    129–30, 179, 180, 188
language, complex use of 112–16,
    128, 166, 181
language deprivation 6, 107–31,
    179
learning at home
  babies, living with 58–61
  cognitive demands 164–5
  counting 36, 37–8, 56, 73–4,
    141, 144–6
  disputes 69–70
  domestic matters 121, 130, 212
  factors conducive to 210–11
  gamesy *see* games
  'geography' 25
  'history' 25
  home as learning environment
    3–5, 76–8, 209–12
  information 24–5

letters of the alphabet 142–3
number skills 36, 37–8, 56, 73–4,
    141, 144–6
parents' beliefs about 22–3
past and future events 61–6,
    151–2, 166, 201, 210, 214–15
playy *see* play
school comparedy *see* home-
    school differences
'science' 24
sex roles 75–6, 144
shopping lists 54–7
size and shape concepts 74–5
special characteristics of 76–8
spelling 142
stories 42–7, 172, 177
survival skills 50–3
TV watching 66–9
window, looking out of 57–8
writing 47–9, 71–3
letter writing 71–3
logical thinking 103–5, 109, 110,
    213
Lotto 37
Ludo 37

Malting House School 220
mathematical skills *see* number skills
meal-times 126
money and work 95–9
mothers
  see also parents
  advice re school behaviour 185
  children's questions *see* questions
  education 111
  ideas about what they are teaching
    their children 22–3, 142, 185
  nursery schools, attitudes to 25,
    142, 185
  play, attitudes to 25, 40–2, 142,
    147–8
  shared world with child 63

working outside the home 2, 111, 132

National Child Development Study 108
Newson, John and Elizabeth 108
number skills 36, 37–8, 56, 73–4, 141, 144–6, 162
nursery school
 communication difficulties 170–1, 199–202
 conversations 153–6
 discipline 152–3
 disputes 152, 183
 home comparedy see home-school differences
 as learning environment 213–15
 mothers' attitudes to 25, 49, 185
 outings 220
 play 185–6
 staff-child interaction, amount of 153–4
 story-reading 172–7, 198–9
 in study 2, 12–13, 20–1
 talking about home at school 183, 199–200, 203–4
 talking about school at home 204–8
 teachersy see nursery teachers
 working-class children at 183–6, 215–16
nursery teachers
 aims and curriculum 150–2, 219
 asking questions 156–62
 attitudes to parents/home 5, 142
 behaviour to working-class children 186–8, 215–16
 children's communications with xv, 2, 153–6, 189–96
 difficulties in 170–1
 flatness of 168–9
 responses 163–4
 educational methods 156–62

language, use for complex purposes 166
reasons for approaching 182–3
relationship with 2
underestimation of children's abilities 6, 130, 160, 186–8, 216–17

observer effect 4, 15–19, 23, 217
outings 220

parents 218–19
 see also fathers; mothers
 education for 5, 223–5
 professionals' attitudes to 4–5, 22, 25, 69, 109, 166, 197, 224
past and future events 61–6, 151–2, 166, 201, 210, 214–15
Piaget, Jean 7, 25, 34, 51, 81, 84, 85, 100–2, 159, 213
play
 at home 26, 27–33, 125–6, 212
 at school 25, 185–6, 214
 bodily contact 40
 gamesy see games
 imaginative 26, 27–33, 125
 mothers' attitudes to 25, 40–2, 142, 147–8, 212
 social class and 125–6, 185–6
 theories of 25
playgroups 215, 219
primary school, preparation for 150, 160, 162, 198
professionals, attitudes to parents 4–5, 22, 25, 69, 109, 166, 197, 224

questions 80–5
 'business' 81, 83, 122, 167, 182
 'challenges' 81–3, 85, 122, 167
 cognitive demands 117–18, 157–65, 186
 contexts 81–5

questions (*cont.*)
  'curiosity'   83, 84, 85, 122, 167,
    182
  home-school differences   167,
    182–3
  'How' questions   84
  intellectual search   91–100, 122,
    167
  misunderstandings not detected
    85–7, 213
    resolution   88–91
  mothers' answers to   122, 123–5
  numbers of   81
  persistent questioning   x, 85,
    91
  'puzzled questions'   84
  social class and   81, 122–3, 180,
    182
  teaching methods   156–62,
    172–7
  'Where' questions   81
  'Why' questions   81, 82, 83, 84,
    122, 123, 124, 167, 182

reading
  learning through stories   42–7
  learning to read   37, 38–9, 86
recording the conversations   13–15,
    85
  timing   19
Robinson, Peter and Elizabeth   118
Rogoff, Barbara   x

sample, selection of   11–13
school *see* nursery school
self-confidence, lack of   183–6
sex-role teaching   75–6, 144
shared world of mother and child
    63
Shipman, V.C.   4
shopping lists   54–7
size and shape concepts   74–5
social class

classification   107–8
comparisonsy   *see* social class
    comparison
language development and
    109–11
reasons for studying   107–8
selection of groups   111–12
verbal deprivation and   6, 107–31,
    179
social class comparison   6, 107–31,
    179
at home
  children's questions   81, 122–5
  cognitive demands   117–18
  control   126–7
  disputes   69–70, 129, 180
  educational priorities   212
  explicitness   116–20, 212
  information and general
    knowledge   120
  intellectual search   91, 122
  IQ scores   127–8
  language development   x–xi,
    109–10
  language, use for complex
    purposes   112–16, 128, 181
  learning environment   212
  midday meals   126
  money and work   98–9
  mother-child talk   112
  mothers' advice re school
    behaviour   185
  mothers' answers to children's
    questions   123–5
  mothers' explanation for control
    127, 129
  mothers' teaching strategies   4
  play   125–6, 212
  questions   81, 122–5
  sex-role teaching   76
  topics of conversation
    120–2
  toys   112, 184

vocabulary   120–1, 179, 212
at school
   approaching staff   182–3
   children's questions   182
   conversations   180, 182–3
   disputes   183
   language, use for complex
      purposes   181
   play   185–6
   self-confidence   183–6
   talking about home at school
      183
   teachers' behaviour   186–8
Stepping Stones   38–9
story-reading
   at home   42–7, 172, 177
   at school   172–7, 198–9
survival skills   50–3
Sylva, K.   186

teachers see nursery teachers
Tough, Joan   112–13, 156–7, 216
toys   112, 184
transcripts, preparation of   20
turns of talk   23, 24
TV watching   22, 44, 66–9

validity of findings   217–18
verbal deprivation   6, 107–31, 179
vocabulary   3, 120–1, 179, 212

Wells, G.   3, 13, 128, 130–1, 218
window, looking out of   57–8
Wood, David   164, 215, 217
word games   37, 41
writing
   as communication   71–3
   learning to write   47–9, 71–3
   letter writing   71–3